Praise for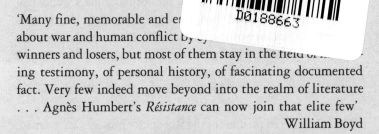

'Many fine, memorable and e[...]
about war and human conflict b[...]
winners and losers, but most of them stay in the field o[...]
ing testimony, of personal history, of fascinating documented
fact. Very few indeed move beyond into the realm of literature
. . . Agnès Humbert's *Résistance* can now join that elite few'

William Boyd

'Her narrative combines evocations of moments of intense suffering with vivid character sketches, ironic asides, snatches of
dialogue and brave repartee to sadistic guards. She weaves all
this together by inventing a narrative voice that is sober and
testifying, sardonic and humorous, always precise . . . This is
a beautiful and powerful work of literature'

Michèle Roberts, *The Times*

'An astonishing work, almost unbearable to read in places, yet
ultimately inspiring. It evokes horror and compels admiration
. . . A remarkable book by a remarkable and brave woman'

Allan Massie, *Literary Review*

She is such a fighter, such a character . . . Her personality
bounces through every page of her diary . . . Humbert's memoir
will remain one of the most valuable testaments we have to
Hitler's policy of "extermination through labour"'

Carmen Callil, *Guardian*

'Astonishin[...] [...]aking
detail her c[...] [...]isoner
and potenti[...] [...]s the
book from [...] [...]k . . .
Rooted in i[...] [...]meless
testament and a timely one   Kamer Hussein, *Independent*

'This is both a historically important document and a fine literary achievement . . . Barbara Mellor has done a wonderful job as translator . . . The name of Agnès Humbert should now join the ranks of Lucie Aubrac and Violette Szabo, women whose bravery and dignity during the occupation deserves to be remembered for many generations to come'

Christian House, *Independent on Sunday*

'A long-neglected memoir of the Resistance provides an intimate view of war . . . It is now translated for the first time in English, and one can only marvel at its 60-year neglect . . . *Résistance* has flashes of self-deprecating humour, and its affirmation of human dignity instils a kind of joy in the reader . . . A marvel of luminous precision and restraint, *Résistance*, beautifully translated by Barbara Mellor, is a book of commemoration as well as a documentary'

Ian Thomson, *Sunday Times*

'A superb account of a warrior in combat . . . [Humbert] showed an astonishing light-hearted courage. She and her comrades faced death almost gaily, accepting the fate they had chosen and glad to have made that choice. Resisters like her are a true elite, different from the rest of us'

Daily Mail

'The book that moved me the most this year was *Résistance*, Agnes Humbert's memoir of her stint in the French Resistance . . . A vivid picture of the cruellest of times, written with an astounding humour, courage and absence of self-pity'

Jenny McCartney, *Sunday Telegraph* Books of the Year

'It is an astonishingly vivid testament to one woman's bravery, humanity and sheer dogged resilience, and, more than any number of academic tomes, it allows us to understand the visceral reality of life in this torrid period of history'

Sunday Times History Books of the Year

Résistance

Memoirs of Occupied France

Agnès Humbert

*Translated from the French
and with notes by Barbara Mellor*

AFTERWORD BY JULIEN BLANC

BLOOMSBURY
LONDON · BERLIN · NEW YORK

First published in Great Britain 2008
This paperback edition published in 2009

Notre Guerre by Agnès Humbert © Editions Emile-Paul Frères, 1946
This edition © Tallandier Editions 2004

English translation © by Barbara Mellor 2008

The publisher and translator would like to thank all sources for permission to reproduce the
following .... page 309 from
Honoré d' .... France Empire,
1999; pa .... e et Jean-Marie
Fitère, Edi .... *Héros de la Résis-*
tance, Rene .... *Gross-Paris, Place*
de la Con .... *bagh!* by Pierre
Sabbagh .... gnès Humbert,

www.bloomsbury.com

Bloomsbury Publishing, London, New York and Berlin

A CIP catalogue record for this book is available from the British Library

ISBN 978 0 7475 9674 5

10 9 8 7 6 5 4 3 2 1

Typeset by Hewer Text UK Ltd, Edinburgh
Printed in Great Britain by Clays Ltd, St Ives plc

The paper this book is printed on is certified independently in accordance with the
rules of the FSC. It is ancient-forest friendly. The printer hold chain of custody.

FSC

Mixed Sources
Product group from well-managed
forests and other controlled sources

Cert no. SGS-COC-2061
www.fsc.org
© 1996 Forest Stewardship Council

CONTENTS

TRANSLATOR'S ACKNOWLEDGEMENTS

When I first came upon *Notre Guerre* – in its evocative 1946 edition – I was unfamiliar with the text or its author. Soon, however, I was overwhelmed by the power and immediacy of the narrative, by the raw intensity of the subject matter, and by the compelling presence of Agnès Humbert herself. First-hand, contemporaneous accounts of epoch-making events are rare; how much rarer, then, to find an account such as this, brimming with life and humour, passion and humanity, generosity and courage? Surely it deserved to be more widely known? Surely it should be made available in an English translation?

Rarely can a translation project and the accompanying research have received such committed support from so many quarters – eloquent testimony in itself to the importance of Agnès Humbert's memoir. First and foremost I am indebted to Rod Kedward, who fired my interest in the French Resistance at Sussex University and who has been a generous and infinitely learned mentor throughout this absorbing venture. To Nancy Wood I owe valuable insights into the essential and often undervalued role of women in the Resistance. Maia Wechsler kindly sent me her moving and illuminating film *Sisters in Resistance*. Catherine Clarke of the Felicity Bryan Literary Agency was generous in her finely judged advocacy of the project. At Bloomsbury, Bill Swainson guided it to publication with vision, discernment and aplomb, and Emily Sweet and Lisa Fiske lent the finished edition clarity and distinction. In France, Julien Blanc was unhesitating in his encouragement; Antoine Sabbagh offered a direct link with his remarkable grandmother and poignant mementos of her life and captivity; and Henri Bovet at Tallandier supported this English language edition from the beginning.

Gwen Chessell, Alison Dufour, Jo King, Ann Mellor, Jo Mountford and Joan Rushton provided greatly valued research and support; Wendy Dallas was as ever a peerless friend and colleague; and Gavin, Lucy and Jim Harding were the best and most forbearing of companions who made it all possible.

It has been an immense privilege to work on this translation; it is dedicated to the memory of Agnès Humbert and her comrades.

Barbara Mellor, 2008

LIST OF ILLUSTRATIONS

Jean Cassou, distinguished writer, art critic and poet. (*Collections Musée de l'Ordre de la Libération, Paris*)

Simone Martin-Chauffier, writer and translator. (*Comité de l'Histoire de la 2e Guerre Mondiale, Paris*)

Jacqueline Bordelet, a young secretary at the Musée de l'Homme. (*Comité de l'Histoire de la 2e Guerre Mondiale, Paris*)

Sylvette Leleu, garage owner in the northern town of Béthune. (*Comité de l'Histoire de la 2e Guerre Mondiale, Paris*)

Honoré d'Estienne d'Orves, aristocratic Free French naval officer. (*From* Les Témoins qui se firent égorger, *Editions Défense de la France*)

The Prison du Cherche-Midi, the notoriously insalubrious French military prison run by the German authorities throughout the Occupation.

Captain Ernst Roskothen, lawyer, Wehrmacht officer and presiding judge at the trial of the 'Vildé affair'. (*Comité de l'Histoire de la 2e Guerre Mondiale, Paris*)

One of the prison huts in which slave workers were held at Krefeld, 8 March 1945. (*Philip R. Mark*)

Two US Army medics help a newly liberated prisoner. (*From* Les Témoins qui se firent égorger, *Editions Défense de la France*)

A spearhead detachment of the advancing US Army, its brief to impose order and American military rule, deals with German civilians, Rhineland, March/April 1945. (*Courtesy of the US Center of Military History*)

Agnès Humbert and other members of the Association France-Yougoslavie with President Tito during his official visit to France, 7–11 May 1956. (*With permission from Antoine Sabbagh*)

'A woman deserving of the highest admiration, unassailable in her strength of character and will, unflinching in her absolute integrity' (Pierre Sabbagh). Agnès Humbert, 12 October 1894–19 September 1963. (*With permission from Antoine Sabbagh*)

PREFACE BY WILLIAM BOYD

Consider this brief thought-experiment: your country is invaded; the city you know and love is overrun by foreign, enemy troops; the occupiers are not going away; you become a powerless, humiliated citizen of a vassal state. What would you do in this situation? What would anyone do? Keep your head down? Adjust to the new status quo, business as usual? Or react in some fashion, find some way of resisting, of fighting back?

This situation is timeless (and contemporary, it hardly needs adding), but for the French such a scenario immediately conjures up World War II and the five years of the Occupation by Nazi Germany. One of the consequences of this remarkable memoir is that it shows us one individual's response to the exact thought-experiment adumbrated above. Agnès Humbert found herself in precisely this terrifying state of affairs in Paris in 1940, and this book, *Résistance*, is the chronicle of her response to it and the consequences she suffered thereafter.

Her reaction was instinctive and spontaneous — some way of fighting back or, at the very least, not yielding had to be found. More intriguingly, more astonishingly, Agnès Humbert was forty-three years old in 1939 when the war began, a respected art historian, left-wing 'intello', and the divorced mother of two grown-up sons. She wasn't a 'firebrand', or young; she was comfortably off and had a reputation, a good job in a museum, yet she simply could not stand by and do nothing. She became one of the first members of one of the first Resistance cells in France, and the journal she kept at the time charts her slow evolution from angry, unfocussed patriot to active Resistance member: disseminating black propaganda, publishing an underground newspaper, passing on military information and sheltering Allied airmen. But the genuine zeal of Agnès and her colleagues was both naïve and amateur.

Her group was betrayed in 1941 after a few months of activity, and the baleful journey that ensued – arrest, imprisonment, trial, execution of her fellow *résistants*, deportation to Germany and years as a slave labourer – makes up the larger part of her wartime story. Liberation, Nazi-hunting and repatriation followed, and in every sense Agnès Humbert (who died in 1963) was vindicated: she had not surrendered, she had fought and suffered to help free her country, she had done the right thing.

Résistance is written in the form of a journal, and this is what gives the book its vivid immediacy and incomparable verve. Written in the present tense (and originally published just after the war's end, in 1946), it benefits hugely from its tone of voice (superbly captured and rendered in English by Barbara Mellor's translation). We live through Agnès Humbert's excitement, danger, terror and eventual ordeal as if we were by her side: her candour, her recall, her eye for detail and her incredibly tenacious sense of humour are conveyed with a freshness that a more considered memoir, adulterated by post-war hindsight, could not have provided.

Agnès Humbert bears devastating witness to her time: here is an insider's account of the germination of the French Resistance in all its fascinating detail – and all the more rare for being written by a woman. But her journal goes further than this: many fine, memorable and enduring books have been written about war and human conflict by eyewitnesses and combatants, winners and losers, but most of them stay in the field of harrowing testimony, of personal history, of fascinating documented fact. Very few indeed move beyond this and into the realm of literature. A small handful of examples come to mind: T. E. Lawrence's *Seven Pillars of Wisdom*, Robert Graves's *Goodbye to All That*, Ernst Junger's *Storm of Steel* and Keith Douglas's *Alamein to Zem Zem*. Agnès Humbert's *Résistance* can now join that elite few.

In memory of my Comrades:

Boris Vildé
Anatole Lewitsky
Pierre Walter
Léon-Maurice Nordmann
Georges Ithier
Jules Andrieu
René Sénéchal

executed by firing squad at Mont Valérien
on 23 February 1942.

Pierre Brossolette

who died by his own hand on 22 March 1944 after with-
standing three days of torture by the Gestapo, during which he
refused to utter a word in betrayal of his companions in arms.

Emile Müller

killed in a Nazi slave labour camp by an
Allied air raid in July 1944.

I

The Fall of the Third Republic

Palais de Chaillot, Paris, 7 June 1940
Rumours are flying, all flatly contradictory, but it seems clear that the Germans are advancing on all fronts. It's only a matter of advance units of motorized troops – naturally – but however they try to explain it away in the newspapers and on the radio, I'm convinced that our position is extremely serious. Life at the museum[1] has become positively sinister. Most of the collections have been evacuated. All that's left is the library. I have just been given instructions to pack up the most valuable volumes – a more or less mechanical task that takes my mind off the turmoil going on all around me . . . The entire population is leaving Paris; we are living in an atmosphere of panic; people seem to have lost all capacity for reasoned thought. Just now on the place du Trocadéro twenty or so people were simply standing there, craning their necks and staring up into the sky – where, so they said, they could see parachutists! Do they even know what a parachutist is, I wonder? My eyes are pretty sharp, and all I could see were swallows . . .

[1] Musée National des Arts et Traditions Populaires, Palais de Chaillot.

Palais de Chaillot, Paris, 8 June 1940

This morning Georges Friedmann came to see me at the museum.
He found me packing the last books into the last case, though
without much enthusiasm as I am perfectly well aware that there
is no longer the smallest chance of evacuating them. Friedmann
wouldn't tell me the current whereabouts of his regiment. It is
not hard to deduce that there has been a major retreat. He is
deeply distressed by the disintegration of the army, and by the
current barrage of orders and counter-orders. What can a humble
lieutenant do, when chaos and arbitrary inconsistency are the
order of the day at every rank, from the highest to the lowest?
He remains admirably calm, and attempts to reassure me without
masking the truth. He doesn't hide the fact that it's all going
extremely badly, though he says the army is organizing a line of
resistance along the Seine. He thinks this might hold the Germans
up for a while – two or three weeks at most – and after that the
invasion could be contained along the Loire. Despite everything,
he has managed to keep his confidence, and I find that contagious.

I forgot all about lunch. Now it's three o'clock, and I am
sitting in my office doing nothing. Every now and again I
pick up the telephone and listen to the news bulletins on the
Informations parlées. The news is depressing, conflicting, faltering. The doors of the Palais de Chaillot are shut. The silence
is deathly. There is nothing to do but wait.

Paris, 10 June 1940

I have catalogued Friedmann's library. His books, manuscripts
and documents are in packing cases stacked in my cellar. I
write to him to tell him that I have undertaken this little
enterprise purely and simply as a precaution against bombing
raids. Against bombing raids . . . oh, but of course. To myself,
however, I can admit the truth: I know full well why I have
moved these precious books – and these compromising

documents – to my house, where no one will think of looking for them. It is as a precaution against enemy occupation. We have to get used to this appalling possibility: Paris may fall. It's one thing to think it, but it's quite another to say the words out loud: 'Paris may fall.' I'm stopped by a superstitious dread: I can't do it. Some things should never be said out loud, for fear they may come true . . .

Paris, 11 June 1940

Never has Paris looked more beautiful, never has it been such a mass of flowers. The Cour du Carrousel looks as if it is ready for a flower show. I gaze at it from the office of the Director of the Musées Nationaux, where we have all gathered, suitcases in hand. We talk in low voices, as though in the presence of death. M. Jaujard moves from one group to another, so calm and controlled. I hear him say: 'I would like my Jewish colleagues to leave first.' The trucks are in the courtyard. We take our places in them, invited to do so by our director with the same unruffled cordiality, the same attentiveness to every detail, the same encouraging smile for each of us as he hands us our evacuation orders. We talk among ourselves. Yesterday I could not bring myself to utter the words 'Paris may fall'; today we say them almost carelessly, confident in the knowledge that the Allied armies have retreated only in order to regroup, to reorganize for the final phase of the war, which will be fought out along the Loire; confident in the absolute conviction that once the harvest is over the Soviet Union will enter the conflict. It's just a matter of holding out till then . . .

With our spirits lifted and our minds almost at peace, we leave Paris for the Château de Chambord. Although the weather is glorious, the sun is blanketed by a thick black fog that leaves greasy black smears on our faces; as we said our goodbyes this morning, my son Pierre explained that this fog is man-made

and designed to offer protection to the people of Paris as they
flee. Then, after a moment's pause for reflection, he added: 'At
least that's what they say . . . but it's much too well done to
be the work of that Civil Defence mob . . .'

Vicq-sur-Breuil, 20 June 1940

Two days I have been here now, in what my head tells me is a
lovely region of rolling hills. My heart, meanwhile, is filled with
the scenes of savagery I have witnessed over the last nine days,
on a journey that defies belief. Paris–Limoges. A speeded-up film
full of double exposures, unreeling at a hectic pace as though the
projectionist were drunk. So many images, chaotic and incoherent,
jolting and jostling for space in my head. Leaving Paris among
so many thousands of others, on foot or by bicycle or in cars –
cars that had to be abandoned almost immediately for lack of
petrol or spare parts. Mothers carrying small children . . . One
young woman, dropping with exhaustion, pushing a strapping
baby squashed into a doll's pram that was far too small for it,
so that it looked as if it would topple out at every step. How
shall I ever forget the sight of her? Such a mass of people, laden
down with the most unlikely looking parcels and packages –
almost invariably including a washtub and a birdcage.

At Chambord, a beautiful sixteen-year-old girl called Emili-
enne was brought to us. That morning she and all her family
had abandoned their farm in the Cher, heading southwards on
foot and without any idea where they were going. A French
army truck in headlong flight from the enemy had run over
this lovely child. We telephoned the hospital at Blois: no reply.
No doctors, no pharmacists. A passing army medic was good
enough to stop off at the chateau for a few minutes. There was
nothing to be done, he told me. We clustered round her, dumb-
struck: a handful of administrators and curators, including Jean
Cassou. I tried to staunch the blood; someone else gave her an

injection of cacodylate: futile gestures that fooled no one. She died, apparently without pain. Jean Cassou and I knew each other already and have a lot in common, but this half-hour together at the side of a dying girl has bound us to each other with deep bonds of comradeship. We both know it.

At La Celle-sur-Cher, amid this impenetrable, heaving mass that choked the road, I saw a French general – a *general* – get out of his car and beg the crowd to let him through in a manner that was truly pathetic. I shall never forget his wheedling voice: 'Oh come *on*, let me through. I have to get *through*.' No one paid him the slightest attention. Only picture the scene: a general of the Debacle . . .

Another sight that will haunt me was that of six haggard soldiers, their uniforms hanging in shreds. They'd abandoned their weapons long before. Between the six of them they had only one possession left: a frying pan.

At Valençay I heard the frantic screams of a mother who had gone out of her mind. She had lost her two little daughters and was shrieking for them everywhere. It was at Valençay that we learned that France was seeking an armistice. All around me, men were weeping silent tears. Jumping out of the car, I stamped and yelled: 'It's all lies, it's all lies, it's the German radio that's saying that just to demoralize us. It can't be true, it's not possible.' I can still hear my voice, as though it were someone else shouting. Within a few hours there was no longer any point in denying it: we had no choice, we had to admit that the unthinkable had happened. The people of France were on their knees, begging for mercy, still fighting here and there, fleeing in all directions, and now all I could hear was, 'Paris has fallen!'

Paris has fallen! Paris is in the hands of the Germans! Somehow we had to make our minds admit this abomination, somehow we had to grasp what it meant, because it was the truth!

At the army petrol depot at Limoges we wait our turn, hour after hour. Six huge Italian bombers fly overhead. I know only too well what would happen if a bomb were to fall on this vast fuel reservoir. But I'm past caring now; I'm too exhausted, too disheartened. I don't feel anything any more, no fear, no anxiety; I'm just numb. Ahead of us in the queue stands an army ambulance. I still have two oranges: perhaps the wounded it is carrying are thirsty? Then, through the half-open rear door, I catch a glimpse of the interior. Strewn on the floor are items of female clothing and a couple of empty champagne bottles. Sprawled in the stretcher berth is a woman in a jade-green crêpe satin slip heavily trimmed with lace, her bloated face mottled with powder and sweat. She is drunk, and dead to the world. Her companion flings his arms about and shouts. He needs petrol, and fast. So this is what our ambulances are carrying, while our wounded are abandoned and left to die.

Vicq-sur-Breuil, 20 June 1940

At last I have found Maman, comfortably installed at cousin Daisy's house in the little village of Vicq-sur-Breuil. The house is filled to bursting with refugees, both French and Belgian. I share a bed with Maman. After so many nights spent in rain-lashed fields, it's wonderful to sleep in a bed. I tell them about my journey, but I can see that no one believes me. An endless stream of refugees troops through the village, all heading for the south, where they hope to find food and safety. I watch this interminable procession from the dining-room window, stupefied. In front of the house a veteran captain directs the traffic, so saving the village streets from becoming completely choked. Where are my sons? Jean was in Newfoundland. Is he still there? And Pierre? Killed on the road, perhaps. People who left Paris after I did have been subjected to terrible bombing, I am told. If I listen hard I can hear artillery fire: so the armistice hasn't been signed. There is still fighting north of Limoges. Oh, how I long to know what is happening! Where are my friends? Shall I ever see them again? What are they thinking? Are they suffering the same torments as me? Or am I 'over-reacting', as Friedmann implied?

I turn the knob on the wireless set, which is tuned to London. By a pure fluke I find myself listening to a transmission in French. A voice announces an appeal to be made by a French general. I don't catch his name. In a delivery that is jerky and peremptory – not at all well suited to the radio – the general urges all Frenchmen to rally round him, to carry on the struggle. I feel I have come back to life. A feeling I thought had died for ever stirs within me again: hope. There is one man after all – one alone, perhaps – who understands what I feel in my heart: 'It's not over yet.' I hurtle outside and across the garden like a lunatic, charging up to the captain – to whom I have not so far spoken a word – panting and breathless. I couldn't care less, I just have to tell him the news: 'Captain, captain, a French general – I don't know his name – has just spoken from London: he says that the French army must regroup around him, that the war will go on, that he will broadcast again to give orders!'

The old captain looks up wearily: 'That'll be de Gaulle, the general. Oh yes, he's a right one, that de Gaulle. Oh, we know all about him, don't you worry! It's all a lot of nonsense. Me, I'm a reservist anyway. All I want is to get back to my business in Paris. Me, I've got a family to feed . . . he's a crackpot, that de Gaulle, you mark my words.'

It is thanks to that 'crackpot' that this evening I decided not to put an end to everything after all. He has given me hope, and nothing in the world can extinguish that hope now.

Vicq, 20 July 1940
Long walks every day help to calm my nerves. If I didn't have the excuse of foraging for food – we still have to eat, after all – I would stay shut up in the house in a stupor, stewing over

the fate that lies in store for us, and how we can continue the struggle and 'pull through'. Jean has telegraphed to say that he is still a naval officer on board the *Ville-d'Ys*, currently in Newfoundland. So he is safe and well. And I've had a letter from Pierre at last. He appears to have experienced all sorts of adventures on the road out of Paris, but was cut off by the German army before he could get as far as the Limousin region. He is waiting for me in Paris, and he tells me that orders to return to my post will soon reach me. Maman remains remarkably calm, and listens to me talking for hours on end. Should I go back to Paris and hand in my notice at the museum? What should I do? I have written to Mme Osorio. Why not go to California? Palo Alto, where she lives, is a university town: surely I could teach history of art there? Or find a job as a curator in a museum or library? Or would it be better to hole up in some Provençal village and live off our savings? At times anything at all seems preferable to living under the swastika, and then just as suddenly I can't envisage any possible alternative to going back to Paris to be with Pierre. This is the solution that is the least creative and the least risky (or is it the most risky?). It is quite likely that I shall waste no time in getting dismissed from my post for my beliefs. The very occasional Lyon editions of *Paris-Soir* that I have managed to read here and there leave no room for doubt (for those still inclined to harbour any) as to the inclinations of the Laval government. But still, this puppet administration can't last for ever. The radio is my sole pleasure. On 14 July there was a broadcast from London of the Romain Rolland play *Le 14 juillet*. What a consolation! This morning we heard that as fast as German posters are put up in Paris they are slashed and torn down again. The people of Paris are rebelling already. So that's decided then: I'm going home!

2

Paris under the Swastika

Paris, 6 August 1940

It's a week now since I got back to Paris. I feel as though I am convalescing after a long and serious illness. I am completely numb and so very tired. The flurry of appointments in so many different offices in Limoges, my return papers being handed from one official to another, from one rubber stamp to the next, left me feeling sick at heart. And then the journey back, the frantic scramble to board the train at Limoges, and crossing the demarcation line at Vierzon at dead of night. I shall never forget the sight of two German soldiers entering our compartment by the dull light of their lamp, punctiliously greeting us with a *'Sieurs, dames'*, doubtless because they think it is the height of courtesy and terribly French. These are the first German soldiers I have seen. They demand to see my return papers, scrutinizing them in minute detail, checking all the dates and stamps before finally waving their lamp in front of my face. Whatever for? My photograph isn't on any of the documents. My appearance evidently proves inoffensive, and they indicate with a guttural grunt that I am in order. Idiotic though it is, my nerves are strained to breaking point. My teeth are chattering: I hope they can't tell, but I'm terrified the Germans will overhear their deafening clatter, like crazy castanets. How sickening it is to have to submit to inspection by these people, when all you want is to go home.

Arriving back in Paris, I find everything so utterly changed
that I wonder if there isn't something wrong with me. I examine
myself in the mirror. The results are conclusive: over the last
six weeks I have aged, and I have lost weight. But what about
my morale? What mirror could show me the ravages there? And
yet I believe – what am I saying? – I am convinced that my
way of thinking has not changed. It is other people, the people
around me, who are different from the way they used to be.
They have acquired a secretive, furtive air, a *je-ne-sais-quoi* of
petty, mean-spirited, smug satisfaction that they are still alive.

At the gates of the Palais de Chaillot a sign has appeared
announcing that entrance to the museums is free for German
troops. The library of the Musée des Arts et Traditions Populaires
has already been reclassified and purged. An edition of Lévy-
Bruhl's *Morceaux choisis*, with a dedication by the author, has
had its flyleaf ripped out. A new book entitled *Les Races* by a
certain Montandon sits near Lévy-Bruhl's works, and already the
shelves are full of works by German authors. A set of photographs
of the strikes of 1936, extremely fine and of great interest, has
vanished from our archive of folk traditions, meanwhile, as has
every trace of documentation from the museums of the USSR.

On its appointed date, a meeting of the 'Folklore Society'
is held. An unaccustomed throng squeezes into a small room
in the Ecole du Louvre. Among this crowd are unfamiliar faces
and – God help us – ladies decked out in all their finery. The
speaker is someone I have never heard of. Fulsome in his praise
of the work of our museum and effusive in his pride in 'the
motherland', he flourishes empty words and sentimental
phrases. Not a word about science. Instead he drones on about
the traditions of France – the *authentic* traditions of France –
regaling us in conclusion with a portrait of the ideal French
village, purged henceforth of the godless schoolteachers who
have brought all our present misfortunes on our heads. I scan
the audience. Most of their expressions register approval. At

the back of the room, however, I notice our great master and
mentor Marcel Mauss. His Semitic features, alert and intelligent, wear an inscrutable smile, timeless like that of the
Buddha, a combination of irony, composure and confidence.
The smile of a great and serene intelligence that floats above
all this, that knows everything, that foresees everything. For
an instant our eyes meet, and in his gaze I find what I have
been looking for. Reassured at last, I know that it is not I who
have changed. It is not I who have taken leave of my senses:
it is they who have gone mad – stark staring mad.

At the end of the meeting I am one of the first to leave. I
hear someone remark that Jean Cassou is back in Paris: I have
to see him, I have to see him now. At the Palais-Royal Métro
station I notice a Paris gendarme saluting a German officer
with obsequious servility. Rooted to the spot, I watch as he
repeats the gesture over and over again for the benefit of every
passing officer – stiff, mechanical, German already.

I find Cassou in his office. He too has aged. In six weeks
his hair has turned white and he appears to have shrunk into
himself. But his smile is still the same. Mme Cassou and little
Isabelle are still in the free zone and will soon be back. We
talk freely, comparing our impressions and discovering that
they are much the same. He mentions Marcel Abraham and
remarks that he too thinks like us. Suddenly I blurt out why
I have come to see him, telling him that I feel I will go mad,
literally, if I don't do something, if I don't react somehow.
Cassou confides that he feels the same, that he shares my fears.
The only remedy is for us to act together, to form a group of
ten like-minded comrades, no more. To meet on agreed days
to exchange news, to write and distribute pamphlets and tracts,
and to share summaries of French radio broadcasts from London.
I don't harbour many illusions about the practical effects of
our actions, but simply keeping our sanity will be success of
a kind. The ten of us will stick together, trying between us

to get to grips with the situation. Basically, it will be a way of keeping our spirits up. Cassou agrees, and says that we can definitely count on Marcel Abraham. I suggest we should include Jean and Colette Duval, who will soon be back in Paris. That makes five of us already. Simply talking about our 'organization' makes us feel better. Cassou is already joking about our 'secret society'. He's been studying the Carbonari for too long. He will be the leader of our group: a leader of huge energy and intelligence and – a necessity in present times – a finely tuned, ironic sense of humour. Within ten minutes he has found us a meeting place: the offices of the publishing company owned by the Emile-Paul brothers. That makes seven. We agree to meet next week, and I return home with a lighter heart.

Paris, 7 August 1940

In early June I spotted Stefan Zweig's latest book, *Spinoza*, in the window of a bookshop on avenue Kléber. Today I hurry over there to buy a copy. The book is no longer in the window, and the bookseller informs me that she is not allowed to sell it any more. I refuse to give up, and in the end she reveals that the Zweig books are packed up in the room behind the shop; after swearing me to secrecy, she eventually agrees to let me have a copy. It appears that the list of banned books has already been drawn up, and that they will be destroyed. So we no longer have the right to read or say what we want in the privacy of our own homes? No doubt they would also take away our right to think if they could. But that they can never do. For the moment they are stronger than us, so let them pulp our best books; but never, ever will they reduce our spirits to pulp! When will the house-to-house searches start, the rifling of private libraries? I suppose the Bible will be classified as subversive because it is non-Aryan! All Jewish authors are banned; we can only be grateful that this will leave us more time to savour the literary delights of Paul Bourget, Henry Bordeaux, Abel Bonnard and their ilk.

Paris, 15 August 1940

From the Métro window on my way home yesterday I witnessed a poignant, painful spectacle. It was near La Motte-Picquet station, where the line runs above street level. In the middle of the avenue de La Motte-Picquet, I saw a column of French soldiers flanked by German troops. They were prisoners-of-war being marched from one camp to another. The man sitting opposite me was also watching them. It's years since I last cried, but yesterday I felt the tears rolling down my cheeks; the stranger opposite me also wept. In a low voice he murmured, 'To see such a sight, Madame, French prisoners in our own country, in Paris, herded like animals . . .'

But today the Métro offered me a scene of consolation. A little French soldier, shabby but clean, apparently free but doubtless in the service of the public cleansing department. Beside him a tall German soldier, big, beefy and pink, tightly strapped into a spotless uniform. He is smoking a cigarette. They all smoke in the Métro precisely because it's not allowed, as they well know from numerous signs in German. For a while he observes the Frenchman with a faintly condescending smirk, almost avuncular. Suddenly he whips out his cigarettes and offers him one. The little Frenchman is gasping for a cigarette, you can see it in his eyes; but without batting an eyelid he refuses, simply, clearly and categorically, with an icy 'non merci'. He will never know how much pleasure he gave me, that little unknown soldier, defeated and betrayed, but still so proud and dignified.

Paris, 18 August 1940

Is it my imagination, or is Jean Cassou less hunched than he
was last week? Now I can see again the Jean Cassou of 1936.
Yesterday Madeleine Le Verrier lent me a tract that she had just
been given, and I made a copy of it. Cassou had already seen it
in several places. Will the people who produced *33 Conseils à
l'occupé* ('33 Hints to the Occupied') ever know what they have
done for us, and probably for thousands of others? A glimmer
of light in the darkness . . . Now we know for certain that we
are not alone. There are other people who think like us, who
are suffering and organizing the struggle: soon a network will
cover the whole of France, and our little group will be just one
link in a mighty chain. We are absolutely overjoyed.

Cassou tells me that when he explained our plans to him,
Marcel Abraham made a joke of it. And – naturally – joined
us without a moment's hesitation. He has been very closely
involved and active in politics for over a decade, and knows
everyone in Paris, so his advice will be invaluable. He has also
made contact with the writer Claude Aveline; we all know
Aveline of old, and have the greatest respect for the sincerity
of his convictions, his intelligence and his talent. He is with
us, as are the publisher Emile-Paul and his brother, whose
offices do not run on German time: refusing to put their clocks
forward was their first symbolic gesture of resistance. Right
from the beginning, since June, they have been committed
wholeheartedly to the struggle, and they are only too happy
for us to meet every week in their offices at 14 rue de l'Abbaye.
So this is where we shall organize our 'conspiracy'.

Christiane Desroches is also with us. She is an Egyptologist
attached to the Musée du Louvre, and she and I have known
each other since 1936, when we worked together in a variety
of organizations under the umbrella of the Front Populaire. I
introduce Jean Aubier: far younger than the rest of us, he will
have access to the student world, and his flawless knowledge

of German will be an invaluable asset to us. I make Cassou laugh when I appoint myself the group's 'runner', like the apprentices in couture houses who run errands between the different ateliers. The telephone is virtually out of bounds to us now, so it will be my job to carry instructions and advice between members. Aveline has already dubbed us the 'Free French in France'. Then we talk shop. From our reading of the signs, Jean Cassou and I have fears – only too well founded, alas – that our positions within the Musées Nationaux hang by a thread. Cassou's past activities – his support for the Republicans in Spain, his contributions to newspapers of the far left, his friendships and beliefs – all conspire to render him suspect in the eyes of our new masters.

As far as I'm concerned the atmosphere at the museum has become absolutely stifling. I have been relieved of virtually every single one of my former responsibilities. My duties are now carried out by 'volunteers' conjured up out of thin air: ladies of considerable charm, elegance and wealth. We'd never heard of any of them before, and they all boast of being at the very least 'close to someone close to the Maréchal'. Raising their eyes to heaven, they prattle about Vichy and a new France, strengthened and revitalized by her ordeal. Meanwhile, I hang around like a blind man at a funfair. They are careful to let me know that *they* know all about my involvement with publications too shameful to mention, about my teaching at the workers' university, about the workers' tours of museums that I organized; and they make it quite clear that my opinions are not those of a society lady, or at least not of their idea of society. The chief curator has thoughtfully advised me to 'play to my advantage' the fact that my son is an officer in the navy. Evidently having a son who is a naval officer is enough to expiate many sins. My declaration that I would not broadcast again on 'Radio-Paris' until the Germans had gone was not exactly warmly received, and I have asked in the plainest possible terms to be excused from any presentations to German officers, who are received by the curator with disconcerting cordiality. Jean Cassou and I carry little weight in the administrative scales of this 'new' France. Laughing (for the sake of appearances), we wonder how on earth we are going to survive after we've been sacked.

Paris, 1 September 1940

Mme Cassou is back. She invited us all to her house today: Jean and Colette Duval, the Emile-Paul brothers, Marcel Abraham, Christiane Desroches, Claude Aveline, Jean Aubier and myself. Marcel Abraham had lost no time in bringing documents to show us, and we could tell he was pleased to have something to fill his days now that his routine has been turned on its head. In theory he should be going back to teach the new term at the Lycée Carnot, but will he be allowed to, being 'non-Aryan', and having worked so closely with so many ministers who are now distinctly out of favour? We are all worried about him. Jean Duval, whose activities and opinions are less widely known, will have no difficulty in returning to his teaching job at the Lycée Condorcet, and Colette will probably carry on with her books for young people. We say 'probably', for what will become of the *Nouvelle Revue Française* or of Editions Gallimard who publish her books, so sound and full of youthful energy? Christiane Desroches is still attached to the Egyptology department at the Louvre, and as the top brass there are unaware of her political activities in 1936–7 she shouldn't encounter any problems, so we have no worries on her account. Jean Aubier, grandson of a major industrialist, is struggling with the many technical problems the business is encountering. Claude Aveline has decided to work for his friends and publishers Emile-Paul. Jean Cassou and I are still (for how many more weeks?) civil servants. So much for our material circumstances. As for our morale, we are all on good form. We all know and respect each other as much as we enjoy each other's company. We discuss our future activities. Idle chitchat is banned, once and for all. We will start by distributing tracts. Colette, Christiane and I will type out as many copies as we can of *33 Conseils à l'occupé.* Then we will start producing our own tracts, and as soon as we can get hold of a roneo machine we will publish a broadsheet. With an air of mystery, Cassou confides that he is on the track of just such a roneo machine. He will vouchsafe more at our next meeting. We agree that all ten of us will meet in the Emile-Paul offices every Tuesday evening at six.

Paris, 22 September 1940

Things are going even better and faster than I had hoped. The mysterious roneo machine that Cassou mentioned last week is none other than the one belonging to the Musée de l'Homme! He has seen Dr Rivet. 'Work' has now begun at the Musée de l'Homme. They have already distributed copies of Dr Rivet's splendid open letter to Maréchal Pétain, in which he expresses all our criticisms in a manner that is at once elegant, considered and firm. Cassou has given us about a hundred copies of the letter for immediate distribution. He has made an appointment for me to see Dr Rivet. The fact that I have an office in the Palais de Chaillot makes my task so much easier. There is even an internal telephone link between the Musée des Arts et Traditions Populaires and the Musée de l'Homme. Luck is on our side!

Paris, 25 September 1940

We have duplicated thousands of copies of our first tract, *Vichy fait la guerre* ('Vichy wages war'). French soldiers have fired on other French soldiers at Dakar: the start of a civil war in aid of our liberation. Cassou is the author of this short tract, scathingly intelligent, witty and extremely concise. Which makes it a great deal easier to copy.

Already we have come a long way since our first typed leaflet of 19 September.

Dr Rivet has put me in contact with his assistant Boris Vildé, who is in charge of all anti-German activities at the Musée de l'Homme. I know Vildé a little from the time when I was secretary of the scientific committee of APECS (*Association pour l'étude de la culture soviétique*), and Vildé gave a lecture on exploration of the Arctic. I already have the greatest respect for his cool and luminous intelligence and his remarkable character. I am happy and proud to be working with him. A Russian by birth – a child of the Revolution, as he is only thirty-three – he has had to support himself since the age of eleven. His life has been one long and extraordinary adventure. As a naturalized Frenchman he was a serving soldier until he was taken prisoner, when he managed to escape, covering three hundred kilometres on foot despite having an injured knee. Now he is a steadfast worker for the cause, as Dr Rivet observes: 'Vildé is a son of the Revolution, he carries the Revolution within him, he understands how revolutions work.'

In spite of his reticence, I gather that Boris hopes to use the American embassy to gain the ear of the Intelligence Service. He tells me that the first thing we must do is start a newspaper. Jean Cassou will be the editor-in-chief. I tell him about my techniques for distributing tracts and capturing the attention of our select readership. The only person who risks arrest is myself, as I am the only person exposed; I pretend that I have received the tract by that morning's post, then I copy it and distribute it far and wide. My most colourful accomplice in this work is a concierge called Mme Homs. Spending her days glued to the radio from London, she nurses a burning desire to 'serve'. From the depths of her little *concierg-erie* she distributes leaflets with professional skill. One of the lodgers in her building then reproduces them in enormous numbers. A pharmacist and his wife have also set up an excellent distribution network, ensuring that the tracts are copied and sent to Fontainebleau for duplication on a roneo machine. We 'accidentally' leave tracts behind us on the Métro, in post offices and in letterboxes. Mme Jean Cassou slips them under fabric remnants in department stores: wherever they lurk, they are found by nimble fingers and read by eager eyes.

There are lots of other people I'd like to involve in the cause. After the museum closes on Thursday, Vildé is coming to the Brasserie du Coq on place du Trocadéro to meet Jean Cassou. Already I'm relishing the delightful prospect of introducing them to each other. Tonight, after dark, I plan to plaster the walls around where I live with stickers that I've made using sticky labels. Using the museum's large-font typewriter, I have typed '*Vive le général de Gaulle*' on them. I've distributed these stickers to all our friends, and they are like excited children at the prospect of putting them up in public urinals, telephone boxes and Métro tunnels. Maurice Braudey, the sole museum guard on our side, goes one better: he pedals up behind German trucks on his bike and carefully sticks small signs on the rear doors reading (again typed by me on the museum machine) '*Nous sommes pour le général de Gaulle*' (we support General de Gaulle). Maurice Braudey also distributes tracts in the suburbs, in the working-class areas where he has been an activist for years.

Paris, 20 October 1940

Jean Cassou has been dismissed, followed a fortnight later by Mme Agnès Humbert. On both occasions M. Jaujard, director of the Musées Nationaux, comported himself impeccably. The orders come from Vichy and no reasons for dismissal are given. M. Jaujard's sole duty is to enforce them. He asks me if I am a member of the Communist Party. I reply that I am not, adding that – as he knows – I was for a long time secretary of the APECS, I have contributed articles to *La Vie ouvrière* and several other progressive publications, and I was secretary of the left-wing Union des Intellectuels Français. 'Along with France's finest,' M. Jaujard responds courteously. Our conversation turns to Cassou, whom he likes and admires: 'His presence is an honour not only to the Musées Nationaux but also to France.' This is his considered verdict. The esteem of our director gives us heart and seems to bolster our confidence. We have a few months' salary to come, and after that, well – 'sufficient unto the day is the evil thereof'. We'll just have to wait and see. Marcel Abraham is going to lose his job. Georges Friedmann has had the course he was teaching at Toulouse taken away from him, and has decided to stay down there for as long as this turmoil continues.

Our Tuesday evening meetings in the Emile-Paul offices are invaluable. We all bring our latest news, snippets passed by word of mouth that are hardly cheering. But the way that Marcel, Claude and Jean tell them they take on an indefinably roguish, Parisian air that reduces us all to giggles.

Jean Cassou has really hit it off with Vildé, and now Claude Aveline has met him too. Like me, they both sense that Vildé is in contact with an organization of major influence. The Intelligence Service? The Deuxième Bureau, or perhaps another French group born out of present circumstances? We have no idea, and we all know that we mustn't ask questions. We have put our trust in Vildé, and we must be guided by him. We inspire our companions who do not know Vildé with our own faith in him. We understand that he collects British servicemen from the north of France and takes them or arranges for them to be taken into the free zone, and from there to Spain and Portugal, and back to Britain. He has also spoken of young Frenchmen following the same route to join de Gaulle's army.

How bizarre it all is! Here we are, most of us the wrong side of forty, careering along like students all fired up with passion and fervour, in the wake of a leader of whom we know absolutely nothing, of whom none of us has even seen a photograph. In the whole course of human history, has there ever been anything quite like it? Thousands upon thousands of people, fired by blind faith, following an unknown figure. Perhaps this strange anonymity is even an asset: the mystery of the unknown!

Paris, 15 November 1940

Last week Boris Vildé appeared in my office, a worried man: he has been expecting two British airmen to arrive any day, and now all of a sudden he's been told to expect five. 'Where on earth am I going to put them all?' he asks gloomily. I explain that I don't live on my own but with my mother. I'm sure, nevertheless, that whatever the threats broadcast over the radio, my mother won't give a second thought to the dangers involved in sheltering a young Englishman.

I'm not wrong. Maman agrees straight away. We will put the Englishman in Jean's room, we decide, and together we make up a story to tell the daily help. Pierre is away on his travels, so will not be compromised by the Englishman's presence. But we impose one condition: the young man must not leave the apartment while he is here; he will be our prisoner. I really couldn't bear the idea of him being plucked like a flower on a stroll through 'gay Paree'.

Paris, 20 November 1940

The Englishman Vildé brought us turns out to be a Pole: a young officer cadet, shy and polite, anxious not to be a nuisance and above all not to leave us out of pocket. Every time we sit down to eat he checks with charming directness: 'No coupons?' We reassure him. 'Not too expensive?' We reassure him again, as always, and only then, his conscience eased, will Leopold tuck in with a twenty-year-old's appetite.

Pierre, who has returned unexpectedly from his travels, has hit it off with our young friend. As they can barely understand each other their conversations are like extended charades. When the time comes for him to leave, both Leopold and Pierre are moved. It is still dark when I usher Leopold to the Métro station where Vildé is waiting for him. Soon he will be passed into the free zone, where he is expected at a chateau near Vierzon. From there he will be guided to the Spanish border, which he will have to cross on foot. In Barcelona he will be taken under the wing of the British consul. So that's it, at last! Now we really are affiliated with an organization, with the real thing! Some of our friends were beginning to have their doubts: now I shall be able to set their minds completely at rest. Last week they were pulling my leg again, with Marcel Abraham pretending to scoff: 'That wretched Agnès has got us all mixed up in this mysterious affair, following Lord knows who – maybe none other than Casimir de La Rocque!'

Paris, 25 November 1940

Vige telephones, asking me to go round straight away. It's clear from her voice that it's urgent. Vige and Jean have a serious problem of some kind. On my way there I wonder what it can be. They are worried to death about their eldest son, Tiapa, a headstrong fifteen-year-old. Last week he insisted on sporting a safety pin in his buttonhole. 'It's my insignia,' he told me, *'une épingle anglaise.'*

He has been in trouble with the police on numerous occasions, and since the demonstrations of 11 November his parents have been beside themselves. Has he got himself arrested? No, it is Tiapa himself who opens the door. Beneath his shock of dark gold hair he wears a strange expression, and he looks older.

Quietly and earnestly, he explains that it is his grandfather, Paul Langevin, who has just been arrested without warning. He was taken away forty-eight hours ago, and no one knows where he is. They have informed the chief of police, who claims to know nothing. Could he have been deported to Germany? Vige and Jean ask me to go round to a number of friends, in case they can find out any information. Above all, they want the French radio in London to know about this arbitrary arrest. I will write at once to Georges Friedmann in Toulouse. He will make sure that those in the free zone know what is happening in Paris. The events of 11 November appear to have been a curtain-raiser. Here comes the Reign of Terror that we have been waiting for . . .

Paris, late November 1940

The editorial committee for our newspaper is settled: it is to consist of Marcel Abraham, Jean Cassou and Claude Aveline. Vildé says we can have three pages. The front page will be written by '*ces messieurs*', the mysterious gentlemen who supply the paper and organize the printing. Our group of ten will receive four or five hundred copies, and it will be up to us to distribute these judiciously, especially to people who have the means to make more copies. The name of our organ? Vildé said they had thought of *Libération*, but since that seemed rather premature they (who? we have no idea) had settled on *Résistance*. Discussion turns to the political line we should adopt. De Gaulle will have all our respect and support: we have to be prudent and give recognition to his political ideals. We should also be circumspect for the moment in our references to that ridiculous old fool Pétain. All of us have got the measure of this small-time Franco, but many other people still have their eyes closed. Events will soon enlighten them. But we risk damaging our own cause if we force it down their throats. From today we start collecting evidence against the 'old man':

passages from Poincaré's *Mémoires*, Lloyd George and
Clemenceau, which we'll put to good use when the time comes;
we'll just push him a little deeper into the mire in which he
is already wallowing. Oh, Montoire!

We are to produce the newspaper at the Martin-Chauffiers'
house, where Claude Aveline is living at the moment. Vildé
tells me that Lewitsky will come to pick up the 'papers' at
the end of the day. Lewitsky? Yes, of course, replies Vildé,
he's been with us from the very beginning. I am delighted. I
have known him since I first started working at the Palais de
Chaillot, and he was always my first port of call whenever I
needed information from the Musée de l'Homme. I love his
impeccable manners, that combination of courtliness and intelligence that is so typically Russian. I'm so delighted that he
is one of us!

Paris, December 1940

Our *canard* has laid its first egg. And oh, our first editorial
meeting!

Jean Cassou, Marcel Abraham and Claude Aveline were quite
emotional, though it was all undercut with typically Parisian
backchat and leg-pulling. We met in Louis Martin-Chauffier's
office, where a minuscule fire was burning. How wonderful it
felt not to be frozen: all four of us were thrilled by this touch
of luxury. Simone Martin-Chauffier brought us a tray of tea –
proper tea – with bread and butter. The atmosphere was snug
and cosy. The men wrote and talked, while I typed up their
articles. Claude has been following military operations in Libya
closely, and will write a few lines on the position of the British
forces. We giggle and call him 'Colonel X'. The thing that
we must get across above all in our first issues, with evidence
to back up our arguments, is that the shortages of food and
other essential supplies that we are suffering are due not to

the British blockade, but rather to wholesale looting by the Germans in all sectors of our economy. Marcel has managed to obtain irrefutable documentation already. Leaning on a corner of the desk and working with enviable ease, Jean Cassou composes phrases of trenchant intelligence, phrases that will carry and be carried from house to house – propaganda, good and true. On the mantelpiece we have propped a photograph of Pétain, agreeing conspiratorially that if the Boches should find us (though how on earth would they?) we'll say that the three friends are writing a play together. The plot is laid out on the desk, ready for all eventualities. I am the typist, naturally. The fire is there so that we can burn any articles in progress. The scene is set. What is there to fear? Claude maintains that I shouldn't walk about carrying my little typewriter. Good heavens above, can a woman not carry a portable typewriter about in broad daylight without it automatically being assumed that she is the typist on an underground newspaper?

Paris, 18 December 1940

Paul Langevin is being held in the Prison de la Santé, in a cell without light or heating. Otherwise he is being well treated. Members of his family were allowed to see him for a few minutes. No accusations have been laid against him. Despite the 'Free Langevin' fliers that have appeared on the walls of Paris, the demonstrations of his students and the petitions of his friends, Paul Langevin remains in German hands. His spirits remain high, needless to say. He confided to Jean that although in his lifetime he had succeeded in solving quite a few problems, this time he had to admit he was flummoxed: however hard he tries, he will never work out why he was arrested.

Paris, late December 1940

I had been thinking about Edouard D., who must be back in Paris by now. I talked to the others about him, and they all agreed that he would be a good recruit. I remembered his activities in 1936, when as principal private secretary to a minister of the Front Populaire he was so easy and straight-forward to deal with, and so generous with both his time and his energies. He is bound to be keen to work with us on the newspaper, and he will distribute it among the circles in which he moves, to which we otherwise have little access.

'Good idea, Agnès. Yes, do go and see him.'

So, *voilà* Agnès with a hundred copies of *Résistance* in her briefcase. Agnès discovers a gentleman who is perfectly cordial, certainly, but with something distant in his manner that she cannot quite put her finger on. A gentleman with one subject of conversation and one only: his grandchildren. He permits her to admire their photographs, he relates every detail of their adorable pranks and their childish mishaps, while Agnès eyes her briefcase bulging with copies of *Résistance*. Edouard D., meanwhile, continues his interminable litany on the Art of being a Grandfather. By now she is convinced that all this lisping sentimentality is designed to prevent her from broach-ing more important subjects, so she asks him straight out what he thinks of current events. 'Events? What events?' he as good as asks. She finds herself obliged to spell it out for him. Victory? A pipedream! De Gaulle? A madman! 'You see,' he says in conclusion, 'I've thought long and hard about it, and I am wholehearted in my support of Pierre Laval and the Maréchal!'

It's people like him that we'll have to watch out for after-wards, when France is free again. We must start drawing up lists of these turncoats, these cowards, these imbeciles. The Fourth Republic will have nothing to do with people like that – or rather it will know what to do with them!

Paris, late December 1940

Quite by chance I bumped into Adolphe Dervaux, the architect. I hadn't seen him for years. He hasn't changed a bit, still as passionate, uncompromising and fiery as ever. We talk about the current state of things, and he feels the same as I do. We have lunch together. Gradually I start to tell him about my 'work'. He evinces interest. He reveals to me that he has a friend, Roger Pons, an air force captain in the last war, who can lay his hands on documents and maps. I become aware of every ounce of blood in my body rushing to my head. At last! Now I can see an opportunity to do something more than propaganda! But can this Roger be persuaded to trust me? Adolphe Dervaux understands the grave risks his friend will run in putting his trust in an unknown woman who can offer him no guarantees. On the spur of the moment, I offer Jean Cassou as my guarantor. Too bad, his name is out of the bag – but for a catch like this it's worth it! Adolphe Dervaux knows Cassou slightly, and says that Roger Pons admires him as much for his political activity as for his work in the arts. Rashly, I arrange a meeting for Sunday morning at Adolphe Dervaux's house: Jean Cassou will meet the airman, and we will have some documents at last. I'm sure of it. Leaving Adolphe Dervaux, I feel absolutely certain of the success of my scheme. As I walk down the rue de Dunkerque I am oblivious to the slush, the mud, the pathetic shop window displays. I'm completely taken up with my idea. What have I achieved up till now? Innocuous propaganda, probably listened to only by like-minded souls. But now I'm going to have maps. Didn't Adolphe Dervaux mention one showing an airstrip laid out just recently somewhere near Paris?

Yes, a map . . . and with that my mood swings abruptly, in a way that is so typical of me, and my heart sinks into my boots. OK, a map – and what will I do with this map? Pass it on to other people, and I know all too well what they will do with it. Because of my meddling there will be widows, inconsolable mothers, fatherless children. Spirits, great minds perhaps, snuffed out before they have a chance to make their contribution to the world. As a direct result of my meddling, people – French people, living peaceful lives – will be killed and wounded, children maimed. Where are all my lofty humanitarian ideals now? Have I taken leave of my senses? How could I ever have wanted to be involved in such a filthy business? I won't go on Sunday. I won't mention it to Jean Cassou.

As I reach the Métro station I look up, and there before me, heading for the Gare de l'Est, are two German soldiers. Trudging in front of them are three porters weighed down with packages: bolts of cloth with I don't know how many shoeboxes tied on to them with string. Suddenly I am reminded of one of those old colonial newsreels – *Afrique vous parle* ('Voice of Africa') or some such – with those long processions of 'native bearers' carrying the baggage of two or three white explorers, or exploiters. A pitiful sight, it always made my heart contract with pain. And now, as I stand in the slush outside the station watching this same spectacle unfold, the same but even more sordid, I am rooted to the spot. We simply have to stop them, we can't allow them to colonize us, to carry off all our goods on the backs of our men while they stroll along, arms swinging, faces wreathed in smiles, boots and belts polished and gleaming. We can't let it happen. And to stop it happening we have to kill. Kill like wild beasts, kill to survive. Kill by stealth, kill by treachery, kill with premeditation, kill the innocent. It has to be done, and I will do it. Later on I'll tell Jean Cassou about the meeting that I've set up for him, and on Sunday we'll go together to meet Roger Pons, who will give us what we need to instigate a massacre. What a filthy business!

Paris, late December 1940

'My dear,' remarks Jean Cassou as we leave Adolphe Dervaux's house, where we have just met Roger Pons, airman of the last war and the Spanish Civil War, 'this Roger will be our right-hand man.' And he's a draughtsman, what's more. He is a member of a group of officers who were waiting for one thing: the link that would enable them to pass their documents discreetly to those who can make good use of them. Roger Pons fizzes with life and enthusiasm like a twenty-year-old, while Adolphe Dervaux has rediscovered all the fervour with which he fought for Alfred Dreyfus as one of his earliest supporters. I think we can say that our morning has not been entirely wasted.

Paris, late December 1940

This evening I arranged to meet Roger Pons at La Closerie des Lilas, where I introduced him to Vildé. The two of them hit it off immediately. Among other things, Roger promised Vildé a map of an underground aircraft hangar that has apparently just been constructed at Dreux. Vildé was full of interest. I offered to put them in contact with some Spaniards who are more or less in hiding. Militiamen from the Civil War, they are experts in the art of blowing up tanks with a well-aimed grenade. This manoeuvre could be taught to our soldiers, since Vildé has stated clearly in my hearing and Claude's that to his knowledge we already have over twelve thousand armed men in Paris. He has even asked us to organize them into squads of ten. Antoine Schlicklin, whom we have nicknamed 'M. de Saint-Maur', is already on the track of physical fitness instructors to train up young men in the suburbs: yet another highly dedicated agent introduced to Vildé and Lewitsky by me. I feel like a huntsman's dog laying game birds at its master's feet.

Paris, January 1941

Yesterday Marcel Abraham pulled a copy of *Le Matin* out of his briefcase. On the front page, a few lines announced the arrest of the barrister Nordmann for distributing copies of *Résistance*. We are all filled with alarm. When I saw Vildé just now at the Brasserie du Coq, he confirmed that Nordmann was indeed one of us, and also that careless mistakes had been made. I could tell that he didn't want to discuss it, so I didn't ask him any more. He left me for a few moments to talk to a short, dark young man wearing a Ford Cars lapel badge. Clearly this lad had been waiting for Vildé; I watched them as they talked. Vildé gave orders, while the young man listened respectfully and attentively. When he came back to my table, Vildé explained in a few words that the young man he had been talking to was known as the 'Kid'.[2]

The Kid passes documents to the British. Tomorrow he is leaving for the free zone, Vildé added. We talk in veiled terms of documents and weapons. Naturally I am not privy to the details, but I have put Vildé in contact with Emile Delion, who introduced Madeleine Le Verrier to me. Any day now, Emile Delion should be setting in train an important new initiative in Marseille. Vildé congratulates me for bringing him into the group. Delighted by this praise, I am convinced now of the truth of a remark he made to me when we first started working together: 'Many of us will be shot, and all of us will go to prison.' There can be no doubt that over the past few weeks our work has become more serious, while our organization appears to be growing.

Paris, 20 January 1941

Vildé has just managed to obtain convalescent leave, necessitated not so much by the state of his knee as by the state of the country. Nordmann is still in prison, and there is furtive

2 René Sénéchal.

talk of other arrests. While Vildé is in the free zone, Lewitsky will stand in for him.

For a few days now our friend Georges Friedmann has been back with us. Having returned discreetly to Paris, he is staying with Jean and Colette Duval. He was present at our last meeting in the Emile-Paul offices, and I just had time to introduce him to Vildé. Friedmann was most impressed, describing Vildé as 'the very image of the young communists I knew in the USSR'. Soon they will see each other again in Toulouse, where Vildé is due to go shortly. Friedmann will take care of the newspaper in the free zone; perhaps he will find a printer in Toulouse? He thinks that propaganda is more important in the free zone than in the occupied zone. Vildé agrees with him: they argue that in the occupied zone the Germans do our job for us, whereas in the free zone the plague is less noticeable to ill-informed eyes, ears, nostrils and – most important of all – minds.

Paris, 25 January 1941

Where was it that they took me? I'll never know, but it was a delightful little Left Bank restaurant, warm and cosy. The streets are so shrouded in darkness that Paris is unrecognizable. Jean Cassou, Abraham, Aveline and I had spent the whole afternoon working. The newspaper is due out on 1 February. Then at about eight o'clock we all met up to take Georges Friedmann – sadly about to leave us to cross the demarcation line again – out to dinner. For three hours we left all our cares behind us and just had fun. Not a single *haricot vert* to be seen in the little dining room chosen by our friends, just true Parisians. At our table were Simone Martin-Chauffier and the three editors of *Résistance*, Friedmann, happy to be surrounded by such affection, Jean and Colette Duval and their son André, suddenly no longer a child but a young man, tall and straight.

The conversation turned to recipes, and I heard Friedmann joking about the meal I had served up to him at home the night before: sautéed swede with black pudding. Never will he know how long I had to queue in the freezing cold outside that wretched charcuterie on rue des Cinq-Diamants before I eventually managed to carry off that miserable lump of black pudding – tasteless and fatless, but 'off-rations' . . .

Paris, 28 January 1941

At some point I suppose we'll have to think about earning a living. Being sacked by the Vichy government is very congenial in terms of the generous amounts of free time it allows us, which we are only too delighted to devote to *Résistance*, but from the point of view of putting food in our stomachs it leaves a lot to be desired. It's always a struggle to scrape together enough money to buy the stamps to mail the paper.

I've hatched a scheme with Iria Deslous.[3] Jean Cassou met her at my house, and at once fell under the spell of her beauty, wit and piercing intelligence. She suggests that we pretend to buy an art gallery belonging to a Jewish art dealer, while drawing up a private contract with him guaranteeing that we will return it to him after the Germans have left. The extraordinary upturn in the art market should enable us to earn a very decent living over the months to come. I suggest calling our new business '*Aux débarqués*' ('for those who have been kicked out'), but Cassou tops me with '*Au débarquement de Cythère*' ('Pilgrims Leaving Cythera'). So here we are, make-believe partners in a make-believe business. Ida Cassou seems pleased with the idea, poking fun at us as though we are a couple of children playing at shops.

3 Project leader at the Musée National des Arts et Traditions Populaires.

Paris, 30 January 1941

Cassou and I have been out in search of an empty gallery. All afternoon it's been nothing but tramping about, discussions and negotiations. We are exhausted.

We go into a café to sit down for a few minutes. There I show Jean my latest project. On blue-and-white five-franc notes, I type in red letters: '*Vive le général de Gaulle.*' No one can afford to destroy a bank note, so they pass from hand to hand, and my mission is accomplished. Cassou laughs, and reveals in the strictest secrecy that he goes round putting up fliers in public urinals. General de Gaulle will surely forgive his humble servants their ignominious means.

Paris, 5 February 1941

The Kid has brought me several thousand envelopes. Four hundred have been given to Antoine Schlicklin (M. de Saint-Maur), along with the *Résistance* file. He has volunteered to organize the typing of the addresses. I have seen a lot of Lewitsky over the past few days, and he has shown me the group's 'mailbox': a shop selling religious articles in Auteuil. This is where we are to leave documents in future. As soon as the envelopes are ready, I must send off the copies of the paper that I shall pick up tomorrow from the Müller bookshop on rue Monsieur-le-Prince. The password? I am to ask if Müller can find me a first edition of *Les Fables de La Fontaine*. Lewitsky has ominous news concerning Nordmann: he has not been freed, far from it. He has managed to send some dirty linen home, with bloodstains all over one sock and the lower half of a pair of underpants. We all know what that means. Lewitsky tells me that it is absolutely imperative that we adopt pseudonyms: from now on he will be Chasal; I meanwhile shall revert to Delphine Girard, the name I adopted in my *La Vie ouvrière* days, after Gaston Monmousseau joked that I should be called the Delphine de Girardin of the working classes! We must exercise the utmost caution, it appears; specialist police have arrived from Berlin. Pass it on!

Paris, 14 February 1941

Iria Deslous telephones: Cassou and I must go to her house immediately. Something is obviously up, but what? We give way to wild speculation. Iria's voice, normally so measured, was utterly changed; it definitely can't be good news.

She tells us straight out: forty-eight hours ago Lewitsky and his fiancée Yvonne Oddon, librarian at the Musée de l'Homme, were arrested. A dozen other colleagues at the museum have been interrogated and set free. Dr Rivet just managed to get away and is safely in the free zone. Iria urges us to destroy all compromising documents as a matter of the greatest urgency. We dash off to do so.

Paris, 18 February 1941

I got home yesterday to find the Kid here. He had just left Vige and Jean. I didn't know they were in contact with each other. He brought me a letter from Vildé, who had already heard about the arrest of his comrades. Vildé asks me to carry on bringing out the newspaper, in order to deflect suspicion from our friends. He didn't need to ask. The 15 February edition is ready: Colette, Christiane and I had it typed up already. The Emile-Paul brothers think they will soon be able to put another roneo machine at our disposal.

But how do we get in touch with our liaison agents? With Vildé gone and Lewitsky arrested, the chain is broken. The Kid, who tells me his name is Sénéchal (his false identity is Raymond Sauvet), seems to know nothing about our mysterious 'gentlemen'. He mentions a comrade whose name I haven't heard before: Georges Ithier, presently in hiding in a highly discreet hotel behind the Gare Saint-Lazare. Jean Cassou has at his house the aviation map that I begged him to collect from Roger Pons three days ago, together with a map and information concerning the submarine base at Saint-Nazaire. Giving the Kid my signature as a password, I send him to get the documents from Cassou's house. By tomorrow evening the Kid will have deposited everything in Toulouse, along with a few copies of *Résistance* and our letters.

Paris, 20 February 1941

Jean Cassou wouldn't let me go on my own to see Ithier, as the hotel where he is living is also a brothel for German soldiers. This is the place where members of our group conceal not only themselves but also British airmen, apparently in perfect safety. The madam and her daughter are ardent supporters of de Gaulle, and English is the lingua franca. Ithier guided Dr Rivet into the free zone, and is forever taking over both British soldiers and French supporters of de Gaulle; soon, he says, he will be making regular trips to Spain. Born in the Republic of Panama, Ithier is as fluent in English and Spanish as he is in French. He is due to leave soon, taking with him a large postbag for the free zone. I have begged Friedmann to do everything he possibly can to ensure that Vildé knows we are carrying on with our work and not giving up, and to make sure he stays in the free zone.

Paris, March 1941

I have just come back from the Cassous' house. I went there to discuss our business plans, but Cassou told me what I had suspected for some weeks now: things are getting too hot for him in Paris. Claude Aveline has already left, urged on by his friends, and Marcel Abraham is obediently getting ready to go.

Cassou and his family clearly have to go too, and with the utmost urgency. This forced departure of my friends and comrades comes as a tremendous blow to me. Roger Pons, to whom I was less close, has gone too. But one of his friends, whom we know as 'Manon', will pass on to me any documents and information supplied by his armed group. Work on that side of things goes on, and the officers have regrouped. But what will become of the newspaper without its three editors? Jean and I come to the same conclusion: we must ask Pierre Brossolette to help us carry on. We met him recently at Madeleine Le Verrier's. In addition to his huge talent as a journalist, we liked everything about him. Has he not given up all his journalism, so as not to have to deal with either the occupying forces or Vichy? He neither writes nor broadcasts now. To earn a living and support his family, he has bought a bookshop and stationer's opposite the Lycée Janson. Behind the counter there a smiling Mme Pierre Brossolette, quite as dignified and uncompromising as her husband, sells pens and Latin grammars to schoolchildren whose parents have no idea of the true identity of the shop's new owners.

Pierre Brossolette accepts the post of editor-in-chief of *Résistance* with great good humour, and we chuckle over the pompous title we have given him. Jean Duval will be his deputy, and I shall carry on with all my humble duties: typist, secretary, go-between and runner. I have recently added many new names to my list of clients, and now dash hither and thither on the Métro, delivering newspapers wherever they are wanted. Communications may be difficult, but with a bit of goodwill and determination nothing is impossible.

Paris, March 1941

The Kid is back from Toulouse, safe and sound. This time he is got up as a mechanic. I scrutinize his appearance with a critical eye: his overalls are far too spruce and clean, as if they are fresh

out of the box. 'Next time,' he laughs, 'I'll come as a curé.' He
tells me how risky the journey has become. The Germans have
now doubled their ranks with fearsome police dogs. Sadly, I
couldn't give him any news of Lewitsky or Yvonne Oddon. He,
on the other hand, brought news of Vildé, who is doing excellent
work in Toulouse, where he sees a lot of Friedmann. The Kid
is to go and meet up with him. The 15 March edition has to
be ready. Mademoiselle B., daughter of the madam of our famous
brothel, is now actively working with us. On my trips to supply
her with paper and carbon paper I have got to know a charming
fellow called Pierre Walter, who is closely connected with Lewitsky and Vildé. For the moment he is keeping his head down in
his discreet lodgings, as he thinks he may have been followed
over the past few days. He is seriously concerned about Ithier,
of whom we have had no news since his last trip: our great fear
is that he might have been arrested at the demarcation line. I
arrange to meet the Kid at Jean and Colette's house, where we
have been holding our Tuesday meetings for the past few weeks.
We feel it is only prudent to change our 'centre of operations'
fairly frequently. I'm quite sure that the whole group will be
glad to meet young Sénéchal, still a child, but so brave and
resourceful!

Paris, March 1941
Today's meeting at Jean and Colette Duval's house on rue
Monsieur-le-Prince was particularly lively. The men were on
good form. Cassou read to us from the underground newspaper
Pantagruel, and we all had various tracts to share with each
other. It is so inspiring to know that there are thousands and
thousands of Parisians, anonymous and unknown, working like
us – often better than us – to organize a resistance movement
that will soon become a liberation struggle. The focal point
of the meeting was young Sénéchal, who knew neither the

names of his hosts nor, among all the people present, who they were. I had simply told him (old hand that I am now in the art of subterfuge) to go up to the second floor and say that Agnès had sent him.[4] Pierre Brossolette was also there, sharp, lively and witty. He is most attentive to all the doings of our little organization, and appears to give it all his full support. For a while now Colette has had her own little project, and a risky one that we all tease her about. She prowls the local markets, slipping leaflets into the shopping baskets of passing housewives. These tracts explain how the shortages of food and other goods are not caused – as the Germans would have us believe – by the British blockade, but are in fact the consequence of their own systematic plundering of our national reserves.

Paris, March 1941

We can no longer be in any doubt that our friend Ithier has been arrested. He has written to Mme B., the hotel keeper, asking her to send him some books. The Boches caught him, probably at the demarcation line, along with three British servicemen, a number of military documents and our letters, including mine to Friedmann. Ithier's position looks very bad, but we know we can count on him not to talk. My letters carried Friedmann's name and address, so now he is slightly compromised too, although only he would understand their contents. All the names I used were false, and I called our organization the Cercle Alain Fournier, a name we fixed upon one day in case any curious Boches should wonder what our meetings were about. Friends and admirers of Alain Fournier, we seek to honour the memory of the great writer in a variety of ways, notably through the publication of his collected correspondence. The idea of this name for our 'brotherhood' emerged quite spontaneously from

4 René Sénéchal spoke about this meeting to Gaveau, whom he believed to be one of the group leaders but who was in fact an agent of the Gestapo.

the fact that most of our meetings took place in the offices of Emile-Paul, publishers of *Le Grand Meaulnes*.

We feel dreadful about the fate of poor Ithier, but as we talk about it we manage to persuade ourselves that this disaster will not have any further repercussions for our organization, and that our friend will manage to emerge more or less unscathed.

Paris, 18 March 1941

The Kid was due to leave this morning, bearing more letters for Friedmann that I'd taken to the hotel in Belleville where the Kid was in hiding. I explained to him that as a safety precaution I have put only Friedmann's initials on the envelopes. These letters chiefly contain information to be passed on to Vildé.

Jean's ship has finally docked at Martinique.[5] He has taken all the necessary steps so that he can marry Monique by proxy, and once they are married my young daughter-in-law hopes to obtain permission to go out there to join her husband. So we have been on a trip to the jeweller's to buy the wedding rings. There we discovered that there is no more platinum to be had, no white gold, no yellow gold. Customers have to provide their own metal. Maman has donated her wedding ring, Monique's mother a signet ring. 'Yes, but,' the jeweller explained after a pause, 'you have to deduct 30 per cent by weight, as this is the cut that has to go to the occupying authorities.' So there we have it: in France today, young couples can't get married until the Germans have exercised their so-called rights over them. I don't want to let my anger spoil dear little Monique's happiness and excitement. It is such a proud moment for a twenty-year-old girl when she chooses the wedding rings for herself and her future husband, and I don't want to be a grumpy old mother-in-law, so I bite my tongue and seethe in silent fury.

5 My elder son, at this point a naval lieutenant.

Paris, March 1941

What a day! This morning I was quietly typing up our next issue when the doorbell rang. I opened the door – and there stood Vildé! A grinning Vildé, totally devoid of make-up or disguise.

'What? Are you mad?!'

A fine welcome he got from me! He knew nothing about my letters to Friedmann, with their warnings of what was happening in Paris and of the dangers of an over-hasty return.

'But I had to come back,' was all he said in return.

The Kid never appeared in Toulouse and has probably been arrested. I continued to scold Vildé, beseeching him to go straight back to the free zone. Poking affectionate fun at me, he simply said that his presence in Paris was absolutely necessary, with no further details.

'Oh yes, and what about when you're in prison?'

'Dear Agnès,' he retorted with a chuckle, 'we're all going to end up in prison, as you very well know.'

He thought the photograph of Pétain that graces my room was terribly funny.

'It's for the benefit of the Gestapo,' I explain, and we giggle like idiots. It's our very own version of the crucifixes that sixteenth-century Huguenots used to hang on their walls to put the Holy League off the scent.

Vildé has lost track of Pierre Walter. With some pride, I tell him that I know where he is, and that I will take him later today to Jean and Colette's house, where we are all to meet up. I give Vildé their address but not their name, and we agree to meet up again at rue Monsieur-le-Prince at six o'clock.

I go to beard Pierre Walter in his den, and – with many a backward glance to make sure we are not being followed – we head off together for Jean and Colette's house, where all our friends are waiting. Vildé reports back on his various missions in the free zone, in Lyon, Toulouse and Marseille. We are all increasingly struck by his extraordinary intelligence, allied with his rare integrity and commitment. We discuss the possibility of printing the newspaper in the free zone. Vildé has many new projects to set in train. I take my leave of him and of Pierre Walter. We arrange to meet again next week, same time, same place.

Paris, March 1941

Pierre Walter telephones. I must go to his hotel urgently. Yesterday he and Vildé were having lunch in a restaurant when Vildé went off for a few minutes to pick up some false identity papers that Simone Martin-Chauffier was arranging for him; she was waiting for him in a café on place Pigalle. An hour later he hadn't come back. Pierre went to the café: there was Simone, but she hadn't seen Vildé. What can have happened to him? We are all beside ourselves. We still nurse the hope that he realized he was being followed, and perhaps managed to find somewhere to hide until he could slip into the free zone.

I rush to share my fears with Cassou and his family, who keep putting off their departure from Paris from one week to the next. I beg them to hurry! Vige urges me to leave Paris. Yes . . . but what about Maman? I can't leave her on her own just now. Her home help can't stay after five o'clock. Domestic concerns quickly make me renounce all thoughts of leaving. Besides, why would anyone be interested in me? I've done so little and been so careful. Why on earth would they arrest me?

Paris, late March 1941

Keeping in touch with our friends in Toulouse is becoming increasingly difficult, except with the aid of formulaic '*familiale*' postcards – though it has to be said that we do manage to make these convey a great deal.

Iria Deslous is going to Marseille for her work and will be there for three days. She has kindly offered to take any correspondence with her. Madeleine Le Verrier is getting ready to leave for the free zone. She hopes to go to South America, and from there to London. Jean Cassou and his family continue their interminable preparations for departure: they are so slow, and I'm so worried about them.

Paris, 28 March 1941

Pierre Walter, Jean and I meet up in a café on rue Saint-Lazare. Walter is a charming fellow, so unaffected and spontaneous. He asks Cassou how he should address him.

'Oh – just "Jean",' replies Cassou.

'That's our reward, you see,' says Walter. 'If I'd met you at some smart do before the war I'd have had to address you as "*Maître*", and now here I am calling you "Jean" straight off!'

There is no news of Vildé. We have virtually given up all hope. He must definitely have been arrested. Pierre is hatching rather far-fetched plans to track him down at the Sûreté or in prison, at Cherche-Midi or Fresnes.

We agree on new projects. I am to introduce Roger Pons' replacement to Walter. For his part, Pierre Walter will put me in contact with a certain Pierre, who on Vildé's orders is to take his place in our group.

Paris, March 1941

Working on the newspaper at my house yesterday, we still managed to find something to laugh about. I had been to Pierre Brossolette's bookshop to collect the 'feature article', a splendid pamphlet in which Pierre sets out what happened to the cod caught by the people of Newfoundland during the campaign of 1939–40.

We had tea while we worked, and then at the end of the day Christiane appeared. She had just returned from Toulouse, and brought with her a magnificent sausage, a present from Friedmann. Without further ado I cut it in three and we drew lots for it, squealing with laughter like children.

Iria is still not back from Marseille. I'm worried about her. Last time she was there she had serious problems with the Vichy police.

Paris, 30 March 1941
Mme D., a friend of Iria Deslous, telephones in tears to tell me the appalling news: Iria is dead! She died of tubercular meningitis, in three days, all alone in Marseille. She has no family, but so many friends, like me, to mourn her. Neither the Cassous nor the Duvals can believe that we shall never again see her beautiful, passionate face . . . Iria is dead!!

Paris, 31 March 1941
Maman is to have her operation tomorrow. The doctor assures us that it's nothing serious, but surgery on an extremely frail seventy-two-year-old is bound to carry a degree of risk. For three days now I have done nothing but look after Maman. Jean Cassou went alone to meet Pierre, our new liaison agent now that we are certain we have lost Vildé. I feel I can't cope with any more sadness: Maman ill, Vildé under arrest,[6] Iria dead . . .

I have tracked down an ambulance: not an easy matter, as there is not a drop of petrol to be had. The operation is now set for the day after tomorrow. Maman is admirably cheerful, confident and calm.

6 Vildé had in fact been recalled to Paris by Gaveau, who had him arrested a few days later.

Paris, 3 April 1941

The operation has been a great success. The surgeon, Dr Lebovici, is a friend of Jean and Vige. He is one of us, and has done everything he possibly can to indicate his sympathies to me. Maman is as delighted with her surroundings as she is with her surgeon and her nurses. But I'll never forget how we left for the clinic on 1 April, with Maman being carried down the stairs on a stretcher and me following behind. It was like a funeral procession: never, ever has my heart felt so heavy. Life at the clinic, stripped to the basics, will do me good. I've been buffeted by so many emotions, so many sorrows over recent days that my nerves are shattered. Why do I keep going over and over this image of us leaving the house, so that it's starting to haunt me? I don't go in for 'premonitions', yet I'm beginning to feel I'm losing my grip. I sleep on a little camp bed beside Maman and go out for just an hour a day, to try and find some little treat or other to tempt her. I dropped in on Müller's bookshop, where I helped the comrades to roll up Ordnance Survey maps and documents that are going to the free zone. Naturally, I asked no questions, but Müller told me with a chuckle that concealed among his books was enough documentation to get an entire regiment shot. He is going to get news of Yvonne Oddon and Lewitsky through their lawyer, with whom he has made contact. He is very attached to Pierre Walter and spoke of him in the highest possible terms. His activities are much more important than I realized. No news whatsoever of Vildé. We don't dare to admit how frightened we are for him.

Paris, 8 April 1941

My brother kindly offered to sit with Maman yesterday so that I could go to our Tuesday meeting, which this week took place at Jean Aubier's. There we welcomed Léo Hamon, who is very active in Toulouse, and who is on a trip to Paris to see how the land lies and to meet us all. He worked very closely with Nordmann, whose trial has just ended. He tells us that he handled himself with great distinction, defending himself with a dignity that impressed even the judges. He was sentenced to just two years. After pleading guilty, he said that he hated Nazism for three reasons: because he is French, Jewish and a socialist. Nordmann has got off lightly. Léo also knows Müller the bookseller; he too is much more active than I realized. Jean Cassou tells me about Pierre, our new leader; he says I will meet him in ten days or so, when Maman is better. We arrange to meet next Tuesday at Jean and Colette's house. By then I shan't be so worried about Maman's health, and we'll be able to have a useful discussion. After the meeting, Pierre Brossolette and Léo take me out to dinner, and we discuss the work to be done after the liberation. What a consolation it is, how good it feels to be planning the early days of a new press under the Fourth Republic! Still no news of Vildé.

Paris, Easter, 13 April 1941

This afternoon I spent my hour of freedom with Léo. He wanted to go to a popular cinema in order to observe the reaction of the good people of Paris to the German newsreels. We both felt the audience was apathetic, no more than that.

Léo gave me the text of President Roosevelt's latest speech. We'll circulate it: it's extremely encouraging.

Maman's convalescence is going according to plan, and she is to leave the clinic next Wednesday. Impossible to find an ambulance to take her home. With huge difficulty I have managed to find an ancient hackney cab, very Belle Epoque. Maman chuckles at the thought of going home in a carriage of similar vintage to herself.

*

On 13 April my diary ends; yet my memories are so clear that I am able to commit them to paper as they happened and in strict sequence. I remember everything as clearly as though it were written in notebooks, one event after another. Slowly turning the pages, I find that virtually every one is illustrated with some barbaric image or other. Many, many women, thousands upon thousands of women, have seen the images described in these pages. Together we are the tiny, insignificant characters in these illustrations to a 'footnote to history'. My memoir will be one among many: its one virtue will be its absolute faithfulness to the truth. My comrades who were there will know that the palette I have used to paint these pictures is deliberately muted, less lurid than the reality. That is my choice. These are images like old prints, clumsily engraved so that here and there the colours leak and run.

Images without art; images of truth.

Paris, 15 April 1941

Why are there some days when we just feel happy, for no particular reason? When everything looks wonderful, and we are pleased with the whole world, including ourselves? For me, 15 April was one of those days.

Maman had asked me to run an errand for her, and as I strode down the street in the sunshine I could feel that winter was over and spring had arrived. How good it was to be alive! On my return to rue Geoffroy-Saint-Hilaire, I noticed a German car parked outside the clinic.

'Well,' I mused, 'do they treat the Boches here as well?'

I climbed the stairs to Maman's room. On the landing outside, two 'gentlemen' seemed to be waiting for me.

'Madame Agnès Humbert?'

'Yes.'

'German police. We would like to carry out a small search

of your house. Please come with us; it will not take very long.'

Why did I look at the electric clock? It said twelve twenty. Idiotically, I said to myself: 'You were arrested at twenty past twelve.' I asked if I could give some instructions to the nurses regarding the care of my patient. This gave me time to reassure Maman, to give her some papers, some money that there was no point in letting them have, and my diamond ring, to which I am rather attached. I swore to her that I had nothing compromising at home, and that I would soon be back.

In the car that took us to our house, the policemen were assiduously polite. One of them looked curiously like Lindbergh, the other had the face of a brute. Only the driver wore a grey-green uniform. I found to my surprise that when they spoke among themselves I could understand them perfectly. I never imagined that my childhood memories would have survived for so many years. Naturally I didn't tell them that I understood what they were saying.

No sooner had they started their search than they took against my taste in books. One of them found the manuscript of Friedmann's latest book, the other his photograph. Immediately they asked if he was Jewish, to which I replied: 'He is a French officer.' With that the tone of our 'conversation' changed abruptly.

'Answer yes or no.'

'Yes, and so what? What's it to you whether he's Jewish or not?'

Doubtless because one of my friends was non-Aryan, they confiscated on the spot my lovely little typewriter, my entire stock of paper, and rough drafts of articles on art and folklore. Then they dismantled my dining-room table, as the mechanism for extending it seemed to offend them. They rummaged around among the dresses in my wardrobe, snorting in triumph as they hauled out a box that they were evidently convinced contained a duplicator. Inside it they found the electric vacuum cleaner.

The chest in which we keep the silverware also got them terribly excited. In Pierre's bedroom they fell upon a tube of Indian ink that was doubtless of enormous interest. From a bowl in my bedroom where I keep small change – some fifty or so nickel coins – they deduced that I had read a tract urging the French people to remove these coins from circulation.

Then, between two sheets of paper, they discovered a third, left there by accident. Clearly written at the top were the words 'Copy and circulate'. It was the front page of *Résistance*, mercifully unfinished. Ordered to explain it, I admitted with a suitable degree of reluctance that it was a copy of a tract exhorting the French people to hoard all their nickel coins. I said I had abandoned the project as I was such a bad typist, but that I had made five copies that I had left on seats in the Métro. All in all, it was a plausible story that would only cost me two or three months in prison. I chuckled inwardly as I thought about the *Résistance* file, with its four hundred names and addresses, lying quietly hidden – together with copies of all the tracts we had published since September 1940 – under the stair carpet between floors. After asking my permission with great ceremony, my gentleman visitors used my telephone to report back to their chief on the success of their mission. Then they hung up, and invited me to leave with them. It was at this point that I remembered the Roosevelt speech that Léo had given me two days before, which was still in my handbag! I asked permission to go to the toilet, which they granted, though not without first snatching my bag from me and ordering me not to shut the door. I heard a cry from our doughty cook: 'What a shame, what a crying shame!'

It is distinctly disagreeable to be taken away by complete strangers without having the slightest notion of where they are taking you. A quarter of an hour later I knew. I was at the headquarters of the Sûreté Nationale on rue des Saussaies. I was taken in at mezzanine level, into a small low-ceilinged office furnished in the turn-of-the-century style of Armand Fallières. On one of the walls was a bad painting of a woman sewing by lamplight. Absurdly, my attention was completely riveted by that painting. They led me through three interconnecting offices. Seated in the last of these was an officer. Asking me if I was Madame Agnès Humbert, he informed me coldly that I was in the hands of the Gestapo, and that I was about to learn that the German police are quite a different matter from their French counterparts. Following this amiable introduction, two or three officers entered the room. I was made to stand in the middle of the space as the Germans circled round me, looking me up and down with jerky, staccato movements, screaming like lunatics all the while, to the accompaniment of some sort of music emitted at top volume from an enormous radio. The din was indescribable. Why did it remind me of that classic from the heyday of silent cinema, *The Cabinet of Dr Caligari*? Perhaps because this idiotic scene, presumably intended to impress me, merely reminded me of all that was most surreal in *Dr Caligari*.[7] I asked a typist, who also seemed to be an interpreter, if she would be kind enough to translate what the gentlemen were shouting at me, as if they were questions I should be happy to answer them. She explained (as I had already deduced) that they were accusing me of lying and threatening me with the full weight of the German law.

Eventually, and for no apparent reason, the scene changes, the minor characters withdraw and I am left alone with the typist and the drill captain. He assures me that he is in possession of my entire correspondence with Vildé, and that he knows *everything*. Since I have never been in correspondence with Vildé, I am completely reassured as to the extent of the damage.

7 Though these techniques seem farcical today, this was how the SS embarked on their 'work' in Paris. When they realized that these ridiculous performances were eliciting no information they improved their methods, so gradually attaining the finesse of semi-drowning in bathtubs filled with iced water, electric shocks and the rest.

Whatever he claims, the captain knows virtually nothing. Naturally, I admit to knowing Vildé, Lewitsky and Yvonne Oddon on a strictly professional basis, following the line that we all agreed upon some time ago. When he asks if I know René Sénéchal, I say no; then I suddenly remember that I have his card in my bag, and realize I must get rid of it at all costs. Taking advantage of a moment when the captain is busy reading the innocuous documents seized from my house, I fold the card up and brazenly stuff it in my mouth. Somehow I carry on talking despite having a mouthful of card, trying to soften it with my saliva all the while. At last I manage to chew it up and swallow it. The sharp-eyed typist informs her superior that I am eating something. Foreseeing this eventuality, I have in my hand a tube of aspirin that some fairy godmother has slipped into my bag by pure chance; showing this to him, I confess that I have indeed just taken an aspirin as I have a slight headache.

Standing in the middle of the room is beginning to get tiring, so I edge towards a capacious leather armchair and rest my knee on one of the arms. A higher-ranking officer, probably a colonel, enters the room. Finding my attitude insulting and wishing to teach me a lesson in German etiquette, he gives the chair an almighty kick, sending it rolling a metre or so away. Caught by surprise, I just manage to keep my balance. A meal is brought for my drill instructor, who scoffs it greedily while carrying on with his work. Now and then he barks some absurd question or other at me.

Then the door leading to the next-door office opens, and I glimpse a number of men in civilian clothes, and in their midst Vildé. Vildé looking thinner and taller. His handsome face is framed by a blond beard, which suits him beautifully! He looks like the young Edouard Manet. He is wearing curious clothes – blue trousers and a black jacket – and his hands are tied behind his back. He has difficulty walking, and appears to have lost his sense of balance. Our eyes meet, and he gives me a long look of inexpressible sadness. A look that will haunt me for ever. Roughly, he is pushed into the third office, and the door closes behind him. The captain asks if I know that man. I reply that I do. With a sarcastic snigger he adds: 'He's changed a bit since he's been with us, don't you think?'

The one I call Lindbergh comes back into the room. He takes me and the typist into the next room to continue the interrogation. I avoid all his traps. Some of the questions he asks me are quite extraordinary. We go back to my childhood and education, meandering off into my tastes, marriage and private life. I wonder anxiously how Vildé's interrogation is going in the next room. Abruptly, I am presented with copies of *Résistance*, two issues with which I am extremely familiar as I was the one who typed them up and made such a mess of them. The carbon paper was too greasy, and they are smeared and smudged all over with my fingerprints. Vildé had these two issues on him: I had given them to him on his last visit to my house. Lindbergh keeps up the questioning. I deny everything indignantly. He has the first few lines of the paper typed out again, using my little typewriter. The results are conclusive; they would be even more so if this imbecile had the sense to compare my fingerprints with those that emblazon the text of *Résistance*!

But Lindbergh is no good at his job. I continue to deny everything, and say I can't type and I can prove it. The lady principal of the Ecole G. will testify that on 1 February 1941 I enrolled in the school's beginners' class. The teachers know that at that point I didn't even know how to load the paper into the typewriter. (In fact it was true that I had enrolled at the Ecole G: wanting to learn how to work a roneo machine, I had thought it more prudent to start the course from the beginning in order not to attract attention.) I was just describing my first faltering steps in the art of typing, when before my eyes there appeared the glorious features of Iria Deslous, and I heard her clear, laughing voice urging me on: 'Go on, go on, be *really* devious!' Why did she come into my thoughts at that particular moment? Who will ever know? She leaves no relatives behind her, and she died just after we published the incriminating article. So I explained how Iria had needed a typewriter to type up some articles on folklore that appeared under her name in the periodical *Visages de France*, and had borrowed mine. She had kept it for over a month, and who knows what it might have been used for during that time? I went on to recount how the typewriter had been returned to me by a perfect stranger on the evening when, frantic with worry, I was getting ready to take my mother to the clinic.

At this point in my story the door flies open again, to reveal the Kid. I had sworn that I didn't know René Sénéchal, but now I realize that he must have admitted to seeing me. In an attempt to save the situation, I explain that I have been in contact with this young man, who was introduced to me as Raymond Sauvet by a certain M. Durandeau. A fictitious character invented on the spot, this M. Durandeau is a plausible one none the less, a regular in the reading room at the Musée des Arts et Traditions Populaires who put me in touch with Sauvet, who used to carry letters into the free zone for me.

I know these lies won't make things any more difficult for the Kid, as I can see my letters that he was carrying laid out on the table in front of me. Taken in by this tale of mistaken identity and with the ins and outs of the Durandeau affair, Lindbergh turns his attention to weaseling out every possible detail about Georges Friedmann. I am not unduly worried about the letters he has found on the Kid, but if they have Friedmann's address it makes it harder to deny that he had at least some knowledge of our activities. My sole aim now, as a matter of the utmost urgency, is to deflect all suspicion from my friend and comrade. I have no idea to what extent the Germans will keep their hands off those who have taken refuge in the free zone: perhaps they send reports on them to the

Vichy police. The grilling goes on for two long hours: Fried-mann, his family, his forebears, his grandmothers, his military situation, his financial situation, his political ideas, his activities. I stand up to the onslaught as best I can.

Then Lindbergh's sidekick in the morning's house search comes into the room and, making strenuous efforts to sound truly terrifying, informs me that I am under arrest. I greet this news with a smile, which sends him into an apoplectic fit. After much whispering and conferring, they ask me if I know Professor Cadou. Of course they mean Cassou! And the fact that they garble his name means that they haven't got him. Naturally I deny all knowledge of him. Then the drill instructor returns, to inform me that I have attended regular meetings at 30 rue Monsieur-le-Prince. I flatly deny ever having visited the house of my friends the Duvals or knowing anyone who lives anywhere in the street. At this point, I deduce that the captain is ordering Lindbergh and his companion to take me with the Kid to the house in question. I clearly hear him say: 'When you're on the spot you'll be able to tell whether or not she knows the house.' And so we set off.

I sense that the only way to save the situation is to stay calm and composed. Then suddenly the terrible realization dawns on me: it is six thirty on Tuesday evening. At this very moment, all our friends will be gathered at the Duvals' house at 30 rue Monsieur-le-Prince, waiting for me to arrive. The full membership of the 'Cercle Alain Fournier'. At each ring of the doorbell, Pierre Brossolette will trot out his usual little joke: 'Look out, it's the Hun!' We'll ring the bell, Pierre will make his usual quip, and this time it will be true: there they will be, the Hun in person, apparently brought there by me! It is extraordinary how, at life's most tragic moments, we are able to stand outside ourselves. I feel an urge to laugh. The Kid remains expressionless. He knows this is our meeting place, and he is bound to realize that I have denied everything.

I can't see how all this is going to work out, but I am
acutely aware of one thing: the freedom of all my friends and
the lives of most of them are at stake here. I have to save them;
what can I do except maintain an icy calm? When I was fifteen
I used to moan about living such a humdrum, everyday life
in such an uneventful century. Just at the moment I feel I am
more than making up for the drabness of those years, with
enough dramas to rival those of 1792. Lindbergh orders the
car to stop at the corner of rue Monsieur-le-Prince and rue de
Vaugirard. The driver adjusts his rear-view mirror so that he
can scrutinize my expression and the other policeman stares
fixedly at me, while Lindbergh gets out and leads the Kid
towards my friends' house. I, meanwhile, concentrate with an
air of total detachment on a corner of the Théâtre de l'Odéon
and a sliver of the Jardin du Luxembourg. I hope I look as
placid as a cow, but my heart is pounding so loudly that I can
hear it. Surely the policeman sitting so close to me can also
hear the slow, dull thud of this rebel heart that will-power
cannot tame? How long do we stay sitting there? Five minutes
at most. The Kid must have denied everything too, as here he
is coming back with Lindbergh. They get into the car, and
Lindbergh barks an order to the driver: '*Nach* Cherche-Midi!'

The car moves off; for the moment at least our friends are
safe!

In the Prison du Cherche-Midi

So here we are at Cherche-Midi. We get out of the car, and Lindbergh rings the bell. Walking towards us in the wan light of early evening I see a city 'gent' in a bowler hat. He is ten metres away. I try to catch his eye, beseeching a look or a smile from him. It's sheer superstition: I crave some gesture of encouragement, however small, from the last Frenchman I shall set eyes on . . . how many months? But the passer-by in his respectable bowler does not smile at me, although he can't have missed my supplication; preferring to err on the side of caution, he swerves across the street and passes by on the other side.

It is eight o'clock in the evening, and I've eaten nothing since last night. Seven and a half hours of interrogation have given me a healthy appetite. At the admissions office I remark, no doubt in too lofty a manner, that I am hungry. Curtly, I am informed that this is a prison, not a hotel: the last meal is served, I am told, at four o'clock in the afternoon. Yet hardly has my cell door shut behind me than I see it open again just a chink, and a hand emerging from a green cuff holds out half a round loaf. Instantly I regret the audible gratitude in the '*Merci*' that slips from my lips, but I'm too hungry to be dignified. I wolf down the brown bread and wash it down with water from the jug in my cell, a hideous enamel object standing beside a slop pail. On the floor in one corner is a

reddish-brown enamel basin, near a small deal table, a stool
and a bed, the springs of which have been replaced by three
planks with a meagre straw mattress on top. Two horse blankets
complete the comforts of my cell. The whitewashed walls are
covered with stains and inscriptions. So cramped is the space
that it seems taller than it actually is: a real broom cupboard.
At the very top of the wall opposite the door, a fanlight allows
a feeble light to penetrate the cell.

For the moment, an electric light bulb hanging from a
flex illumines the scene. Fortified by my meal, I start to
laugh — hysterically, probably — at the thought that the
others are safe for the moment. Tomorrow Cassou will hear
that I've been caught and will make himself scarce. Pierre
Brossolette will lie low for a while; only Jean and Colette
Duval are compromised, but the Boches don't know their
names and everything at their house is well hidden. They
might be searched, but they probably won't be arrested.

I think about Maman, about how worried she was, and Pierre
too. I lie down on the pallet fully dressed, as I imagine they
will continue my interrogation later on tonight. It's what they
usually do. I must be slightly feverish. I have a thought that
I can't get out of my head. This cell must be about the size
of a burial vault. I have been laid out in a sepulchre. Above
me, high up, is a tablet, and on it this inscription: *Here lies
Agnès Humbert, died 15 April 1941*. There are flowers, too, yes,
flowers . . . *Here lies* . . . No, this is ridiculous, I mustn't think
such idiotic thoughts.

I stand up and put my ear to the cell door. I hear whisperings
and a man's voice: 'Good evening, everyone.'

And women's voices: 'Good evening, Jean-Pierre.'

The man's voice goes on: 'We have to be quiet tonight, it's
Fernandel on guard.'

Somehow I don't think our famous comic actor has become
a prison guard; it must be a nickname.

The light is turned out. I lie down, and again I see: *Here lies Agnès* . . .

No, that's enough, I must sleep, I'm exhausted. I doze off, but every hour the light is switched on and the guard peers at me through the spyhole: probably they're worried I will have dark thoughts. The heavy clang of the guard's boots, the jangling of keys, the metallic clash of rifles: despite it all, I drift back to sleep.

Cherche-Midi, 16 April 1941

The light penetrates my cell through the fanlight high in the wall. It all looks even filthier than it did last night. I'm aching all over, but at least I've had some sleep.

I become aware of whisperings, which gradually become clearer. It is a quarter to eight. Women's voices, light and clear, some almost like children: 'Morning, Sylvie; morning, Renée; morning, Josette. Did you sleep well, Line?'

It all sounds so bright and young. Am I in a prison or a boarding school?

Then a man's voice: 'It must be time . . .'

And all together, the voices – perhaps twenty or thirty of them – chorus: 'Good morning, Jean-Pierre.'

And the man's voice replies: 'Salute the colours.'

And he whistles a bugle call. After a silence, the same voices that earlier wished Jean-Pierre good morning launch into a muted chorus of 'La Marseillaise', followed by an enthusiastic cry of: '*Vive le général de Gaulle!*'

There are many people here, but prison life is a complete mystery to me. All these people talk to each other, know each other's names, seem even to see each other. And where is the flag? Are they all in one large room, with me in a cell off it? The conversations start up again, then the clash of boots and the sudden jangling of keys. Someone whistles the tune of 'Au clair de la lune', and my companions fall silent like a flock of sparrows at the approach of a cat.

It is eight o'clock. There is a tremendous commotion as doors are flung open, cell by cell, and an NCO invites me to bring out my jug and slop pail. A young woman hands me a small brush and indicates that I should use it to sweep out my cell. I glance quickly down the corridor, which is lined with doors in a hideous shade of brown. There is no large room; prisoners must evidently talk to each other under their doors or through their fanlights. A German woman in a black shirt embroidered with the insignia of the National Socialist Party comes into my cell. I deduce that she is the individual in charge of this establishment. She is pleasant, too pleasant, positively unctuous. I point out that I have neither comb nor soap nor linen; she retorts that there is nothing she can do about it, and that doubtless my family will soon take care of my needs. She suggests that I should write home, then returns to tell me that I am in solitary confinement and that I do not have the right to either send or receive letters.

The Gestapo officers who brought me here last night relieved me of my handbag, identity papers, personal items and fifteen hundred francs. They let me keep my handkerchief, saying that it was all I would need in prison. This handkerchief, ridiculously small and embroidered with a childish pattern of roses, is my only possession.

People here are reduced to the absolute basics, I can tell already, subordinated to the physical necessities of life: eating, washing, defecating, staunching blood. 'They' have it in their power to prevent us from doing any of these things, as we are locked up in broom cupboards, entirely at their mercy. They can do anything and everything they want with us. How can we have any redress? And it's a strange feeling to be completely in the power of these soldiers. Before, the idea of being assaulted by a man would never have entered my head, I'd never even thought about it; but if by some remote chance something monstrous had ever happened, I knew that (always supposing I couldn't defend myself) I could call on my sons, the law, the emergency services and I don't know who else. In here we are utterly defenceless, with only our dignity to protect us!

I am not yet ready to introduce myself to my companions. I listen, and try to get my bearings. I read the rules over and over again. They say that whenever a German deigns to speak to us we must stand up. Every time I hear steps approaching my door, I jump up from the bed. I don't mind if they find me standing up, but I'm damned if I'm going to let those people think that I'm standing up for them. I keep expecting my interrogation to start again, but nothing happens.

What are my friends doing? How is Maman? Has she managed to get home without too much difficulty, without too much pain?

Between noon and two o'clock there don't seem to be any guards in the corridor, and you could almost imagine the prisoners gossiping between cells. At ten o'clock I am given a tiny cup of vegetable soup and half a round loaf of brown bread. At four o'clock it is margarine and a piece of sausage. At six o'clock the guards give another turn of the key to the locks in everyone's cell doors before evidently leaving our corridor, with only the occasional round now and then. Whenever the clanging of boots is heard on the stairs somebody whistles 'Au clair de la lune'; when the coast is clear it's 'Cadet Rousselle', and immediately everyone starts talking again. Gradually I get to know the prison noises, like those of an unfamiliar hotel.

I deduce that Jean-Pierre is a naval officer; he seems cultured and witty. In the next cell to mine is Jean, a Breton seaman to judge from his conversation.

At seven o'clock we all chorus the house chant: '*Notre France vivra*' ('Our France shall live') repeated three times. At about eight o'clock the chatting subsides, and then Sylvie, Line,

Renée, Josette, Jeannot, Henriette and all the rest wish each other goodnight. Finally Jean-Pierre bids goodnight to us all, adding a few discreet words of advice for those who are expecting an interrogation the following day. In addition, he asks the believers among us to pray for a reprieve from execution for our comrades Catherine and Christian. He says this as if it were the most natural thing in the world, as though it were a matter of saving them from some tedious interrogation or some sort of punishment. So it's true then, the executions have started, and the first execution in Paris, of Bonsergent, this mysterious execution that we have talked about so often among ourselves, is now a fact, a fait accompli.

Cherche-Midi, 17 April 1941

The second day has been a long one for me. Nothing to read. Nothing to do with my hands. I estimate that my cell measures one metre sixty by two metres forty. Stretched out on the pallet bed, I daydream. I think about the members of the group. Up until now, I don't think I've uttered a single word that could make things awkward for them. That's my sole ambition: not to cause any problems for them. I make up cover stories in my head and work out answers to any questions I might be asked. All my little fantasies seem to fit together and be quite plausible. It's tricky without pen and paper, but I'm reasonably sure that my stories will stand up to scrutiny. Certainly I never stay lying down for more than about ten minutes: every time I hear boots approaching my cell door I stand up, and every time – it must be a hundred times now – I wonder who will carry out my next interrogation? When will it be? These gymnastics, physical and emotional, cannot help but strain my nerves. I listen out for all the voices in the corridor, and others that I can hear in the yard, but I can't hear Yvonne Oddon. She certainly doesn't seem to be on my wing; is she at Cherche-Midi at all? Where are Vildé, Lewitsky and the Kid? What torments are they having to endure?

I keep myself amused by tracing the patterns of marks, stains and cracks on the cell walls. With a bit of imagination you can find anything you want to see. Here is the unmistakable profile of Jean Cassou, over there a patch of damp becomes a panther on its hind legs in a style that is pure Antoine Bourdelle. Meanwhile, the sun creeps slowly across the wall, a parsimonious patch of light measuring a few square centimetres at most. Now and then a small shadow passes overhead and is outlined against the wall. It takes me a long time to work out where these come from: they are the shadows of birds as they flit over the yard. The shadow of a bird is a thing of beauty, especially against a sombre prison wall.

This evening I shall introduce myself to my companions. Their conversation is enjoyable, with Jean-Pierre setting the tone. It will do me good to talk, and take my mind off my hunger pangs, for already I am very, very hungry.

Cherche-Midi, 18 April 1941
Jean-Pierre was warm – very warm even – in his welcome, managing in a few sentences to make me feel that I am one of the 'gang', that from now on I will never be alone, that I am no longer an isolated unit, that I am no longer one of the 'outsiders'. Since they can't see me, the others ask me, through Jean-Pierre, how old I am, if I have any family, and what I have been arrested for. Conscious of the dangers of speaking too freely in prison, I offer a slightly oblique account of the events that brought me to Cherche-Midi. From the chuckles of my fellow prisoners, and Jean-Pierre's 'Ah yes, quite so,' I can tell that they understand the reasons for my reticence. I embark on a series of experiments to work out how best to make myself heard. The most effective technique

seems to be to lie flat on my front, projecting my voice underneath the heavy cell door. My companions ask me for the latest news from the BBC. I tell them that Peter II has seized power in Yugoslavia, and that there have been mass demonstrations outside the Russian and British embassies in Belgrade. We carry on talking for a while; then, after our battle cry, 'Notre France vivra' three times, silence falls and everyone seems to go to bed.

I imagine all the different cells. They must all be the same as mine, and every one of them contains its own drama, every one of them houses a human being who is enduring his or her own ordeal. Physically we are all alone, but none of us will ever before have experienced the solidarity that cocoons us here.

Through the snatches of conversation that I hear, through our muffled singing of 'La Marseillaise', we know that we are all in this together, and that in unity lies strength.

A tall, burly individual in civilian clothes comes into my cell. He reads out the prison rules that my interrogators have drawn up for my benefit. I learn that I am not allowed any 'privileges': I am not allowed any letters, visitors, books, manual work, cigarettes, newspapers or food. In sum, he intones with a particularly solemn flourish, I am to be subject to a 'regime of extreme harshness'. The only thing I am allowed is clean linen from home. Given that all I have by way of linen is my one tiny handkerchief, I find this largesse a bit of a joke. I use a hairpin to comb my hair, and in the absence of a mirror view my reflection in the water of my basin, unclouded as it is by any soap bubbles. Before he shuts the cell door behind him, the large individual repeats, 'No more privileges,' in what is evidently his most imposing and fearsome voice. 'Oh, that's such a shame,' I quip, 'especially since you took me to the pictures last week.' He looks deeply affronted. Really, these people have no sense of humour.

René Sénéchal is here. Lewitsky is on the third floor. On

the prison grapevine, whispered from one cell door to the next, I sent a message to tell him that I am close by and in good health and spirits. In reply he sent me a kiss. The amount of kissing that goes on in this prison, with all of us securely locked in our cells, is quite remarkable. I know now that Yvonne is in the corridor on the opposite side of the yard, where I can't communicate with her. Vildé is not here. We assume he is at Fresnes. Jacotte, the young secretary from the Musée de l'Homme, has just been brought in; I didn't know that she was one of us. She makes her presence known to me, and very cleverly gives me to understand that she has never seen me. She tells me that Pierre Walter is also in prison, following a dramatic arrest. They were captured together. It was the same Gestapo men who picked me up, and apparently they roughed him up and threatened to throttle him with his scarf. Müller will soon be next, we imagine. I think back to our last conversation as we were rolling up those big Ordnance Survey maps, when he told me with a chortle that hidden among the books in his shop he had enough documents to have an entire regiment shot. Where did the Germans find the vital lead that has brought them to us all?

There is no news of the Duvals, the Cassous or the others. If the Germans had arrested them they would have confronted me with them. Is Friedmann really safe from arrest? He knows nothing about all the stories I have invented. I don't want to think about it, and I think about it all the time.

Today Jean-Pierre initiated me into the art of seeing my fellow prisoners between noon and two o'clock, when the guards are off duty. The procedure is as follows. You take your spoon in your right hand, equip yourself with a piece of string (a shoelace or similar), then climb from the bed on to the table and from the table on to the stool. When you have located the shutter on the fanlight above the door, you jiggle the back of the spoon against the trigger mechanism until the fanlight opens. You must take care at this point to attach the string so that you can close the fanlight in case of danger. It all goes smoothly, and before me I see Sylvie, who has such a pretty voice. At the moment she is on a punishment regime, which means that she has no mattress, they have confiscated all her clothes except for her skirt and jacket, and she is on a diet of bread and water. She throws me a strip of cloth that she is using as a bandage, to which I attach some sugar I was given this morning, and we entertain ourselves with my attempts to throw it back. You need a good aim at Cherche-Midi. All night I could hear poor Sylvie moaning in her sleep, 'I'm cold, I'm so cold.' Inside these ancient walls where the sun never penetrates it is literally freezing. The view from my fanlight makes me giggle. The row of cell doors along the corridor is too good to be true: if you saw them on stage you would think they were hopelessly overdone. Are those massive hinges and locks Louis XIV or Napoleon? I can't quite decide.

Cherche-Midi, 24 April 1941

My cell door bursts open, and Mme Blumelein – for so I discover our lady governor is called – tosses toilet articles, linen and blankets any old how on to my bed, then walks out again without a word. I did not think to be so moved at the sight of my clothes, of things from my house. So at last people know where I am. I can't allow myself to think about my family. You have to anaesthetize your feelings, but all these familiar objects disarm me: this softening of feeling is dangerous and to be avoided. You have to be hard. This evening I shall try to throw some underwear and stockings to Sylvie, who is so cold. The lives of my fellow prisoners intertwine with my own like vine tendrils. I've only been in Cherche-Midi for nine days, and already prison life looms larger than my personal life, my house and family, which seem to be gradually fading into the background. In the fever of my first day I said to myself: *Here lies Agnès Humbert, died 15 April 1941*. When I come to think about it now, I realize that it's true in a way: it's another life that begins in here; a different life, or rather a living death. People on the outside live in a different world, speak a different language. We have our own jokes, our own joys and fears. Selfishly, we keep this new life to ourselves.

The reception of a 'new girl' has become a ceremony, almost a ritual, of great significance for us. Every time we hear a commotion in the corridor we know that a new girl has arrived; in the evening, when we are left to ourselves, Jean-Pierre will ask her questions, formally welcome her as one of us and offer her a few words of essential advice. She in turn will relate the latest news from outside, doubtless with a few embellishments. Today's new girl weeps inconsolably; we hear her sobbing and hiccuping. We implore her to calm herself. We assure her that as long as she keeps a tight grip on herself and refuses to admit to anything it will be all right, but she just howls even louder. Eventually, Jean-Pierre manages to extract her story. She is a war widow, twenty years old, with a three-month-old baby. She had dashed out to buy milk for the baby when she was picked up and brought here. She pleaded with them, told them that she had left her baby all alone in the house, screamed and begged, but all to no avail. So now here she is, powerless, helpless and locked up in a cell. It's too dreadful. No one says a word. Just silence.

At last Jean-Pierre ventures hesitantly: 'Um, the Red Cross, you know . . . sometimes in such cases . . .'

But then he stammers to a halt, realizing that there is nothing he can say, and the young mother sobs: 'What can the Red Cross do? No one knows I'm here, that the baby's all alone; nobody, not the concierge, not a soul . . .'

Cherche-Midi, 30 April 1941

The incessant jangling of keys prompts Mimi, the life and soul of our little group, to remark: 'When I get out of here I shall simply *have* to buy a bunch of keys, I shall *so* miss the pretty tunes they make. Only I'm not sure you can buy such big, heavy ones in the shops – *such* a pity.'

As for me, I can't get out of my obsessive habit of jumping up every time I hear footsteps approaching my cell door. But this morning it was not in vain. The door was opened by a fair young man who gestured me to follow him, with a gutteral '*Dribunal*.' My lucky day! I'm going to court! I'll only get three months for distributing the little tract about hoarding nickel coins, the only sin to which I have admitted.

In the guardroom I find Lindbergh's sidekick waiting for me like a bull mastiff, though this time in uniform. His forage cap sports the SS skull and crossbones. On his epaulette are the letters GFP. So he's the genuine article, as one might have guessed from his brutal features. Without a word, he takes me to the Sûreté on rue des Saussaies. At the time of my arrest I had adamantly refused to sign any statement written in German. This morning my deposition is translated for me. Briskly I write out the fifteen pages of this charming work of fiction and sign it, declaring it to be the truth, the whole truth and nothing but the truth. Lindbergh is also present. He asks me my opinion of General de Gaulle. For once I tell him the truth. I reply that until the end of June 1940 I had never heard of him, but that after the ignominy of our defeat, after all that I had witnessed on the roads out of Paris, one voice and one voice alone had given me the will to carry on: the voice of General de Gaulle. I let myself go rather, speaking with genuine feeling and conviction, and then I look across at Lindbergh. I am not imagining it. Lindbergh is moved. Getting up out of his chair with tears in his eyes, he paces the room, blows his nose and says: 'That's very good,

Madame, what you just said is very fine. Add it to your statement.' What a triumph! I've made an SS officer blub! Who would ever have imagined that I possessed such powers of persuasion?

Before we leave the Sûreté, I ask to be allowed to have books to read. I had no idea my request was so hilarious; amid bellows of laughter the reply comes: 'Books, for *you* . . . Oh, no! No books for *you* . . .' Why is it that all my fellow prisoners are allowed books to read? What is it that entitles me to such special treatment?

Viewed from the car that brings me back to prison, how strange and remote life in Paris seems. I've been locked up for a fortnight now, and this feeling of no longer belonging to the world of the living grows ever stronger and more defined.

Cherche-Midi, 11 May 1941

Dexia[8] gets news from outside: I gather her friends slip it in among her linen. Today she announces that General de Gaulle has called for an hour's silence from three o'clock this afternoon. I am the only one on our corridor with a watch: I still don't know why they let me keep it. So I propose that I should announce the time for us all, and that Jean-Pierre should ask Sylvie to sing 'Le Chant du Départ' at three o'clock. Then I suggest that we should all observe the hour's silence, before together raising a chorus of 'La Marseillaise' as it has never been heard before. Jean-Pierre approves the idea, and passes it to the next floor up (I suspect him of having a hole for such communications). Renée, 'switchboard operator' for the yard, yells the command at the top of her voice. In the communal cells, on the ground floor, on the third floor, there can't be a soul who hasn't heard.

At three o'clock I bang my spoon against my enamel basin

8 Elisabeth, Comtesse de La Bourdonnaye.

three times, and in her beautiful voice, warm and untrained, Sylvie sings: '*La Victoire en chantant nous ouvre la barrière.*'

Never before have I found the words of the old battle hymn of the Revolution so moving. The final words — 'for Her a Frenchman must die' — fall on a thoughtful, total silence: a silence that will last, unbroken, for an hour. For any rule to be observed so scrupulously is unprecedented! At four o'clock I give four bangs. All the windows are opened so that people on the outside can hear us. At Jean-Pierre's request we sing the final verse of 'La Marseillaise', the one that people sang on their knees in 1792: '*Amour sacré de la Patrie . . .*'

I hadn't realized there were so many of us. This 'Marseillaise' seems to swell, becoming a tangible, palpable presence. Soon it will expand too far upwards, too far sideways to be contained by the prison walls; soon, it seems, the walls will burst apart and the roof will fly off. I know that the feelings that choke me are shared by us all. What beauty! What power of shared emotion! The guards, bemused by our prolonged silence followed by this musical explosion, try in vain to shut us up. But where to start, who to blame? The 'din' is ubiquitous! Then the sounds of boots kicking doors, shouts and oaths. The singing dies away, and all is silence.

On Saturday and Sunday our cell doors are always carefully locked and bolted from midday, and there are no more guards in the corridor. Occasionally they decide to do a round, so if someone hears them coming and we are about to be caught on the hop they give a quick shout of 'Watch out!' or whistle a snatch of 'Au clair de la lune', and silence falls. For the week-end, Jean-Pierre organizes 'Radio Cherche-Midi'. During the week he works out a programme, with everyone taking turns to contribute a personal memoir, anecdote or traveller's tale. Anyone who can sing is pressed into service. Sylvie is our true *chanteuse*, with 'Le Galoubet' as her party piece. Renée always enjoys a rousing success with sea shanties such as 'Jean-François de Nantes' and 'La Marie-Jésus qu'est un bateau', while Léa, with her pure, clear voice, never tires of singing 'Brave marin', which Jean-Pierre invariably requests along with 'Solveig's Song' from *Peer Gynt*. Jean-Pierre is the compère, deftly alternating musical turns with spoken numbers. He often entertains us with stories from his travels. Our friend Dexia, a raconteur with an elegant, eighteenth-century wit, relates amusing anecdotes about the prominent figures she has known. Preparing our 'chats' without the aid of pencil and paper serves as a major distraction for us all. Some of us talk through our open fanlight and others through the spyhole, while those who have a large gap under their door sprawl flat on their stomachs on the floor.

Last night Jean-Pierre was singing duets with Mimi through his fanlight. To our delight they trawled their memories for snatches of all our old favourites. After 'Viens, Poupoule' and 'Elle était souriante', they embarked on 'La Petite Tonkinoise'. We were having such fun that none of us heard the warning. Two German guards crept stealthily down the corridor in their stockinged feet. Suddenly they burst into Jean-Pierre's cell, and we could hear the thuds of the beating they gave him. How insufferable it must be for this French officer to have to endure such a cowardly attack from a pair of German soldiers. I am burning with indignation, as are all my companions, I know. When all is quiet again, I tell Jean-Pierre how we feel. With sublime dignity and composure he replies: 'No, no, Agnès, honestly, they didn't lay a finger on me. What you thought was the sound of blows was actually my books falling to the floor. They just shouted a bit, that's all.'

'They' wasted no time after that: the other evening, the night before his trial, we heard noises coming from Jean-Pierre's cell. It was his first visit from his officially appointed lawyer, a German officer. He spent barely five minutes with his client. I could hear their exchanges, with the German officer posing questions along the lines of 'Have you ever sought to harm the Third Reich?', and Jean-Pierre parrying with 'You surely don't expect me to say no?' Poor Jean-Pierre! Happily, he nurses no illusions regarding his defence lawyer's competence on his behalf.

Tomorrow I am to wake him for the sentence.

It was a great drama when they came for him, with soldiers in helmets and armed to the teeth. I managed to glimpse the escort through my spyhole, but I couldn't see our friend.

We follow the progress of Jean-Pierre's trial day by day. Today he rounded off his court report with a cheery: 'Well, folks, every day I'm that little bit closer to the Fossés de Vincennes.' When he returns from the day's hearing his first concern is for us. Who has been interrogated today? Who has been punished? Only then will he consent to talk about himself. Just now he had the great joy of seeing his wife and learning that his fifth child is a boy. Philippe d'Estienne d'Orves is six months old already.

The death sentence came as no surprise. On his return we sang 'La Marseillaise'. The guards said nothing.

The disinfection service has just attempted to get rid of the vermin. I am moved without warning to the cell next to Jean-Pierre. It is more or less in darkness, the window being blocked by the chevet of a convent chapel that must stand on rue de Sèvres. I inspect my new lodgings. On the wall at the level of my forehead is a small bloodstain; some forty centimetres away another one, wider and darker; then further on, three more, each wider and darker than the last. It doesn't take much effort of the imagination to picture the scene. Grasping their prisoner by the back of the neck, the Boches smashed his or her forehead against the wall. Five times they pounded it, until they produced this large, blackish stain. This is the Nazi way: we've read about it in the official reports.

After six o'clock, Jean-Pierre and I talk to our hearts' content.

Knowing that we can't be overheard, we are able to talk openly
for the first time. The wall is thin, and our conversation carries
on late into the night. I tell him about our 'work'. He too
thinks I will get away with it, as there is no serious evidence
against me. I've already more or less served my sentence for
the tract about hoarding nickel coins. Jean-Pierre has seen a
copy of *Résistance* in London. He tells me who to contact in
order to carry on with the work as soon as I am freed. This
time I will go to the free zone, where there is sure to be plenty
of useful work to be done. For himself he expects the worst.
He tells me that everything is against him and he doesn't
think his sentence will be commuted. He advises me not to
tell anyone that it was on General de Gaulle's orders that he
returned to France. Everything he has done he has done freely,
on his own initiative. He assures me that the mission he
undertook was successful in part; that his sacrifice and that of
his comrades will not be in vain. He has the great joy of
knowing that he has protected many friends and avoided many
more arrests. He gives me some instructions, and asks me to
pass on his gratitude to a retired naval officer whom I used to
know and who is now living in Egypt. We make jokes despite
everything, describing our appearance to each other so as not
to be too disappointed when we meet at my house when it's
all over, to 'talk about old times'. For I can't bear to believe
that he will be executed – I simply can't bear it – and I sense
that this game amuses him, this musing on a future that he
may not live to see. I ask him whether he thinks that General
de Gaulle will lead the government after the liberation. He
has asked the General the same question. De Gaulle replied
that he was a soldier and nothing more.

He has a sense of foreboding that they will transfer him to
Fresnes. He knows that his departure will be abrupt and
without warning. So he bids us all a cheery farewell. He has
a few special words for each of us. He thanks us for keeping

up a brave front, and for all we have done to distract him and to take him out of himself during his darkest hours. Not a word of bitterness, nor any hint of sadness.

Cherche-Midi, 15 May 1941

This time it was after supper that the gentlemen sent for me. In the guardroom I discover an individual in bourgeois civilian dress whom I don't know. He grabs me roughly by the wrist, wrapping a heavy chain around it and holding the two ends as though I were a dancing bear. Recovering from my surprise I remark: 'At least like this people in the street will see that it's not for pleasure that I'm stepping out with a German.' He appears not to understand French and drags me roughly to the car, which takes us once again to the Sûreté, where the captain who interrogated me on the first day is waiting for me. He starts by asking me if I understand German. Without giving the game away, I wait for the typist-cum-interpreter to translate his question before replying that I don't understand a word of his language. He motions me to a chair, insisting that I should take this one and no other. I smell a rat. Naturally, the chair in question is on the verge of collapse. Had I sat on it I should have ended up on the floor, and this flower of Teutonic chivalry would have split his sides laughing at my discomfiture. I draw his attention to the fact that his chair is broken and go to fetch another one, pausing to admire my reflection in the over-mantel mirror, and to remark to the typist how pleased I am to see myself again and to find that I don't look at all bad after a month in prison. The exasperated captain orders the typist to inform me that I am not there for my amusement. I reply that I have already worked this out for myself.

The interrogation starts with a string of questions devoted exclusively to the subject of Jean Paulhan; I deny all knowledge of him, or of the street where he lives. Rue des Arènes? I didn't even know there was such a street in Paris: it sounds more like Nîmes, surely. When the captain tells me via the typist that he knows that I know Paulhan, I swear that I have never even heard the name – but wait a minute, isn't Paulhan a make of aircraft? But then I've always been so stupid about aeroplanes. Finally he realizes that I'm making a fool of him, and threatens me with all the terrible might of the Third Reich. He informs me that Paulhan is in prison, which I doubt, as the details he has given me seem so sketchy. Eventually he sends me on to the officer who arrested me, who continues the interrogation. Having given me the third degree, he finishes with the traditional threat with a revolver, at which I just laugh. This makes him awfully cross. I know that so far these threats have always been just empty words, which is why I dare to put on such a show of bravura.

Leaving the prison and going back to it are always times of high emotion. Everyone on the corridor is anxious: as you pass on your way out you hear, 'Remember the most important thing: don't give in, deny everything, admit nothing,' and on the way back, 'How was it? No nasty surprises?' You have to be careful what you say, but back in your cell you can tell your friends the truth via the fanlight. The comrade opposite reads your lips and passes it on to the person in the next cell.

Yesterday morning the whole place was turned inside out and upside down, with every surface swabbed down, scrubbed and swept – though without any apparent effect on our bug population. We are informed that the general has ordered a regime of daily exercise for us. We are therefore to be let out of our broom cupboards. The population of the corridor goes down to the yard, where we trudge round and round in slow, silent circles. We walk in single file, a metre apart from each other. Many of us stumble and totter. We are not used to walking in the open air; even the air of this squalid yard seems too sharp, and the daylight hurts our eyes. I feel numb all over, and I can imagine how Mimi and Christiane must feel after their three months inside. They look so pale, and their hair is so lifeless. It's strange to see all these young women without make-up. They look like death. Our great amusement this evening will be working out who's who:

'Who's the one in the black suit?'

'Dexia?'

'Oh, how funny, I didn't imagine her like that at all! I thought she'd be plump with glasses.'

Then I hear a young voice: 'Who is it in the brown suit with the fur trim?'

'Agnès.'

'No, it can't be: Agnès is old, she's got a son who's about to get married.'

I feel absurdly flattered by this tribute to my sprightly gait from Jeannot,[9] a slip of a girl in a white blouse, just seventeen – though she still manages to acquire two death sentences all by herself.

The days fill themselves as though by magic. Dreams assume a place of unprecedented importance here. We have all become soothsayers, offering more or less creative interpretations of the previous night's dreams. Hearing people talk in their sleep can be very disturbing. Sometimes at night I hear men's voices through the open window, incomprehensible snatches of phrases in strange, troubling voices. Occasionally they laugh, which is macabre. Generally speaking, we all sleep soundly, a tribute to the bromide administered lavishly in our soup, which we absorb without knowing it. I have the answers to all possible questions clearly sorted out in my head now, and I try not to think about the 'affair'. In my mind I go back to places I have visited – Greece, Yugoslavia, Turkey – reliving in my head those happy, crowded days I spent with Yugoslavian friends

9 Jeanne Poulain.

in Dubrovnik. What will have become of them, those boys so full of enthusiasm and conviction? Are they fighting, or are they raging uselessly within prison walls, like me?

I think back to all the happy times in my life. Just the happy times. The rest you have to forget, especially in here: you must forget, or else you get wrinkles. Wrinkles on your face are bad enough; in your heart they are even worse. Hour by hour, I relive my unforgettable travels in the Soviet Union, my visits to Kiev, Moscow and Leningrad. I should like to tame some mice, but there aren't any on our floor. It's teeming with bugs, though. If it's possible to train fleas for flea circuses, surely you must be able to tame bugs. I study flies at close quarters, admiring them as they clean their legs with such elegance. In normal circumstances we never have the time to appreciate the precise movements of a fly. In my mind I wander through the galleries in the Louvre. I try to piece together the image of some of the paintings that I love best; but already there will be a corner, a detail or even an entire figure that has become blurred, or even worse that has vanished entirely from my memory. To tell the truth, even without books or work of any sort, it is still possible to fill one's days.

'*Les épinards, les épinards, les épinards sont là*' ('The spinach, the spinach, the spinach is here'), sung to the tune of 'Les Montagnards' every time we hear a suspicious clang of boots on the stairs, is our latest flash of inspiration.

We are overjoyed, as Catherine and Christian have had their sentences commuted; they will soon be deported to Germany, but their lives have been spared.

Young Philippe the sweeper, who sings messages from cell to cell, is going to be let out. I have written to Maman, using for notepaper the tissue paper that was wrapped round the lemon we had for pudding last Sunday. With a pin I prick holes in it to form the words: 'Clothes received, in good health, case not

serious, kisses.' Then the name and address. I give the paper to
Philippe, who instantly hides it inside his shirt.

The hunger is unbearable. I can't get used to this hunger,
and all my friends roar with laughter when I scream that I'm
going to consume my mattress. From what they tell me, I gather
that I am being more or less deprived of my soup rations, of the
soup that forms our staple diet. The other prisoners have large
bowls that hold a litre; I have just a plate and a beaker about
the size of a teacup. Jean-Pierre says that they are trying to
weaken me physically by reducing my rations, and morally by
depriving me of books and manual work. He gives me too
much credit, but when all's said and done I think I prefer this
method to the one chosen for little Yeyette.[10] Though her
rations haven't been reduced, she has spent a fortnight in the
punishment cell, which is a black hole. On her twentieth birthday, as our cell walls were stippled with meagre patches of
sunlight, we heard her asking in her pretty, shrill, childlike
voice: 'Is it a fine day?' In the opinion of her interrogators,
Yeyette's memory needs a severe jogging.

I have also made up some games. I play interminable rounds
of spillikins, using straws, naturally. This was how the game
was invented in the Middle Ages, I believe, using the rushes
that were strewn on floors in winter. I have used this week's
lemon paper to make a ball, tying it into shape with strands
of wool pulled from my blanket. This ball is an inexhaustible
source of pleasure. I play table tennis with it, using my plate
as a bat and pressing the wall into service as my imaginary
partner. Then there is real tennis, with the ball coming sometimes from the left, sometimes from the right. Another pastime
consists of counting the number of planes that pass overhead
in a day. Odd or even? And so it becomes a game of patience.
Then I count the floorboards in my cell again and again for

10 Henriette Dauquier.

the thousandth time – one, two, three, four, five, six, seven – knowing full well that there are seven, a lucky number.

One day my ball games must have become too riotous. Mme Blumelein flings open my cell door. She finds it reprehensible that I should still be playing games at my age. She scrutinizes the ball, interrogates me regarding its provenance, then makes me undress and searches me from top to toe; she runs her fingers through my hair, presumably to be quite sure that I haven't concealed more games in it. From all this I conclude that playing ball games in Germany must be an extremely risky business. As punishment for this disgraceful activity she summarily transfers me, pushing me roughly into a cell that is truly disgusting. Cardboard has been shoved into the broken window panes, and the floor is scattered with putrid scraps of food that look as if they have been there for weeks. Bugs scuttle about undisturbed, and it is pitch black.

It happened just as we thought it would: in a few moments they had taken Jean-Pierre and he was gone. Despite rebukes from the guards, he just had time to bid us a collective farewell. To the tune of 'Auld Lang Syne', someone started to sing, '*Ce n'est qu'un au revoir, mes frères . . .*'; I hope he heard.

Earlier today Mimi had the rare and enviable good fortune to be taken to the bathroom. This offers the dual pleasure of an opportunity to wash, while at the same time observing life on rue du Cherche-Midi. Mimi spotted a man on a balcony opposite the prison. Hoping to get some news, she spoke to him but got no reply. She tried again, and was rewarded with the following gallantries: 'Shut your face, you little slut. If you hadn't slept with a Kraut you wouldn't be in there, would you?'

'So that's what they think of us out there,' sniffed Mimi furiously.

Cherche-Midi, 6 June 1941

It's fifty-two days now that I have been walled up alive, with no news of Maman or home. Sometimes I think that Maman is dead, and then I imagine every conceivable disaster raining down on members of the group: Jean Cassou arrested, investigations, searches, arrests, torture. Could I have unwittingly put my foot in it? Have I said anything that could rebound on them, that could incriminate them? I pace my cell, from the door to the window, from the window to the door. Three paces there, three paces back. My upstairs neighbour paces his cell for ten or twelve hours a day. Poor fellow, he has no idea just how much his pacing like a caged beast gets on my nerves.

Léa, my neighbour when I was first brought in, has promised to pass news to Maman via her sister. Léa is only a witness in an 'affair'; she is allowed to see her family from time to time, and often passes on messages. Now I am separated from Léa by the whole length of the corridor. Although communication between us is virtually impossible, she still manages to let me know that everyone at home is well, that they send me kisses and are doing all they can for me. Heavens above, what on earth can they possibly do for me? All I ask is that they should carry on living – carry on living as best they can. I lean my head against the door, my ear pressed against the spyhole. My head is spinning; I feel hot and then so cold my teeth are chattering. Everyone at home is well: could this just be an empty formula to set my mind at rest? But then Léa adds, 'Your mother's having her usual problems with her eyes.' So her sister really *has* been to my house . . . and everyone really *is* well!

Cherche-Midi, 8 June 1941

What lies in store for me, I wonder? This is all just too good to be true. Yesterday it was news from home; today Mme Blumelein half-opens my door, and with a vinegary smirk

hands me a book: *La Tragédie de Ravaillac* by the Frères
Tharaud. From today, it seems, I am allowed books. But the
danger is that this joy will make me forget my job, the only
thing I have to do all day, which consists of ringing the hours
and half-hours. I'm the only one in the prison with a watch.
All the time I used to hear plaintive voices asking, 'Agnès,
what time is it?' So I resolved to take on the role of prison
clock, banging out the hours with my spoon against my
enamel basin. It's a small thing but it helps to divide up the
days for my fellow prisoners, who tell me they are grateful
for this aid to counting the hours . . .

I am not particularly prudish by nature. Mme Blumelein's
perpetual body searches, from the top of my head to the soles
of my feet, long ago destroyed any remaining vestiges of the
modesty I might once have had. But just because I'm not prim
it doesn't necessarily follow that I am immune to feelings of
revulsion when, every time I wash, a click warns me that the
guard has pushed up the small metal flap covering the spyhole
in my door. Alerted by the sound of water being poured into
my basin, he treats his blue German eye to the sight of a
Parisienne washing, using cold water in a hideous brown enamel
bowl. A toothbrush in an army issue mug is her one and only
toilet requisite. For form's sake I am determined to ignore this
presence, but I find it exasperating.

Cherche-Midi, June 1941
The heat is intense, and the bugs unbearable. Blumelein,
whom Dexia has just nicknamed 'Florida', tells us that the
temperature in our cells is forty-five degrees. She wonders
how we do not suffocate. The stench from our slop pails is
abominable, and there is no escape from these receptacles for
our daily ablutions. To add to our joys, most of the lids don't
fit properly. The nerves of some of the women are giving

way under the strain. Hedwige, who is Polish, has one fit of uncontrollable screaming after another. She howls like a dog, and we hear her rolling in all directions on the floor, crashing into the table or the stool. In the silence of the night the noise takes on a sinister air. Marie, another Polish girl close by, hanged herself using a skein of knitting wool that she had tied to the hook on her window.

Cherche-Midi, June 1941

I've tried everything. It appears to be completely impossible to secure the momentary loan from the 'occupying authorities' of a pair of nail scissors. My nails are so long they would be the envy of eighteenth-century Chinese ladies. The job is now far beyond the capabilities of my teeth, and although I try to make a joke of it, both my fingers and my toes are really painful. I point out to Mme Blumelein that my nails are so long that they have become veritable weapons, and that I am considering hatching an escape plan with the aid of these magnificent tools. With the ghost of a wan smile, Mme Blumelein assures me that neither she nor those responsible to her has any scissors available. And so the cell door is firmly closed on Agnès-of-the-long-nails!

Cherche-Midi, 22 June 1941

Today the prisoner who ladles out my soup tells me through the half-open door that at five o'clock this morning the Russians entered the war! It was the Germans, it seems, who launched an offensive. I don't know any more, but I am delirious with joy. I can't keep still for a moment. I walk, jump, sing . . . How can I pass the news to my comrades before noon? I'll have to wait a whole hour! Let's hope that Paul, the young German from the International Brigades, has heard the news. Any day now he's to be shot; if he knows about this I am sure his death will be easier. At last the Russians are coming to the aid of Civilization!

All day in my head I've been going over and over, for the hundredth time maybe, my travels in the USSR. My thoughts turn to Maria X., curator at the Museum of Ethnography in Leningrad, who following the regulations had hung her gas mask from the window catch in her office, just as I did at the Palais de Chaillot, where my ugly mask still hung when I left. 'You see, we're the same, you and I, we'll fight together on the same side,' said Maria. That was on 14 August 1939. Now she has joined the struggle, and I am stuck in this ridiculous place, bound hand and foot.

This morning I was given a normal-sized bowl at last, so now I can drink my soup like a big grown-up girl. Without the scraps my companions have been sending me, especially Dexia, I don't know how I would still be standing upright.

This evening we heard a woman's glorious voice rising from the street outside. She clearly wasn't singing for money, but for one of the prisoners. How I hope he heard her! I try to imagine how he would feel. She must have chosen that particular song for a reason. The other day a group of Breton musicians treated us to a concert of bagpipe music and singing. They weren't doing it to raise money either.

Cherche-Midi, 9 July 1941

Soon it will be dear Maman's birthday. How I would love to write to her! For nearly three months now I've had no news of her, except that she is still alive – me, who's always been so keen to keep in touch with those I love, through letters, telegrams and telephone calls! It's like a hunger strike: the first few days are torture, and then gradually you get used to it, the pain deadens, you go numb. Today my thoughts turn with unaccustomed intensity to my aged Maman. At that moment Blumelein pushes open my cell door. With a sickly smirk that indicates she's up to no good, she holds out an envelope, a sheet of paper and two pencils, 'in case one should break'. She explains rather vaguely that, because of my exemplary conduct and the high opinion he has formed of me, the 'captain' wishes to make a gesture that will give me pleasure. As a token of his esteem, I am to be allowed to write to my mother. Furthermore, she tells me, the soldier on guard duty has been given special orders to collect my letter at five o'clock. This unaccustomed concern for my well-being makes me uneasy. I write a letter consisting of innocuous good wishes and a few enquiries about health matters.

At five o'clock, as arranged, the guard comes to collect my letter. Ten minutes later they come for me. In an office below, two men are waiting for me. They say: 'It's the same handwriting, not a shadow of a doubt.' And they show me some of my letters to Friedmann. I recognize them immediately. They are the letters I gave to Georges Ithier in February. They were found on him when he was arrested at the demarcation line. In them I discuss every topic of interest to us: only the names are disguised. They order me to decode them. What is the 'Cercle Alain Fournier'? Who are Vige, Tiapa, Jean and Léon? Who is Maurice? They snigger. Of course, it's Vildé, whose first name is Boris. Who is Jacqueline H.? And who are M. and Mme Lucien F.? The last two are not directly involved in the affair, but if I say who they are the Gestapo will go to their house, and perhaps find a tract or something else I don't know about. My only option is to remain silent. They shout, they threaten to have me taken out and shot. I try to remain impassive. Then they tell me that if I don't talk they will arrest Maman. This is no idle threat. My only hope of saving her from execution is to feign indifference. 'Well, what do you expect me to do about it? Go on then, arrest her.' Maman is seventy-three, in poor health and virtually blind.

'Go on then, arrest her,' I had said. When they left me, they said they would go straight to our house. Last night I hardly slept. What sleep I had was shattered by terrible nightmares. I had visions of Maman being dragged away by the Germans, dressed all in white, her eyes yawning black holes streaming with unquenchable torrents of blood. I can't stop thinking about Anatole Lewitsky's father. He is seventy-six years old and knows nothing of his son's activities. For two months they imprisoned him in Cherche-Midi to make his son talk. Did he so much as turn a hair? Of course not.

The days go by. I ask a nurse, 'Sister' Lia, an exquisite creature from the Baltic States, if she knows of a very old and almost blind woman anywhere in the prison. She says no, and I'm sure she is telling the truth; but there are so many other prisons. I can't say my fears are allayed, but gradually I become less frantic with worry.

What is this stuff that we are made of? In the midst of the cruellest mental torment we still manage to laugh, and I mean really laugh. This morning, outside my cell door, I was treated to a scene that was truly farcical. Our guard was showing the ropes to a 'rookie', initiating him into the challenging task of guarding women prisoners locked up in fetid broom cupboards. He was explaining that whenever he approaches we shout '*Vingt-deux!*' ('Watch out!'), which (he explains) means '*Zwei und zwanzig*'. Why do we shout '*Zwei und zwanzig*'? A mystery! The first guard puts forward a number of ponderous hypotheses, none of which proves satisfactory. At last he concludes: 'Well, they just do, that's all. "*Vingt-deux*" is French for "Here comes the sentry".'

It's the little things that bring home to us the breadth and depth of our physical isolation, which as a general rule doesn't bother me too much. Yesterday, however, as we were going down for what they like to call our 'walk', Jacotte squeezed my hand as she passed; she squeezed my hand on the stair rail.

I can't get it out of my mind: this warmth, this feeling of human flesh brushing my own. A caress after three months of total isolation is not something that is easily forgotten; and the pleasure that it gives underlines the stark contrast with the barren wasteland that surrounds us here. The same is true of the ugliness and squalor all around: after a while you just don't notice it any more. Yet when the warder (a decent fellow) brought me two flowers from Jacotte, I of all people – I who never cry, I who have not shed a single tear since my arrest – found myself sobbing like a child. A red rose and a cornflower: the colours of Paris! It's over three months since I saw the smallest scrap of greenery, the tiniest corner of nature; all it takes is two flowers sent by a kind young friend and my equilibrium is shattered, my feigned indifference in shreds.

The girls on the corridor are despondent and forlorn: the setbacks on the Russian front have crushed their morale, which had been so high. Six weeks ago they glimpsed an immediate Russian victory, something approaching a miracle. And now we know it's true that Smolensk has fallen. Kiev, that lovely city that I adored, is lost for the moment. The march on Moscow and Leningrad is inevitable. Even if Moscow were to fall, we know that the war would go on. Victory will be longer in coming, but will be no less complete. We know this, the older ones, and we try to convince the girls, whose feelings of fear and helplessness are so easy for us to understand.

Dexia has been freed. She conducted her own defence with remarkable aplomb. She bequeaths me some of her 'treasures': tweezers, Cerebos salt and some pharmaceutical products. Everyone who goes free makes a similar bequest to those they leave behind them in the shadows.

The news from the Eastern Front may be disastrous, but we still do our best to keep up the spirits of even the most despondent among us. Yesterday another 'new girl' arrived, in absolute floods of tears. After an entire night of her wailing and sobbing,

Mimi could take it no longer and yelled: 'If she doesn't shut up I'm going to put my head in my pail and jam the lid on!' Immune to all attempts to soothe her, the new girl refused to answer any of our questions and carried on sobbing convulsively. Then someone slipped in the *coup de grâce*: 'They don't execute women, you know – or not so far, anyway.' Even this didn't calm her down. It was morning before she could eventually be persuaded to talk: 'Well, it was like this you see. I had this pig. I live out in the suburbs, and I didn't know you weren't supposed to keep a pig without telling "them". And then, well, I decided to call him "Hitler" – well, how was I supposed to know that there was a law against calling your pig Hitler? Anyway, that's why they brought me here. And whatever's to become of me now?'

But answer came there none, as we were all doubled up with laughter. She found out soon enough, poor woman. Calling your pig 'Hitler' still only gets you nine months: a small price to pay, some of us maintain, for giving so much pleasure!

Cherche-Midi, August 1941

For a few days there has been talk of transferring us to the Prison de la Santé. The entire corridor is plunged into a fever of excitement. There is talk of better conditions, a less stifling atmosphere. The prospect of doing the journey in a police van delights the girls beyond all expression.

4

In the Prison de la Santé

Prison de la Santé, 27 August 1941
It's twenty-five years since I last saw the Prison de la Santé.
The ivy has grown since then, lending a homely, provincial
air to the prison yard that I found so forbidding in 1917.
When I came to the Santé to visit my father[11] during his time
in prison, I little imagined that a quarter of a century later
I'd be back again, but this time in a police van and surrounded
by German soldiers.

I am assigned to cell thirty-two, large and airy, in section
one on the ground floor. There is a latrine instead of a pail,
but I still have the regulation stoneware jug and brown enamel
basin. Because it is attached to the wall by a heavy chain, I
immediately christen the stool 'Medor'. But I can still detach
it easily enough whenever I want to sit by the window, from
which I can see the yard.

Silence reigns in the cells at La Santé, as communication
among ourselves is practically impossible here. Sometimes we
manage to send messages via the 'trusties' or exchange a few
hasty remarks in the yard, but conversation is now out of the
question.

On my first evening here Florida appeared in my cell, like

11 Senator Charles Humbert.

an attentive hostess anxious to ensure that I was quite comfortable. She had been drinking; I was in bed. She sat on my bed, and started to stroke my hair. I am not particularly brave, and it took all my courage to control my terror, keep my head and make her understand in no uncertain fashion that if that was what she wanted she had better look elsewhere . . .

Prison de la Santé, October 1941

The days pass pleasantly enough. I have received wool and fabric from home; I knit, I sew, I read. In the evening I listen to conversations between the men on the opposite side of the yard. I try to join in, but they can't hear me. I learned of the assassination attempt on Laval, who, alas, survived! On Sundays a rather aristocratic-looking gentleman exercises in the yard. His guard is easily distracted, and he takes advantage of this to throw me delicious chocolates and to tell me the latest news. According to him, the situation in the East is improving.

I have been interrogated by the prosecuting officer. Telling me that he wishes to become acquainted with me before the trial, he pays oafish compliments to the women of France. He assures me that if the French army had been composed of women instead of men, the Germans would never have got as far as Paris. He tries to make me believe that I have been denounced by Pierre Walter, and informs me that I am accused of passing military information to the enemy. This makes me laugh, as I know that there is not a shred of evidence against me on that count, and I have absolute faith in Pierre. He asks me about Jean Cassou: naturally, I have never heard of him. There can't be too much damage done in this direction, as he knows neither his first name nor his profession. He makes no mention of the Duvals, Friedmann or Pierre Brossolette. So they must all still be free: how wonderful! He tries to get me to talk about young Renée Guitton, who was in the next cell to me at Cherche-Midi, and shamelessly catalogues to my face some scraps of malicious gossip about me that his spies have managed to rake up in the prison corridors. In sum, he is unctuous, obsequious, oily and stupid.

I had a visit from Maman, and we were allowed to talk for a quarter of an hour. She is much stronger than she was this time last year, both physically and mentally. She seems convinced that I will soon be freed. I dread the terrible shock to her system when she realizes that I will not be back quite as soon as she imagines.

Prison de la Santé, November 1941

It's four months now that I have been at La Santé. One day follows another, silent and virtually indistinguishable. We have had a few great joys, such as America's entry into the war and much better news from the Russian front. I managed to see Yvonne Oddon briefly in the yard, and she told me that our trial keeps getting put back from one week to the next. It's all extra time for the men, who, alas, will not get off as lightly as we shall.

I heard someone shouting in the courtyard that Jean-Pierre was executed in August. I simply can't believe it: my mind has developed a curious way of refusing to accept bad news. I just find it all unbelievable. And yet – can it really be possible that d'Estienne d'Orves is dead? That all his quiet heroism should have come to nothing? My thoughts turn to all that he told me about the appalling treatment inflicted on him in Berlin, where they dragged him straight after his arrest. Still in terrible pain from the head injuries he had received during his traumatic arrest at Nantes, he was flung in a cell with no mattress, table or stool, just a pail with no lid. You have to have been in prison to understand the significance of a lidless pail in a tiny, airless cell. They kept him in Berlin for about a month before sending him back to Paris. On the train back they put him in first-class accommodation and the officer escorting him offered him cigars. Then at Cherche-Midi, without any explanation, they put him in the punishment cells for a month or more, before moving him to the cell where we had the great joy of hearing his voice so often.

Prison de la Santé, 15 November 1941
The cold is intense, and my only source of warmth is a small stock of private jokes, the ultimate in self-indulgence, for my own pleasure and mine alone. A female guard, pencil and note-book in hand, comes to ask me if I am Jewish. Three times in three successive weeks she returns, and I note that this particular question invariably comes at ten o'clock on a Monday morning. After my third denial I add: 'Honestly, Madame, I simply haven't had the time to convert to Judaism since last week.' Eyeing me warily over her spectacles, the poor woman turns on her heels without even a flicker of a smile.

I have had a visit from the lawyer whom Maman has chosen for me on the advice of friends. She is quite ravishing to look at, with an ostentatious and eccentric elegance. Perhaps my dear ones think that she will seduce the judges with a flash of her beautiful eyes? With a peal of laughter she tells me that she has seen the prosecuting lawyer, and that he intends to demand the death penalty for me. 'But we don't need to fuss about *that*,' she adds condescendingly, 'as they never execute women: they'll just send you to Germany, nothing more than that.' I reply that I have done nothing to deserve such a heavy sentence, but my lovely lawyer suddenly adopts a severe expression and demands to know what on earth I thought I was doing in compromising myself by association with such people . . . 'with English agents, Madame, with numbered –

numbered – agents.' Evidently, I should have sought the advice of the highly dubious Mme Christo before even considering working against the Germans.

Prison de la Santé, 20 December 1941

This morning I was told to pack my bag immediately, as I was being transferred to Fresnes for the trial.

In the police van, Yvonne and I enjoy a good chat; her spirits are magnificently high, and she sees the funny side to everything.

5

In the Prison de Fresnes

Prison de Fresnes, 20 December 1941
We are now installed at Fresnes, in the men's quarters, section one. I am in cell fifty-nine. The cold is arctic and relentless. At lunchtime I hear Pierre Walter and René Sénéchal talking to each other. How I would love to join in, but since I have denied all knowledge of Pierre and have admitted to seeing the Kid only once, I decide it is more prudent not to – and all the more so since the cells to either side of me are empty, so could be used to house informers at any time. I hum to myself the last stanza of a song that Yvonne Oddon composed at Cherche-Midi:

> If you've a secret to keep (repeat)
> Don't let vigilance sleep. (repeat)
> Keep it close to your chest:
> Swarming here is a pest.
> There's a rat here that tells
> All it hears in the cells.
> For its masters it stores
> All it hears at the doors;
> For its masters it stocks
> All it hears through the locks.
> Tra la la, tra la la, tra la tra la
> Tra la la laire . . . Tra la la! (repeat)

Prison de Fresnes, 25 December 1941
The cold is simply excruciating. My warder, an Austrian veteran of the 1914–18 war and a former political prisoner himself, tries to show his sympathy for me.

This morning he told me that it was Christmas Day, and that although like him I probably had children, I should try not to be too sad. As he spoke he proffered me two detective stories, which he said I must promise to read in order to take my mind off things. At midday, the soldiers on guard duty launch into a Christmas carol. The adjutant barks at them to shut up. He's the perfect little Nazi, piously *Heil Hitler*-ing at the slightest opportunity. Clearly in his view it is positively obscene for his men to sing in celebration of the birth of a dirty Jew.

Prison de Fresnes, 1 January 1942
The young lad who passes me my food bowl and clears out my sweepings every morning cheerily wishes me 'a happy new year, liberation and victory'. With the warder's consent I shake his hand and give him some chocolates, as for some time now I have been allowed provisions from home – though I hate to think of Pierre and Maman going short for my sake. Pierre Walter gets nothing, poor fellow, and I hear him complaining that he is starving, adding with a laugh: 'Let them shoot me quickly, but don't let me die slowly of starvation.' I can't bear not being able to do a thing to help him!

My sympathetic warder transfers me to cell number seventy, which he thinks is marginally less glacial. I can't see that there's anything to choose between the two, however. When he comes into the cell he makes a great show of shivering with the cold, despite his gloves and greatcoat, and sometimes summons a friend to show him the luxury in which the Third Reich detains its political prisoners.

Water seeps from the walls and turns to ice. The number of slugs is impressive. Organizing slug races is a great entertainment, laying bets against oneself on which one will be first to reach a particular mark, inscription or hole in the wall. My bed is not just damp, it's positively wringing. Despite my woollen socks, my toes have turned black. I imagine this is the beginnings of frostbite, but it doesn't hurt. I smear them with the lard we were given for supper last night and I expect they will soon be better. I'm starting to wonder whether our trial hasn't been postponed indefinitely. With each new day you wonder 'Will it be today?' and it plays havoc with your nerves. There is no library here, but the good Austrian brings me books. At the moment I am immersed in an incomplete set of the works of Alexandre Dumas. I find their thrilling intrigues all-consuming.

Prison de Fresnes, 8 January 1942
My warder pokes his nose through the door hatch and tells me that the trial is about to begin. At last!

At half past eight the corridor is still dark. A few light bulbs scattered here and there shed a blue light, eerie and melancholy. One by one we are brought out of our cells and placed on both sides of the corridor, two metres apart from each other. There are so many of us! Many people I don't know at all. There is a man I have never seen before who appears to be severely disabled; he can hardly walk and Pierre Walter is even allowed to help him; he is called Andrieu, and I have never heard of him. In the gloom I make out Vildé, who gives me a smile. He has aged, and his beautiful golden hair has fallen out in handfuls. Lewitsky has grown thinner; Müller the bookseller is just the same, elegant as ever with his grey hair, grey jacket, grey tie. Yvonne Oddon looks well, and I catch my second glimpse of Sylvette Leleu, a very pretty woman of whom I know little except that she runs a garage in Béthune, that she has done admirable work and that she is exceptionally courageous. The adjutant counts us over and over again. We are eighteen in all. He is a busy man and – naturally – discharges his duties with absurd pomp and gravitas. He announces that M. and Mme Simonnet (who have not seen each other for a year) are to be allowed to kiss. Turning to the interested parties, he tells them to await his order. There is silence, then at last he orders them to fall out and kiss each other. The order is duly obeyed in full view of their sixteen accomplices, all of us roaring with laughter. Utterly nonplussed, he glares at us in a fury.

So here we are, surrounded by armed soldiers. It is all too apparent that 'they' are keen to make an impression on us. Through long dark corridors we are frogmarched to a small courtyard containing a building that looks brand new. Inside, it is decorated with hideous green wallpaper in a Louis XVI pattern. The Nazi flag shrouds the end wall, in front of which stands a table – probably reserved for the officers – also draped with a flag. At right angles to this is another table, this one bare, for the lawyers. Set out in front of these two tables are eighteen chairs, hideous light-wood affairs in a pretentious 'moderne' style, perfect for a respectable provincial dining room. In the middle of the building stands a stove, huge and brand new. There is no photo of Hitler on the walls. An oversight, perhaps? There is, on the other hand, a map of France, on which a number of itineraries have been traced in different colours: those of Vildé and the Kid, no doubt, and perhaps those of Ithier too?

Our judges make their entrance amid a terrific din of boots and clashing of rifles, while the lawyers bustle about in a flurry of activity. Amid this crowd of people I notice a French soldier in a uniform of such an immaculate cut that it must be made to measure. He is decorated with the Croix de Guerre. He carries two briefcases – containing our files and the evidence for the prosecution – with scrupulous care, and he bows and scrapes to the Germans while studiedly omitting to so much as glance in our direction. Aren't there enough flunkeys in the German army? Do they really have to look for them in the ranks of the French army? I imagine that in civilian life this natty little lapdog must be a well-heeled young man of private means.

By bending down and pretending to tie our shoelaces, we manage to exchange a few jokes and the sort of quips that students trade before exams, to do with 'Romantic literature' or 'French architecture in the thirteenth century' or whatever. On this occasion, however, the subject matter is neither literature nor art, but the lives of men – the outstanding lives of remarkable men. Although we all know this, none of us cares to admit it: neither to ourselves nor to each other. The Kid looks well. His lawyer (who is also mine) tells him that he will be spared execution because of his youth. The officers take their seats behind the table draped with its black swastika on a red background. It was Claude Aveline, I recall, who used to say that it was swimming in blood. The officers are four in all: the presiding judge, young, tall and slim, with an intelligent and distinguished air; the prosecutor, whom I find no less offensive here than at the Prison de la Santé; and two assessors, both of them old, fat and fleshy, with shaven heads and faces like pigs. An interpreter and a clerk complete the team.

Jacotte, Yvonne and I risk a few whispered jokes about this 'game of hangman', which make us giggle. The prosecutor observes that we will soon be laughing on the other side of our faces. He is apoplectic with rage because we remain obstinately unimpressed by the scene before us. Stationed all round the room are armed soldiers. A woman dressed in mourning smiles at me. I don't know who she is; then all of a sudden I realize that it's Dexia, but so much healthier-looking than at Cherche-Midi that I simply didn't recognize her. I suppose she's here as a witness, or have they arrested her again? By the door a German nurse, a picture of dignity, seems to be waiting for something. What is she here for?

Today's sitting is devoted to formalities, and we are escorted back to our cells before soup.

Prison de Fresnes, 9 January 1942

The same drill as yesterday.

The identities of the accused are read out, and the presiding judge presents our cases to the prosecutor. On trial, he says, are eighteen French 'nationalists'. I find the notion of being a 'nationalist' – not a term I ever thought to hear applied to myself – highly entertaining. The judge stresses the fact that out of eighteen of us, ten have false identity papers. Then he delivers an astounding eulogy in praise of the men, paying particular tribute to Vildé. He draws attention to the fact that Vildé has shown remarkable strength of character in devoting his time in prison to learning Sanskrit and Japanese. Turning to face us, he informs us of his great respect for all of us. He understands, he says, that we have conducted ourselves as good Frenchmen and women, and that it is his own harsh duty to conduct himself towards us as a German. He adds that he imagines that we have been able to gauge for ourselves the esteem in which we are held from the regime under which we have been kept in prison. At this point I think we must all have registered (mentally of course) a large question mark; if we have been lavished with any favourable treatment so far we have failed to notice it.

Prison de Fresnes, 14 January 1942

The same performance again today, but this time all in aid of reading out the charges against us. None of us is disappointed, I think. We all got what we were expecting, and I got slightly more, perhaps. I am accused of the 'offence' of writing, printing and distributing the anti-German newspaper *Résistance*, and of the crime of espionage.

The nurse is still in her corner, and the judge courteously asks 'the ladies' whether they desire the presence of the 'sister'. It is only at this point that we all realize that the nurse is there to bathe our temples in case we should swoon under the emotional strain of cross-examination. We all burst out laughing, and reply that we are sure that medical attendance will not be necessary; with a smile, the judge observes that he is of much the same opinion.

Prison de Fresnes, 20 January 1942
The days go by, dismal, dark and freezing cold. The trial must be continuing, as every evening at six o'clock on the dot I hear Yvonne calling out to Lewitsky 'Goodnight, Toto', with a few remarks about the 'affair', offering advice or encouragement. Her words cut through the deafening silence like the tolling of a bell. They can't talk any more after that, because as soon as they hear a voice the police dogs in the yard start howling. Then the vicious curs in the other yards join in the barking, and the din alerts the guards.

Yesterday I heard the screams of a man being tortured. When the screams died down, they were followed by deep, throaty laughter. All day I have been haunted by these two sounds: screams and laughter. I don't know which was the more terrible. The laughter, I think.

Sometimes (doubtless when the dogs are elsewhere) I overhear conversations between the men on the other side of the yard.

'Paul's not talking. Have you banged on his wall?'

'Yes, but there's no reply.'

'So . . . do you think he's had it then?'

'Suppose so. Poor bloke, he was a really good sort.'

'Hey, guess what, Louis says that tomorrow it's sardines

again – you know, the salty ones that take the roof of your mouth off . . .'

At night, to take the edge off the bitter cold, I pull a corner of my blanket over my head so that my breath acts as central heating. This really annoys my guardian angels, who think I am dead. Two or three at a time they burst into my cell brandishing torches, waking me up with the clatter of their boots. When the corpse moves they all groan and pretend they've come to adjust the window blackout.

There are a lot of suicides.

Prison de Fresnes, 3 February 1942

I am fetched from my cell at last. On stage for act three. My cross-examination begins. I have to find answers to the same riddles as on 15 April last year; happily I have a good memory. The judge asks me all sorts of questions about the meetings on rue Monsieur-le-Prince. I deny all knowledge of them. He quibbles at great length over my letters to Georges Friedmann. I tell lies that might just appear plausible. The espionage charge is dropped for lack of evidence. The bag left at Jean and Colette's house proves more of a problem. Getting rid of that wretched bag is a struggle, but in the end I manage it without too much harm done. Finally, he comes back yet again to the meetings at the Duvals', before moving on to more general questions. I hear him say to the prosecutor: 'I've studied this *Résistance* affair so closely that I can say in all sincerity that I know the lives of these people better than my own. Much better than my own.' If he had caught sight of my smile at that moment it might have dented his confidence.

At last I am taken back to my cell. This is how the cross-examinations will continue, bit by bit, so that none of us will be able to hear what the others say.

Prison de Fresnes, 4 February 1942

This morning I was brought face to face with Müller and Lewitsky. To ensure that their stories stand up, I realize that I must admit to having been to Müller's bookshop to collect four hundred copies of *Résistance*, before putting them in envelopes and posting them in various different postboxes. I can see that my two friends are hugely relieved by this confession. The judge then informs me, with rather emphatic solemnity, that he is asking me for the last time to tell the truth about the meetings on rue Monsieur-le-Prince; that if I admit the truth it will count in my favour, and that my friends at number twenty-eight or number thirty will not suffer as a result; that in any case their activities are probably not worth considering and they have nothing to fear. Again I deny all knowledge of them. At this a lawyer, a Frenchman, leans towards me, all suave and insinuating: 'You are mistaken in maintaining this position, Madame,' he says. Furious, I spit back: 'I suppose you think it's better to shop your friends?' A sweeping gesture from an arm emerging from a lawyer's robe is my only answer.

It must be Jean and Colette Duval who sent me the works of Descartes this week. Could there be a more perfect place in which to read the *Discourse on Method*?

'And in general to accustom myself to the belief that we hold nothing entirely within our power except our thoughts . . .'

Never, ever has Descartes been so true; never has he had such a fervent follower!

Prison de Fresnes, 11 February 1942

On the way to the courtroom this morning I manage to exchange a few words with Nordmann, to whom I have never spoken before. We have a mutual friend, Louise Alcan. I explain to him that she used to distribute *Résistance*, and tell him about

all the unassuming courage she has shown since June 1940.
He was unaware that Louise worked with us, and seems pleased.
We exchange views about our little problems, and I say, 'After
all, we were old enough to know what we were doing when
we went into this . . .' This undeniable truth appears to amuse
him greatly.

Today it is the summing up for the prosecution.

At Cherche-Midi, I often used to think how unbearable it
would be to hear Vildé, Lewitsky, Walter and the Kid
condemned to death, but now we seem to view things differently, and I don't feel anything any more. We are in a state
of euphoria, and everything seems unreal. The prosecutor
demands five years' imprisonment for me, on top of the time
I have already spent in custody. Müller, who has conducted
his own defence with consummate skill, gets only five years
for lack of conclusive evidence against him. The prosecutor
directs his vitriol at Nordmann, stating that the 'Jewish lawyer'
has been despicable enough to denounce the Comtesse de La
Bourdonnaye, who gave him shelter. Nordmann's lawyer inter-
venes to protest vehemently that his client has never talked,
and that Dexia was betrayed, like the rest of us, in exchange
for 'blood money'. This interruption sends the prosecutor into
paroxysms of rage, during which the judge, a decent and fair
man, nods his head to the lawyer and replies, 'Perfectly true.'

It is hard to credit the state of mind that we are all in. As
we arrive we are seated according to the severity of our sentence.
In the front row are Dexia, Jacotte and the others who are
going to be let off, then Jean-Paul Carrier, Müller and me, all
of us wondering among ourselves at what point the death
sentence begins. It's a bit like the queue at a vegetable stall:
at what point will the cabbages and carrots run out? I am
outraged at my lack of feeling, but forgive myself as apparently
we are all in the same state.

Before we leave the building I find a moment to grasp

Nordmann's hand. I can still hear him saying, with a lovely, unclouded smile, 'They may shoot me, but my honour is intact.' Then his smile broadens: 'You were right when you said we were grown up enough to know what we were doing.'

On the way back to my cell I am able to thank Georges Ithier, who has never implicated me. He says simply, 'I shall go to my death with my head held high. I didn't talk.' Then he tells me about his arrest at the demarcation line, and how they staged a mock execution for him in order to try and panic him.

Prison de Fresnes, 12 February 1942

Today it was the turn of speeches for the defence, about which the less said the better. For the rest, the prosecutor observes that the trial has been going on since 8 January and that he wants to get it over and done with. He orders the lawyers to hurry up. He won't even bother to listen to them, of course, and his pair of bovine assessors invariably look as if they are half asleep. Probably their function is purely decorative.

I exchange a few words with Jules Andrieu. His severe disabilities are the result of wounds from the last war, and the Germans show him the utmost deference. A leather surgical corset holds his trunk upright, but he can no longer move without assistance. He did admirable work at Béthune, where he is headmaster of a primary school. We discuss the likelihood of his execution, and I say they wouldn't dare to shoot him. 'Oh, Madame,' he replies with a kindly smile, 'there's nothing they wouldn't dare do!' Then, quite simply, he adds that it would be for the best anyway, as he can feel himself becoming totally paralysed. He has endured such terrible cold during this last year in prison, and being cooped up and unable to move in a cell has been disastrous for his health. Although he has asked many times to see a doctor, he has only ever had visits from nurses. Then he shows me photographs of his children. This very morning he received a new picture of his daughter. He is so proud of her beautiful looks and glowing health. A happy man!

Prison de Fresnes, 17 February 1942

The verdict at last!

The judge is pale; I've never seen a man so pale: he has said that his duty as a German is harsh. Today it is clear that his words were genuine. Passing these sentences is painful to him. He respects and admires the men whom he is about to condemn to death.

We are placed in the same order as for the summing up of the prosecution. The judge indicates to those who are to go free that they will be able to walk from the courtroom. Then he turns to those of us who have a sentence to serve: Müller, Jean-Paul Carrier and myself. Last of all come the death sentences: Yvonne Oddon, Sylvette Leleu, Alice Simonnet and the seven men. Jean-Paul Carrier escapes with three years' imprisonment. Müller and I get five years each.[12]

The judge asks if there is anything I wish to say. I reply that, as he must be aware, over the last eleven months I have not uttered a word of truth; but that the purpose of this web of deceit was to protect friends whom the Germans would never lay their hands on, and not to exonerate myself. And since he is an army captain I add: 'Despite my lies, I believe I have conducted myself with honour as the mother and daughter of officers.' He bows his head in response.

In a few clear sentences, Vildé makes an eloquent, humane plea on behalf of the Kid. He asks to be held entirely responsible

12 Jean-Paul Carrier escaped from Clairvaux prison, spending seven months in Spanish prisons before he reached North Africa; Müller was tragically killed by bombing in Germany.

for René Sénéchal's actions, as – he assures the judge – the lad had no idea what he was carrying into the free zone. He begs for Sénéchal's youth to be taken into account. For himself he utters not a word. All his efforts are concentrated on one end and one end only: getting René off, saving René's life.

Jules Andrieu, speaking briefly and with great dignity and nobility, avows that he bears no personal hatred towards the German people.

Pierre Walter, born in Lorraine but a Frenchman by election, gives one last cry of '*Vive la France!*'

Yvette Oddon declares that she is the daughter of a colonel who died of his wounds, and that she has acted as the daughter of a French officer. With moving pride, Sylvette Leleu proclaims that she acted to avenge the death of her airman husband, shot down and killed in 1939.

The judge orders the three future deportees to leave the court. Then he calls me back and allows me to wait in a small adjacent room, where I will be able to make my last farewells to my friends. He says 'last farewells' as though he believes it, but I – we – cannot!

Half an hour later we are all together again in the courtroom. Vildé is convinced that whatever happens he will be shot as a hostage, as there was another anti-German attack in Paris last night. He says this with a detached air, as though he were talking about someone else, someone of no particular importance. He jokes with Pierre Walter, who tells him, 'You know, I've just heard that Gaveau has sold twelve more of us down the river in Lille.' Then Pierre examines the palm of his left hand, tracing the life line with his right index finger: 'It's a long one, we'll be fine.' And he laughs. Then he asks me to pass on his best wishes to Simone Martin-Chauffier, who was so kind to him. But I retort that we'll see her together when we get out. Suddenly solemn, he replies: 'No, you know I'll never see her again.'

Vildé asks whether my family have enough to live on, adding: 'My wife knows everything; go to her if you need anything. Your families will be looked after while you are in Germany, until victory comes.' Then he adds: 'Victory in 1944.' (This seems so far away that I feel a pang of anguish. He predicts it with such certainty!) Then, taking my hand and looking at me with his blue eyes, sparkling with mischief, he says, 'There'll be plenty of work for you, Agnès, when you get back.' And we kiss each other. Then I embrace Lewitsky, who is smiling and chatting with Yvonne. We are taken back to our cells. In the corridor I turn round to catch one last glimpse of Vildé. The clerk – a German soldier – is telling him, his voice faltering with emotion, that he hopes he will soon be given clemency. Vildé laughs, shakes him by the hand and, as if to distract the German from his pain, swings his arm to left and right as though he were a child, and the pair of them roar with laughter.

Lewitsky, Nordmann and Ithier have been taken away, leaving me with Pierre Walter, the Kid and Jules Andrieu. I embrace Pierre and the Kid, then I hesitate: I hardly know M. Andrieu! But then, sounding like a naughty child who has been punished, he asks, 'And me? Don't I get a kiss?' With this kiss I return to my cell, while the adjutant yells at us to hurry up and my good Austrian warder, his eyes filled with tears, whispers in my ear: 'They've got no heart, those people!' As he shuts the cell door behind me I hear him murmur again: 'No heart.'

I have had a visit from Pierre. They put us in separate cubicles covered in chicken wire, with a space in between in which a German officer sits, pretending to read a newspaper. It is ten months since I last saw my son. A slanting light falls on his face. On his forehead and in the corners of his eyes I see the beginnings of fine lines. This time last year Pierre was only a child. Now I see a man before me, a man whom I hardly know.

We talk quickly, about nothing in particular. The quarter of an hour is soon up. Pierre asks if he can kiss me. Permission is granted. For an instant he squeezes me so hard that it hurts. Then the adjutant appears, shouting as always. Quickly I make for a corridor, realize it's the wrong one, and double back to where I started from. I see Pierre still standing where I left him. He is looking at me. The adjutant starts yelling again, this time even louder. Pierre must think that he is about to hit me: his expression hardens and he turns pale. Brutally, he is told to leave. I shall never forget his expression. It must be terrible for a child to see his mother abused without being able to do anything to stop it. I wish now he hadn't come!

Prison de Fresnes, 18 February 1942
This morning at eight o'clock my Austrian warder comes to fetch me. I am wanted in Paris, he says. No, I don't need to pack my things. What do they want me for? He doesn't know. I am put in a truck with an escort of soldiers. They are exuberant and good-natured; we are driven to the Hôtel Crillon. What a joy it is to see the place de la Concorde again! If only that shameful flag weren't flying over the Navy Ministry. I am taken into a small office, where two officers are waiting for me with the prosecutor. He is oily and ingratiating. Pulling an armchair up for me, he offers me cigarettes, which I naturally refuse. In a few words, he informs me that I am about to leave for Germany, and that life there will be hard for me, very hard. But, he adds, my sentence is not definitely decided, not definitely decided at all, and he makes heavy weather of trying to convince me that it is entirely up to me. He reminds me that I claimed not to have written *Résistance*; so, if that was true, who did write it?

I must know who wrote it: they are quite convinced that I know everything about it. Why yes, of course, I reply, I know exactly who wrote it.

'So?' he asks, with an expression of triumph in his evil little eyes like lottery balls. 'So . . .?'

'So, what would you do in my position?'

He smiles.

'You're smiling, so I'll do the same. I'll smile too.'

'You don't want to change your mind in any respect?'

'Absolutely not.'

'Well, bringing you here was a complete waste of time then!'

'By no means. I saw the place de la Concorde, and I am grateful to you for giving me this pleasure before I leave France.'

But this wasn't the only useful thing to emerge from my trip to Paris. All afternoon I was left more or less to my own devices in the waiting room. There I was able to offer assistance to an English member of the order of White Fathers, and to give advice to a Jewish silk stocking salesman, who managed to deal very well with a few little difficulties he had been experiencing. I made the acquaintance of a pretty palm-reader who had been brought in for announcing the imminent victory of General de Gaulle rather too enthusiastically. And finally I was able to have a longish talk with Pierre Walter's lawyer, who was there quite by chance. He assured me that there was no question of them executing Boris Vildé. Petitions for clemency were pouring in from both the free zone and the occupied zone. The Germans could not ignore demands for clemency for Vildé from distinguished names such as François Mauriac, Paul Valéry and Georges Duhamel. And once Vildé's sentence was commuted, the others would automatically follow. Gaveau, the despicable informer on whom I have never clapped eyes, would be found wherever he might be and 'dealt with'. Maître Wilhelm is convinced of it. It was with this assurance ringing in my ears that I returned 'home' to Fresnes.

Prison de Fresnes, 19 February 1942

This morning at eight o'clock the Austrian comes to fetch me again. He bustles around busily, telling me that I have thirteen minutes (such military precision!) to get ready. The door to Yvonne Oddon's cell is half open, and she is finishing her packing. Lewitsky is there! Our kind warder has been to fetch him so that he can say goodbye to his fiancée. He is even allowed to help us carry our parcels to the bus. I have time to embrace him, to tell him of yesterday's excursion, to convey to him Maître Wilhelm's absolute conviction that Vildé will be granted clemency. What a wonderful, confident smile when Lewitsky hears this!

'So in that case none of us will be shot, neither me nor the others.'

And on those words we parted.

6

In the Communal Cell

Prison de la Santé, 19 February–16 March 1942

For my last month in France I was put in a communal cell: section four, cell twenty-two. There were four of us: Rachel Zalkinoff, Jeannette Février, Andrée and myself. After so many days and weeks of biting cold and silence at Fresnes, I can't begin to describe the warm camaraderie of cell twenty-two! We weren't four separate beings; we were one entity. We shared the same thoughts, the same joys, the same sorrows. When one of us received a parcel it was 'our parcel'. The cell was heated. We were like a harem without a sultan. We tried out new hairstyles, did each other's make-up, altered each other's dresses, read, told stories and swapped recipes. Life was good. Between noon and two o'clock one of us would stand watch while the others chatted with the men on the other side of the yard. With Henri especially, Henri the young communist electrician (and Jewish to boot, just to annoy them, as he used to say). To take his mind off the cold and hunger he used to make up songs. He used to sing one using our names, which made us giggle, especially when he came to the verse starting, 'And what did you do, Agnès?' And then there was Jean, Jean the student, who was forever asking how to get rid of the bugs that were eating him alive. This gave rise to endless dubious jokes on the theme of Jean the student and his crabs.

Andrée was there for distributing Gaullist tracts; Jeannette, who worked in the Citroën factory, was accused – not without reason – of being a communist. Rachel was the heroine of the dorm. She was recovering with difficulty from her frostbitten feet, which were black to the ankles. It was thanks to the incessant demands of the nurse, 'Sister' Lia, that Rachel had been transferred to the heated fourth section from the freezing cold first section. When she arrived at La Santé, Rachel was haemorrhaging badly. Naturally, according to the custom here, she was not given so much as a scrap of cotton wool to mop up the blood, and for five days and five nights she had nothing to either eat or drink. None of which prevented them from dragging her off every day for interrogations. She was forced to watch as her elderly father and her brother were beaten up by French policemen. Rachel never gave in, never talked. Her brother Fernand Zalkinoff was a group leader and a remarkable character. He was eighteen and there were seven in his group, all the same age. They derailed trains carrying German soldiers going home on leave and set fire to the fodder for German horses, before they were caught, tortured and shot. I was there when the captain came into our cell to inform Rachel officially of the death of her beloved brother. It was he, the German, who was forced to lower his gaze, deeply moved by this admirable little Jewish communist, just twenty-three years old. The German would have preferred tears, screams, insults – anything rather than this contemptuous silence. When the cell door closed behind him, Rachel said simply: 'I can't believe that Fernand isn't thinking any more.' She didn't say another word.

Maman came to see me on 10 March. I asked her if the petitions had had the effect we hoped for. Maman replied that there was nothing more to be done now. They were all shot on 23 February. On Vichy orders, Jean Cassou has been put in a concentration camp in the free zone. I don't know why.

Rachel has been taken away. She said she was sure she would find her parents again. It seems that they are gathering all the Jews together at Drancy. Rachel thought they would take her there too: 'I'll be able to comfort my parents.' That was all she said. Never did I imagine that I could feel so much respect for a child of twenty-three. Respect: that is my overwhelming feeling when I think of Rachel.

Prison de la Santé, 16 March 1942

Pierre and Maman came to see me this morning. It appears that I am being sent to Germany tonight. Maman was terribly brave, cheerful even. I was inexpressibly grateful to her for concealing her feelings. Pierre coped very well too. We asked the Germans for permission to embrace each other. They refused.

I have told Jeannette and Andrée that they are not allowed to cry. They help me to pack my case. The men shout all sorts of nice things, and a chorus of other voices joins in.

'Big Lulu' – who is wonderfully brave, as all the men in her family are to be shot – takes my case down to the yard. She says, 'Me, I'm an orderly, so that's why I can see you for a bit longer.' A warder, fat Herr Matz, sobs into his checked handkerchief. I say to Lulu: 'He must be drunk, the fat *haricot vert*.' Far from it, it appears: he is shedding tears for us. 'Such fine women, it's disgusting taking them away like this.'

Yvonne is with me. We travel in an ordinary third-class carriage with bars at the windows. We talk right through the night. Sometimes old clichés come into our heads, and we giggle. *Michel Strogoff* made a huge impression on us both when we were girls. The departure for exile. Has it been written about in literature? It's much simpler than you'd think. It's the people we leave behind us who will surely suffer more than we do . . .

7

Forced Labour

Anrath Prison, 31 March 1942
We finally ended up at Anrath.[13]

During this improbable journey – which took a fortnight from Paris to Anrath – we were able to talk to a French comrade. The best of our conversations took place in the police van that took us from Düsseldorf station to the prison.

Armand Schmidt already has long experience of German prisons: for seventeen months now they have dragged him around like this from one prison to another. We can't remember the name of the place we are heading for. As we rack our brains Schmidt remarks, 'Just as long as it's not Anrath.'

'Yes, that's the place: Anrath. Is it really that bad?'

A short pause, then Armand goes on: 'I might as well tell you now, Agnès, there isn't a more terrible forced labour prison in the whole of Germany. It's better that you know from the start. The food isn't too awful, but there's hardly any of it . . .'

'Do they let you have books to read?'

'Yes . . .'

13 At this period political deportees were not taken straight to extermination camps, but were automatically sent to do forced labour in Germany alongside common criminals. This explains why my own experience, and that of all other deportees in early 1942, differed so greatly from that of deportees who arrived in Germany after us. Their fate, alas, was far crueller than ours.

'Well then, it can't be that bad. What about the work?'

'You'll be making cardboard boxes for shops.'

'Doesn't sound too dreadful to me . . .'

'No, but the prison director is a sadist; you'll need to grit your teeth, Agnès . . .'

On this piece of advice we at last get out at the station serving Anrath, a village apparently a long way from the nearest town – reassuring from the point of view of air raids.

From the outside the prison looks like a fortress; inside it is pleasant enough, with ochre-coloured tiles and house plants in the corridors, all spotlessly clean and silent as the grave. As we go in I hear someone say my name. It comes from an upper floor, probably from a woman prisoner I don't recognize who is pinning out laundry. Who is she?

We are stripped without further delay. Yvonne and I are split up . . . to be allowed to stay together would be too much to hope for! Showered, searched and dressed as convicts, we look like ancient and impoverished peasant women. My dress was originally made from a light woollen material. Now it's a patchwork of different black fabrics, with embroidery in the form of a few machine darns. The left sleeve sports a yellow armband, the colour of shame. I thought I would get a jacket, but I'm not allowed one. But I do have a white cook's pinafore. By way of underclothes I have a heavily patched chemise and a pair of long drawers that fasten below the knee . . . very risqué! Around my throat is a small blue-and-white-checked cotton scarf. My hair is plaited in pigtails, secured with elastic bands. As my hair is quite short and my plaits no more than ten centimetres long, this makes me look just like Bécassine. But the shoes are the best thing: a pair of black mules, though I use the word 'pair' loosely, as one must be a size 37 and the other a 41. With all my things stuffed anyhow into a large sack, I am dispatched to my cell. Thus the 'robing ceremony' is completed swiftly and efficiently, to the accompaniment of

a magnificent air raid. The prison walls shake, so the anti-
aircraft guns must be close by. Our British friends have not
forgotten us – but you can't help wondering what on earth
they can find to bomb in this dump.

My cell is fairly big, but I have it all to myself. Still that
deathly silence reigns. If I climb on top of the table I can see
the countryside and a small factory that must be attached to
the prison. I wonder what they make there?

The soup seems well made, but unfortunately there is so
little of it that I have stomach cramps already. A French orderly
announces under my cell door that the British are in Paris. I
disabuse her, to her evident disappointment. I dampen her
enthusiasm again when she tells me that the British have landed
in Belgium, and are thirty kilometres – no more, no less –
from the German border.

I am at leisure to study the decorative style of my cell.
White walls, naturally, with inscriptions. I can't understand
all of them. But here as everywhere there are notches to mark
the passing days, or possibly hours. The iron bed has a reasonably good mattress and clean blankets wrapped in a blue-and-
white-checked pillowcase. The bottom sheet is white. The table
and stool are of deal, the jug is Alsace stoneware, and the wash-
bowl is metal. The slop bucket is ceramic with an aluminium
lid. The floor is of ochre-coloured tiles. Against the wall is a
small cupboard containing a white enamel food bowl, a glass,
a small mirror and a poster showing physical exercises. The
cell is heated. All things considered it's a distinct improvement
on my French cells, and solitude holds no fears for me. If only
I had some manual work or a book to read, how good life
would be! Henceforth I have just two personal possessions: my
toothbrush and my comb.

I am taken from my cell to be introduced to the female
director. We form a queue outside her office. Yvonne is next
to me; she has a cotton dress and tells me between clenched

teeth that she is absolutely frozen. They have taken everything woollen away from her – and she is so delicate and feels the cold so cruelly! For a moment she forgets to stand to attention and slips her hand up to her hair. A wardress orders her to stand to attention according to the rules. Yvonne does not obey absolutely immediately, and the wardress strikes her hand with a key, tearing the skin on her thumb. Yvonne draws herself slowly up to attention, and I notice blood dripping from her thumb on to her hand and then on to her pinafore. The wardress calls for a strip of plaster and bandages Yvonne up without a word. I'm fuming. This is a fine start: Germany certainly looks promising! That a nasty little brat of a twenty-year-old should dare to lay a hand on Yvonne, to make her bleed!

The female director asks my name and, after ordering me unpleasantly to behave well and work hard, sends me back to my cell under escort. Once inside, I pass the time by singing.

I am allowed to write to Maman with my news, but only in six months' time. Perhaps the war will be over in six months! September – yes, surely the war will be over before the winter!

I am taken to see a doctor. A nurse of some kind asks me beforehand if I can read and write. When I say I can, she asks how many years I spent at school. Modestly, I begin to list my university degrees, but she remarks that if Frenchwomen are to be believed they are all 'professors'. Then, moving on to a different line of questioning, she asks if I have already been in prison in my own country. At which I bristle and inform her that if she cares to consult my file she will find that I am a political prisoner, not a common criminal. She dismisses me with a sarcastic laugh. The doctor listens to my heart for at least ten seconds, asks me if I have any 'diseases', and when I say I haven't tells me that I am fit to work. I stress that I am perfectly willing to do sedentary work, but that my doctor has always told me to avoid any physical strain, strenuous sports or prolonged periods of standing. A snort of laughter even more sarcastic than the nurse's effort gives short shrift to the views of the Paris Faculty of Medicine.

A week later, a prisoner who seems gentle and intelligent brings me some socks to knit. If this is what they call work it's not bad. Hideous grey socks with a red band round the ankle, the distinguishing mark of prisoners. In a mechanical fashion, this little job helps to pass the time. Meanwhile, my thoughts wander. Life here looks bearable. I sing. I pace the length and breadth of my cell. Then suddenly one day a wardress tosses me a pair of enormous clumsy shoes: I can't possibly wear shoes like these! The soles are wooden and very worn, evidently by someone with a limp in her left leg, and the leather uppers are as stiff as a board. My ankles will never withstand great clodhoppers like this. Their only redeeming feature is that they are not too short. In fact they must be at least size 44. I try to console myself with the thought that they could equally well have thrown me a pair of size 36s. Clearly any complaints, however amply justified, will not be tolerated. With all the tenderness of a bull mastiff, the wardress orders me to be ready first thing tomorrow, as I am to go 'on kommando'. I am still bold enough to ask what a 'kommando' is. She tells me that it's where I'll be put to work. I try to discover what kind of work, and am told that I'll find out soon enough – a truth accompanied by a snort of laughter that I'm starting to recognize.

Anrath, 10 April 1942

There are about forty of us in the corridor, standing in two ranks. It is time for soup: a watery swede purée, so thin it's virtually transparent. I'm absolutely famished. For the last two days I've had dysentery, with black specks flitting in front of my eyes. But these don't prevent me from examining the features of my companions, the other women who will make up this mysterious 'kommando': wretched faces, vicious and primitive. In among them, though, is one charming face, a young blonde woman with blue eyes. Our eyes meet, and with a deft manoeuvre we manage to get next to each other. Between clenched teeth I venture: '*Française?*'

'Belgian, political prisoner.'

I squeeze her hand and whisper: 'Let's stick together, you and I, whatever happens.'

She seems as anxious as I am not to be on her own, all alone among this pack of German women with their depressing faces.

They put us in a bus. Kate, my new friend, tells me that we are going to Krefeld, an industrial town a few kilometres from Anrath, where we are to work in a factory. We are both implacably determined not to work in any industry connected – however remotely – with the war.

The bus stops in front of a small and extremely dilapidated building that stands at the far end of a yard. The façade still bears a sign indicating that it used to be a furniture workshop: a humble establishment that must have belonged to some poor unfortunate Jew. The living arrangements and refurbishments that are planned for the building are far from finished. The stairs are filthy and ramshackle, and the rudimentary zinc wash-basins are more like a horse trough with small taps every now and then. The toilets are still at the planning stage. The dormitory is ready, jam-packed with bunks like berths on board ship, with hardly room to move. The wardress orders us to assemble in the dormitory, then double-locks us in – though not without providing us with a lidless bucket for our basic needs.

Kate and I grab a pair of bunks that appear to be relatively well placed. I take the top one, she takes the bottom one. She tells me that she has been sentenced to three years' forced labour for 'aiding the enemy'. Her husband is a prisoner too.

She has had no news of him, nor of their little boy, Freddy. Kate and her husband ran a hotel on the border between Belgium and Germany which was used as a 'mailbox' by a client and friend, a German Jew who was a member of the Intelligence Service. They both knew and approved of his activities. Denounced by the village postmaster, they were arrested as soon as the Germans invaded, on 10 May 1940.

Kate has been treated passably well so far. I tell her that I have been sentenced to imprisonment, not forced labour. Apparently the Germans make no distinction between the two. All prisoners are automatically made to do forced labour, whether or not they have been sentenced to it. A German woman with finer features than the rest joins in our conversation. In halting French she explains that she is a pure Aryan by birth, who committed the crime – after 1933 – of marrying a Jew. They thought they could live in peace in Belgium, poor things. Hunted down by the Gestapo, her husband was arrested and beaten, and they were both sent to do forced labour.

We are very worried about what sort of work we will have to do. Kate and I stretch out on our bunks to calm our nerves. When we open our eyes after a few minutes, we discover beside our bunks a magnificent steaming turd that was certainly not there earlier. The German women howl with indignation, accusing us (naturally) of being responsible for this pretty gesture. In mute accord, Kate and I both close our eyes as if to show that we are above all this pandemonium. A woman called Elsa, a very pretty girl whom I hadn't noticed before, springs to our defence, deciding that we can't be responsible for the mess as we have been on our bunks all the time, and that it will only mean trouble for us all if the wardress sees it. So she arms herself with a scrap of paper and courageously sets about cleaning it up. We meanwhile take no notice.

We have realized that there is another dormitory across the landing. A noise on the stairs alerts us to the return of our neighbours in the opposite 'apartment'. A few minutes later there is a scratching at the door and a voice asks: 'Are there any Frenchwomen in there?'

I call out.

'What luck!' comes the reply. 'It's you, Agnès! It's me, Denise, Denise from Cherche-Midi!'

It's dear little Denise! I'm so happy to hear her cheerful voice. I ask her straight away about life here, and above all about the sort of work we will have to do. We won't be doing war work! We'll be working in a factory making artificial silk, spooling the rayon on to bobbins eight hours a day. The work isn't too hard; the factory supervisors are kind. The rayon is used for making lingerie and stockings. It's all good news. The living arrangements are primitive, but they'll soon be better. The factory food is good and reasonably plentiful, nothing like the watery slop at Anrath.

This is all very well. But when I look around at my companions I am left speechless: we have to share our lives with these women! There are constant arguments and threats of violence. A particularly vicious-looking Polish woman confides in me, with a smile that is meant to be friendly but just looks depraved, that her speciality was picking pockets on public transport in Berlin. She points to the woman in the next bunk. Her name is Gertrude, and from a distance she looks like one of those faces you see in so many early German paintings: pale and anaemic looking, with blue-green eyes and tow-coloured hair, a huge bulging forehead, sensual lips and a long neck. Gertrude married a widower, and this widower had a little boy, nine years old. Gertrude abused him so badly and for so long that he died. She is serving ten years' forced labour. Over there is Annie, twenty years old and completely toothless. Her laugh is blood-curdling, her face an eruption of spots, and her legs a mass of suppurating sores. She carried on working in the full knowledge that she had syphilis, so infecting three of her male clients. As a result of their complaints she got two years' hard labour. Just how contagious *is* syphilis, I wonder? My, what fun we are going to have here!

A natural optimist I may be, but I still find my companions deeply dispiriting. Thank goodness that Kate's clear, pretty face is always there, and that we speak the same language and share the same views. Educated at the *lycée* in Aix-la-Chapelle, she is a cultivated woman; I am so unbelievably lucky to be with her. The thought of being on my own with all these gallows birds sends shivers down my spine. Lisa – witch-like and deeply lined before her time – will not be deterred from telling me her story. She is here, she says, because of a French soldier, a very nice prisoner of war who worked where she lived. She had amorous assignations with him in the cellar, where she was very careful about the basement window and the neighbours who might see what was none of their business. So careful was she that she would block the view through this wretched window with an open umbrella. One day the umbrella toppled over and a neighbour peered in; she told the Gestapo about what she saw, and hey presto, the French soldier was arrested and Lisa with him. So one precariously balanced umbrella added up to two people sentenced to forced labour and one unhappy husband obliged to work on his own while bringing up four children. 'Life is stupid,' concludes Lisa philosophically, with a pressing warning to me to watch out for umbrellas; you can't be too careful. There must be some very singular cases among all these women, psychological case studies laid out for first-hand scrutiny: what a gold mine for a novelist of the realist school, a sociologist or a psychologist . . .

For meals we have to go downstairs to a room known as the 'kitchen', doubtless by virtue of the ancient gas stove that stands in one corner. The women from our dormitory just about manage to squeeze on to two tables set along the walls. Each of us is given a reddish-brown enamel bowl and a wooden spoon. The soup is good. The women appear delighted, and wolf it down greedily and messily, squabbling noisily among themselves the whole time, despite warnings from the wardress.

Krefeld, 11 April 1942

At about one o'clock we are told to get ready. In the yard we are put in three ranks and marched off by two wardresses and two men who are apparently factory policemen. They make us walk down the middle of the street, like soldiers. It's impossible to speak to Denise, as the two dormitories are not allowed to mix. We pass in front of a dress shop. It has a large mirror, and I catch sight of myself in it. That old crone, limping along in her preposterous clumping shoes and with her hair scraped into such a grotesque style – that old crone is me. I have to raise my right hand to convince myself that the reflection in the mirror is really me. Yes, it must be me: the old crone in the dress-shop mirror is holding up her right hand, just like me. So I look just like all the others, just as wretched and destitute. It's so ridiculous to feel humiliated at being made to walk through these sunny streets looking like this. Other women, ladies on the pavements, are wearing pretty dresses with an air of spring about them. This feeling like sadness that rises in my throat, choking me, is just absurd. Why should we blush at being paraded through the streets of Krefeld like this? Yes, of course, my internal dialogue continues, but if only we had something – Kate, Denise and I – to mark us out from the German thieves and murderesses we have been thrown among, something small like a tricolor rosette. But then, I reflect, men (and women) are truly petty creatures if all it takes to allay these feelings – to rescue us from this weight of crushing humiliation – is three little lengths of ribbon sewn together!

They make us get into a tram that has been reserved for us.

The journey takes about half an hour. I find what I see of the town interesting. The houses look prosperous and attractive. The windows are beautifully dressed, with perfectly arranged curtains and masses of flowers. The road takes us out into the countryside, where the fruit trees are in bud. This glimpse of nature is hugely comforting. We pass through an old village with the tower of its feudal castle still standing. It is crowned with a temporary wooden structure, an anti-aircraft battery, no doubt. After the village we are treated to another vista across fields to the fringes of a distant wood. How lovely this all looks to eyes that have not contemplated nature for so long.

Eventually, we reach the factory. It is vast, ringed by workers' housing and more factories. In the distance is a massive suspension bridge. This, we gather from the street signs, is the Adolf-Hitler-Rheinbrücke. The factory complex consists of several large red-brick buildings, all of them very modern and harmonious in design. The first courtyard is embellished with flowers and a lawn. The largest building has an immensely tall tower that reminds me, though on a much larger scale, of the tower of the Palazzo Vecchio in Florence. I am so overjoyed to see something new – and something new that is a pleasure to look at, as everything here speaks of order and harmony – that I forget about my appearance. The courtyard around which the buildings are grouped is criss-crossed by railway tracks, and several railway wagons stand there. One of them is from France: '*Hommes: 40; chevaux en long: 8*' ('Men: 40; horses lengthwise: 8'). It contains neither men nor horses, but tons and tons of good French potatoes. There are so many that the Germans just walk over them. Why worry, when they are to be had so cheaply? My sudden anger is checked by the sight of two large glasshouses behind the factory. The factory grows its own flowers. I don't think there is anything like this in France, and yet there should be. All these flowers give such a cheerful, lively, humane look to the rational, austere architecture of the

buildings. The name of the factory is 'Phrix. Rheinische Kunst-
seide Aktiengesellschaft', but Kate has already found out that
it is known for short as 'Rheika'.

It is two o'clock in the afternoon. We go in. On the stairs
is a notice board. Later on I'll try to read some of the notices;
some of them are in French. We find ourselves in an enormous
hall; it has a metal structure, painted green throughout. The
floor is of beautifully polished wood. And everywhere, all
around, are spools of rayon in every shape and size, heaped in
gleaming white piles, reminding me of brides in their thousands. The hall is a symphony in white and green.

On every side spools are whirling. Evidently our job is to
divide up the skeins of rayon and wind the thread on to the
spools. Someone leads me to a machine of which every part
seems to be spinning and whirring at hectic speed. They explain
the work to me; there doesn't seem to be any great secret to
it. The female supervisor is friendly. My feet are absolute agony,
and we'll be standing for hours. I have a brainwave: I ask
permission to take off my awful shoes (my insteps are bleeding
already) and wrap my feet in the lengths of rayon that are scattered all around. Used to sheath the skeins, these look a bit
like the legs of stockings. The supervisor agrees to my request
without hesitation, and even seems to feel sorry for me. I work
under the supervision of a German female worker. Staying on
my feet all the time is going to be hard, but apart from that
I think I can cope with the work. Kate signals to me that she
is all right too. I see the civilian workers drinking from bottles
of sparkling water: it certainly is thirsty work, doubtless because
of the rayon dust that we swallow with every breath, which
dries our throats. Not far off I spot a little water fountain,
ingeniously and hygienically designed. The wardress informs
me curtly that this fountain is not for the use of prisoners: I
am not to leave my machine for any reason whatsoever. She
will take me to the toilets twice during the working day, and

that's all. Drinking in the toilets is out of the question. There too it is forbidden.

Passing the notice board, I manage to read one of the notices printed in French. This is what it says, word for word: 'At 46 Mittelstrasse, Krefeld, is a brothel (house of prostitution) with foreign girls. ALL other brothels are out of bounds to Phrix workers.' There follows the illegible signature of some big shot in the management. In the three hours that I have been at the Phrix factory I have let myself be carried away by the external appearance of the place, by the visual harmony that has such a powerful effect on me. For three hours I have forgotten that we are in Nazi Germany, where alongside the plants that decorate the factory there also flourishes a prostitution industry raised to the status of a municipal – if not national – institution: prostitution and racism. 'Foreign girls': we all know what that means. For three hours, I have forgotten where I am. I won't let it happen again.

We are allowed to stop for a meal break, and we are marched in three ranks across the courtyard to another building. There we climb a handsome staircase, with excellent woodcuts illustrating folk tales on the walls. The dining hall is vast. At the far end is a raised stage with two grand pianos. The space doubles as a cinema. It is virtually without walls: on both sides rise glass walls veiled with white curtains decorated with a Tyrolean-style design in red. It is quite beautiful. Rather less beautiful is the outsize portrait of Adolf hanging above the stage. On the walls, in charming lettering, are the same Adolf's exhortations to the workers. These texts and the portrait together form the only decorations in the far section of the hall. To the left, beside the door, is a kitchen, visible through glass walls, where meals for thousands of workers are prepared in huge electric cooking pots. The kitchen staff are dressed in white. Flooded with light and spotlessly clean, it is like some tremendous laboratory. One after the other, we file past a serving hatch. We are each given a bowl of excellent soup, which we take to one of the solid great wooden tables that are washed down after each sitting. All this is very fine, certainly . . . but there is still that notice in the stairwell on the other side of the courtyard: '. . . a brothel (house of prostitution) with foreign girls. ALL other brothels are out of bounds to Phrix workers.'

It would all be fairly tolerable were it not for the portrait at the end of the hall, the exhortations to the workers, the prostitution, the racism – in other words, were it not for Hitler. I mustn't let myself be seduced by this outward show that flatters my craving for culture and beguiles my sense of aesthetics. The Nazi jamborees at Nuremberg that I saw in the cinema were magnificent, but the obverse of these celebrations is war, the murder of men and the crushing of the human spirit.

At eight o'clock we are given more soup. The portions are generous, and the German women wolf down three or four bowls each; I wonder how they can possibly absorb such quantities of food at such astonishing speed!

Kate has been told to warn me that the director of Anrath is going to carry out an inspection, and that I should stand to attention when he arrives. The promised visit is not long in coming. I see an individual in a grey jacket and felt hat with the Nazi insignia in his buttonhole. He is short and dark, with an oriental look about him. His features are fine, his expression intelligent. He stops in front of me, asking me viciously why I have taken off my shoes. I explain. He replies: 'Very good. You will be severely punished.'

And with that promise he leaves me.

Our working day finishes at ten o'clock at night. They make us wait for the tram in front of the factory. Sleet is falling and we are freezing cold. And inside the factory it is so hot! I don't have a jacket. Kate pretends not to need hers – it's not true, I know – and is so insistent that in the end I give in and gladly put on what was once, it would appear, a nightshirt, a little grey cotton jacket with short sleeves.

The sky is lit up all around. Despite the sleet, they must be expecting an air raid.

My legs are very painful and swollen. For a year I have been confined to a cell, lying down most of the time, and now suddenly I am flung into a factory and doing this unaccustomed work . . .

When I stretch out on my bunk, I fold my clothes into a pile and put them under my feet, together with the sack of straw that serves as my pillow. I hope I'll be better tomorrow.

Krefeld, 21 April 1942

Yesterday was Hitler's birthday. Every shop is adorned with his photograph, every window with the Nazi flag. But we hear rumours of riots. Could this be the first breath of wind that heralds the revolution? Throughout our journey from Paris to Anrath we witnessed so many signs of genuine discontent.

The people of Krefeld watch our pathetic procession pass by with a kindly air. The day before yesterday a man positioned himself on the pavement and took a photograph of us. A witty German woman – and they do exist – remarked that the photograph would doubtless appear in a German illustrated magazine above the caption: 'How the Bolsheviks treat their female prisoners'.

Three days ago a new and much more promising batch of women arrived.

Elfrida is a butcher's wife. The mother of four young children, she swapped meat for shoes for her children, a crime that earned her two years' forced labour. Her husband, who is fighting on the Russian front, was brave enough to write to Hitler to tell him that he would fight much better if he knew his wife was free, his business prospering and his children cared for.

Frau Kaiser is elderly. She is devoted to her husband, and

to give him a treat on his birthday she bought him a box of fine cigars. The supplier of the cigars was a French prisoner, who used Frau Kaiser's money to escape. Frau Kaiser was sentenced to eighteen months in prison – time enough for her to learn that she should be more careful in her purchases.

Ingrid is implicated in the same 'affair': she has a sweet tooth, and couldn't resist buying half a pound of French chocolate, for the sum of five marks, from the same prisoner. Ingrid got two years. She is a glorious creature, elegant and diaphanous, the image of Walt Disney's Snow White. She speaks good German in a gentle voice. Just looking at her makes me feel better.

At the washbasins this morning, as we perform our hasty toilette while being jostled on all sides (like on the Métro in the rush hour), one woman asks me: 'Why are you bothering to wash your feet? There aren't any men here!'

Afterwards, we return to the dormitory, where we are locked in. But the wardress is constantly spying on us, searching us and generally making a nuisance of herself, never missing any opportunity. Yesterday she accused me of thieving because, with the supervisor's permission, I had taken a few scraps of waste rayon from the factory. Sanitary towels are very rare commodities here, and I had pinned my hopes on these scraps – but my hopes were dashed. Our wardress is called Frau Vicom. Frau Vicom is a Rhine maiden: she would be amazed, I'm sure, if I were to tell her that she could have been the model for the beautiful figure of 'Synagogue' on Cologne Cathedral, with the same cold purity and distinction. Sadly, she also has both heart and spirit of stone. She really can't be bothered with us, and takes us to the toilets only twice during the working day, when she feels like it. The change of routine and diet have upset my digestive system, and I ask to go on my own, urgently. No doubt I look very comical, as Vicom calls her colleague Frau Krefradt over, makes some remark to her about the face I am pulling, doubles up with laughter, and finally sends me roughly back to work. Ten minutes later I am back, by now in desperate straits, and this time I insist. The pair of them chortle long and loud. I had no idea I was so entertaining. Eventually, in her own good time, Frau Vicom takes me to the toilets. Another prisoner, Elsa Hartmann, a poor retarded girl with a squint, is suffering from dysentery. They refuse to take her to the toilets, so she relieves herself in the box meant for rayon waste. Betrayed by the smell, she earns herself a couple of hearty slaps round the face.

The weather has got colder. Our teeth start chattering as we leave the factory; it's been snowing, and I've got a nasty dose of flu. I ask for an aspirin. Vicom gives me one, but the next day I have the temerity to ask for another one. Vicom's room is on the landing. She decides to show me how she deals with unwelcome visitors. After telling me that it is not the administration's job to keep me in aspirin, Frau Vicom gives me a hearty punch in the stomach, and I go flying down the stairs. I manage to grab the stair rail halfway down and so save myself from injury. I spend the rest of the day reflecting on German remedies for flu.

Our charming Vicom has noticed that Kate and I are always together, and that we enjoy each other's company. It doesn't do, as a forced labourer, to show that you have found something that brings a little gentleness, a little pleasure into your life. Vicom summons Kate and orders her to move into the other dormitory. So for all practical purposes I'm now on my own, as even if I manage to see Kate, I'm officially forbidden to speak to her. No more of our endless chats: they were too good to last! But I shall still have the pleasure of seeing Kate's pretty face on the journeys from Ritterstrasse to the Rheika and back again – which is a lot to be thankful for.

Krefeld, April 1942

The rumours of rioting must be true, as our wardresses have just received their marshal's batons – in other words, the administration has issued them with adorable little coshes, known here as *'gummi Knüppel'*. These are a source of great pride. In the street they swagger about with them just like Marshal Goering. They inform us that from now on they have the power of life or death over us; this comes as no great surprise.

In the three weeks that I have been here my feet have been agony because of those wretched shoes, but mercifully my legs are better. Sadly, the other women are not so fortunate. This standing without moving for eight hours a day is causing all sorts of problems, from varicose veins to ulcers, and the legs of those with heart conditions have swollen up alarmingly. When consulted about this, the wardress makes a dismissive gesture and says, 'Well, there's nothing I can do about it.' And we have to carry on, naturally. There are many nights when we have to carry our companions from the tram stop to our quarters on Ritterstrasse.

I get the distinct impression that it's not a good idea to be ill here! A young French girl, Luce, has moved into the other dormitory, ruled by Frau Krefradt. Like me she has had the flu but has had to carry on going to the factory regardless. But she wasn't made to work and they gave her aspirin. She was granted the much-coveted right, moreover, to replace her non-existent coat with a blanket. Back at the dormitory, the poor child fell into an exhausted sleep in her bed, a bottom bunk. The German woman who sleeps above her is incontinent: all of a sudden, without warning, Luce found herself drenched.

A fine tall girl by the name of Annalisa is suffering from an acute infection of the fallopian tubes; when she came back from the factory yesterday she was unconscious, out cold. This time it was policemen who carried her back. As long as we're still alive we have to go to the factory. When the woman in the next bunk to me developed scabies, however, Vicom had her sent back to Anrath.

Yesterday a civilian worker, a Flemish woman who doesn't speak French, slipped me a packet of sugar – a gesture of camaraderie that gave me so much pleasure. I don't suppose I'm exactly glowing with health, and the good woman clearly thought I must be hungry. In fact I suffer much less from hunger than from my surroundings. Every woman here is a 'case', a tragedy caused by the creation of the hellish monument that is Nazism.

Take Annie, a decent German housewife who must once have been pretty. She has been married for twenty-six years. Her husband is a greedy man and very fastidious in his tastes, so she forged some food ration tickets to get him what he wanted. She was denounced, and sentenced to three years' hard labour. Her husband is a Party member, and she has just heard that he has divorced her, as a Nazi cannot afford to have his honour blemished by a worthless woman. And of course he has a younger and prettier replacement lined up. Annie never stops crying, dissolving into one fit of helpless sobbing after another. I try to look after her, to calm her down, but what can you do when the only remedy available is fine words?

I'm intrigued – and amused – by another woman. What sort of underbelly of society produced her, I wonder? She is here for stealing a sausage from a butcher's window display. She calls herself a pedlar, and answers to the name of Baker. Baker is very musical, and gives charming performances of arias from comic operas. Draped in a blanket, she also gives stirring recitals of classic verse. She is a fortune-teller and also reads cards (although this forbidden activity could earn her another month's imprisonment). Her deeply lined and crumpled face makes her look older than her forty-five years, but it sparkles with intelligence. The day before yesterday she got it into her head that she wasn't going to work, and simply abandoned her spools all over the place. The wardress noticed; the foreman, the female supervisor, the police, everyone screamed and shouted. Baker was taken away, and we know that there is a prison cell in the factory. Yesterday Baker reappeared with a black eye and her face all swollen. It appears that it's not so very advisable to refuse to work as a forced labourer under the Third Reich.

We are all in the toilets. Vicom orders us all to remove our drawers and file past her, proffering them for her inspection. Vicom examines the gusset of each pair of drawers, none of them freshly laundered, alas. We've been wearing the same underwear for two or three weeks now, and we are strictly forbidden to wash it. I wonder what sort of whim this parade could possibly be intended to satisfy? And lo, the answer comes! Vicom has spied clots of blood under some of the machines, and she is scrutinizing our underwear for fresh bloodstains. Who among us, I ask you, could have had the temerity to stain the sacred factory floor with her blood? None of us, of course! Vicom, imbecile that she is, had failed to notice that the red clots were in fact gobbets of the grease used to lubricate the machines. And so the incident is closed . . .

Krefeld, May 1942

There is talk of nothing but Russians, of how we're going to be replaced by Russians! Are these Russians men or women, and what will happen to us when they arrive? Where will we go? What will become of us? The German women weave fanciful scenarios in which they are invariably to be released, with Russians taking their places. Meanwhile the days pass and nothing changes.

As we leave the Rheika in the evening, we often pass the

next kommando arriving. Among the women I notice one – a Frenchwoman – with a twinkle in her eye. She shouts out the 'news' to me. Apart from the fact that she is from Tourcoing I know nothing about her – except that she has a wonderful spirit and energy, and that she wants to share her natural cheerfulness with everyone around her. One day it's Pétain who has fled to Algeria, the next it's Italy on the verge of surrender, and the latest is that Sikorski has spoken from Poland – and the proof is that there are no Polish workers left at the factory; they've all gone home. Then there's the landing by British and American troops: just wait for the fine weather and they'll be here in no time. I don't believe a word of it, but it cheers me enormously. I know that the war can't go on much longer, and that Nazism will be destroyed from within as well as without. As soon as the Russians cross the border, revolution will break out in Germany. For years we have been told that everything is ready – weapons stockpiled, blueprints for action drawn up, watchwords prepared – and just waiting for the sign, when rebellion will spread throughout the country like wildfire. I know all this, and yet the 'bulletins' provided by the lady of Tourcoing still make me happy. I love to see the flash of her eyes as she arrives and shouts out to me: 'It's all going *so* well,' with an unaccountable stress on the 'so'.

Krefeld, Whit Monday 1942

Oh, what a great and wonderful feeling! It's a magnificent day. Just before we leave for work, I go back up to the dormitory. In the quietness I hear the drone of an aeroplane, and instinctively I look up at the sky, so blue and with not a cloud to be seen. And yet – what is that white shape there, that the aeroplane has just traced? A hammer and sickle! Will he ever know, that unknown airman, how many hearts swelled with joy on this spring day because of him? Will he ever know how much this emblem of work – of work freely consented to – means to a humiliated prisoner exhausted by slave labour?

Krefeld, May 1942

I have become quite skilled at winding rayon. So now I am applying myself to the art and technique of sabotage.

We are supposed to tie flat weavers' knots, as ordinary knots apparently make the machines break down. I see! The insides of my spools are studded with lumpy knots that will create a fine mess, while the outsides are neat and correct. That's the main thing: what the eye doesn't see . . . I feel much happier now that I know that not a single one of my spools is any good, not a single one will be of the slightest use to the Third Reich!

The Russians have arrived. They are Ukrainian girls, so young they are still virtually children. Naturally, we are forbidden to approach them, speak to them or even look at them. Even so, we discover that they have been forcibly deported, that they have been made to sign contracts to work in a chocolate factory, and this is where they have ended up. Most of them are quite beautiful. They all wear their traditional scarf or a white kerchief around their heads, and they have a shy, timid air like a flock of little sparrows. The German women crowd round to look at them. Many of the new girls wear little crosses round their necks, a matter of great surprise to the German women, who are having to rethink some of the rubbish they have been fed about life in the Soviet Union.

The Russian girls have a label sewn on their clothes, a little rectangle of blue material with the word '*Ost*' in white. You sense that they are proud of this distinction, of a little sign of the sort that I have lobbied for (mentally, obviously) since I have been here. The Polish women, by contrast, seem to be ashamed of the yellow lozenge with a dark-blue 'P' that they have to wear, using every possible stratagem to get rid of this identifying mark. Why are they ashamed to be Polish? As I wind my rayon I watch all these young Ukrainian girls, torn from their country and their families. They are so pretty, so innocent, so naïve, with their cheap jewellery and their shabby little dresses. These were the girls that I saw in the collective farms around Kiev in 1939, singing from sheer *joie de vivre*, and now here they are shackled in slavery.

Krefeld, May 1942

There was a great concert last night! A terrific air raid over Cologne. The bombers – British or American, we couldn't tell – flew over Krefeld on the way there. I knelt on my bunk, near the window, to watch the flamboyant spectacle of the searchlights, their luminous beams intersecting in the clear night sky; suddenly an aeroplane is caught in a shaft of light. Anti-aircraft shells explode all around it. Like a trapped moth, so white in the light, the aeroplane bounces up and then down, avoids the shells and at last – at last! – escapes from the treacherous light. Wildly, I scream, 'They missed him, the swine!'

The women's nerves are shredded by the din of the anti-aircraft guns, and they know that we are right beside Krefeld station – not the best position. There is no shelter. The wardresses have gone and hidden themselves the devil knows where, though not without first locking us inside. A thoughtful gesture if the building should catch fire. The windows are barred. I try to lie down on my bunk, but someone is already on it. It is the ineffable Baker, who takes me in her arms and calls me her 'sugar dove'; fear has made her amorous. With a thump I send her to look elsewhere for whatever it is that she needs to get her through the night. Alone at last, I doze off to the sound of the intensive bombing of Cologne, musing mournfully on how many people's lives will be extinguished tonight. Yet this massacre has to be . . .

Krefeld, June 1942

All of a sudden it's hot, and our thirst has become absolute torture. The food is highly spiced – with synthetic spices, of course – and we are constantly swallowing dust from the rayon. We are not allowed to drink water at the factory. At four o'clock a pot of some tepid infusion is passed round. We are permitted a quarter of a pint each. We all drink from the same enamel bowl, passing it from mouth to mouth: a charming habit that includes the tubercular and the syphilitic. I only hope the germs all cancel each other out. There have been several cases of tonsillitis and one of diphtheria. That one at least was evacuated to the hospital in Krefeld.

Only too well aware of our thirst, Vicom decides to make sport of it. We are caught talking in the tram? 'You will be punished: three days without drinking,' and for three days she watches us. When we go to wash she spies on our every move to make sure we don't drink, then she locks the door after us. When we come back from the factory she is first into the building, putting her cap over the tap on the stairs in case we should try to filch a few drops of water. Then she locks us in the dormitory. Maddened by thirst, the women beat on the door, begging for water. Vicom doesn't give an inch. I had always heard it said that thirst is more terrible than hunger, and now I know it's true. But Vicom has forgotten one thing: the water in the toilet flush! Of course she doesn't realize that when your tongue is swollen with thirst, you lose your sense of revulsion. So coolly I pull the flush, and quickly catch a little water in the hollow of my palm; two or three times more and my thirst is a little less unbearable.

Krefeld, June 1942

As we pass them in the street, two small boys stare in wonder at our wretched appearance. One asks the other where these poor women come from? We hear the older boy reply that his mother has told him that we are refugees, and that our houses have been bombed. We have been given these ugly dresses just for the moment, but we work at the factory and soon we will have pretty clothes and smart shoes like everyone else. These children are the exception. While adults tend to look on us with kindness, the children almost always shout abuse and throw stones at us, though as yet there have been no serious injuries.

It's my lucky day! By some arrangement that we don't even try to understand, the '*dame de Tourcoing*' has arrived in our dormitory. Her name is Betty Spriet, and she radiates energy. She runs her own small business and she's a true Frenchwoman, a true citizen of the Republic. I tell her that she must definitely have been at the Bastille on 14 July 1789, no question about it, urging the men on to storm the prison. We make a joke out of everything, Betty and I.

She has a fine sense of the comic and the ridiculous, and I'm no slouch myself. When it's my turn to slop out in the morning we do a rather good line in barrack-room humour. What I love about Betty is that she understands the importance of French propaganda. Unfailingly courteous to the German women, she earns their affection – affection and respect – as they all know why Betty is here. Her sterling work with the British in Tourcoing and Lille was rewarded with interrogations of particularly refined brutality, in which beatings with coshes alternated with psychological torture. Betty never weakened. Her beloved husband and her elderly mother are waiting for her at home. But not the slightest hint of sadness, the faintest sigh of regret ever escapes her lips. Her company consoles me for the loss of Kate, who now that she is in the other dormitory can only exchange the odd hurried word with me.

The German women have nicknamed me 'Angelica'. Oddly enough, it doesn't take much to gain the trust of these simple women, pig-headed and bigoted though most of them are. They are entirely devoid of any sense of solidarity. If one of them is ill, it never occurs to the others to come to her aid. I wonder if the same is true of women of their class in other countries?

When we wake up in the morning we are allowed a ration of what is pretentiously known as 'coffee'. I take some upstairs to the women whose legs are bad, a tiny attention that they find very touching. The 'coffee' is brewed in a large brown enamel pot that serves a dual purpose: once a week we use it to boil up the sanitary towels that the most ingenious among us have been lucky enough to acquire.

A new girl arrived today. Nora is twenty years old and quite beautiful. The sight of such a lovely face does one good. She is Dutch, the daughter of a tulip-grower near Haarlem, and she helped her anti-Nazi fiancé to escape. Her smile is exquisite, and her blue eyes sparkle as she declares in her pidgin mixture of Dutch and German: 'Hitler has taken my country, my home and my fiancé, but he will never take my thoughts. My thoughts are mine and only mine.'

This simple young girl sounds like Descartes.

There is a good and venerable institution in the Judaeo-Christian tradition known as the day of rest. My respect for this institution has grown to the point of reverence since I have been doing forced labour. Here not only is Sunday not a day of rest, but it is even more shattering than the rest of the week. On Saturday we do our normal shift, from two o'clock in the afternoon to ten o'clock at night. By the time we get back to Krefeld and into our bunks it is nearly midnight. We then have to get up at four o'clock on Sunday morning in order to work from six o'clock to two o'clock. At two o'clock the tram is never there, moreover. We have to stand in three ranks and wait in the blazing sun, sometimes for an hour, sometimes longer. There are invariably some of us who pass out. But the wardresses are all right, which is what really matters. A bench under an awning in the shade makes the perfect place for a little light dalliance with the factory police. It is rare for us to get back to the dormitory before four o'clock on a Sunday, by which time our bare feet in our ill-fitting shoes are exquisitely painful.

Krefeld, July 1942

Excavation work is going on in the courtyard and – joy of joys! – the work has been allotted to two French prisoners of war. One of them, from Provence, has promised to pass on our news to our families. With great ingenuity, Luce has contrived to pass him our addresses, and we carry out our verbal nego- tiations from the toilet windows while the wardress enjoys her siesta. Yesterday the other prisoner, a spirited young fellow from Belleville, had a good go at Vicom on our behalf. She was tearing us off a strip, just for a change. We were standing in the courtyard in three ranks, waiting for the order to march off. The silence that followed the reprimand by our guardian angel was broken by a chirpy voice: 'You starve them, dress them in rags and make them work like slaves, but that's not enough, I suppose. Oh no, you have to shout at them too. Why don't you just put a sock in it, you old bitch!'

It was like a blast of fresh air straight from the streets of Paris – the streets of Paris taking their revenge! We set off with a new feeling of serenity. One of our men had sprung to our defence; we felt protected and less abandoned.

Krefeld, early July 1942

The whole kommando is in a fever of excitement at the great and wonderful news: Vicom is leaving! Our joy knows no bounds. When we get back to Ritterstrasse in the evening we celebrate by going straight up to the washbasins and drinking – drinking ad lib.

Her replacement is Fräulein Oberlack, a fat blonde girl, gentle and good-natured. The women tell her what fine times we have been having. Our new wardress informs us that the bad times are over and that she will try to help us to forget them. She is full of good intentions, and we sense that she really has a heart. Betty knows her and speaks very well of her. We can breathe at last!

There is talk of nothing but our move. From one day to the next, it appears, the kommando will change lodgings. Betty has already seen our new home and describes it to us. It is a large house called Kölping Haus, a Catholic youth club and social centre before the rise of Hitler, comprising a boarding house, theatre, gymnasium and restaurant. The theatre has been turned into a dormitory where some two hundred of us will sleep. There is free access to a courtyard, where it appears there is a large tree. Now that the heat has arrived it will be a pleasure to be in the fresh air. It's over fifteen months now since I last sat outside in the sunshine . . .

Krefeld, early July 1942

We are now installed in the famous Kölping Haus. It's just as filthy as Ritterstrasse, but the courtyard is a great plus for us. We are allowed out there in the morning. For the first few days I was intoxicated by the fresh air, and so very tired. The standard of the food is not as good either, and the rations are noticeably smaller.

The only parcels we are allowed consist of a comb and a toothbrush. I have just received mine from home. How I would have loved to see the handwriting on the wrapping paper, but my comb and toothbrush were unwrapped before I got them.

My new supervisor orders me to wind sixty spools, which

is practically impossible. I tell her that when my German neighbour manages it I will endeavour to do so too. My young madam raises her hand to slap me, but something about my attitude makes her change her mind, and she vents her spleen on a poor unfortunate creature with a goitre as big as her head, who weeps and sobs that she can't possibly do any more. Seeing that this pitiful old woman is more abject and vulnerable than I, she takes her anger out on her, shaking her and showering her with insults. When she goes to bed tonight our fine young lady, a Party member, will be able to congratulate herself on serving her Führer well today.

We have virtually no news, just wild rumours. Betty and I draw our own conclusions on the political situation from the mountains of merchandise stockpiled in the factory garages. Enormous bundles of rayon bound for Finland and Norway are stuck here. Are the lines of communication cut? As long as supplies are suffering, our morale is high.

Krefeld, early July 1942

We live and eat in the courtyard. Everyone has found their own spot. The one that Betty and I have chosen is very comfortable: with four bricks and a small board we have made a small bench a little apart from the others. There we can chat away with Rosette, our great German friend from Cologne. Rosette Weiss is a woman to be admired. The Nazis are unaware that she is a militant communist: she is here merely for having left Germany after 1933 without permission. Her husband is Jewish to boot. She was arrested in Belgium, but fortunately her husband managed to get away. She has no idea where he might be: in Portugal, or perhaps Russia? She spends her entire time trying to sort out other people's problems to the best of her ability. Her knowledge of the regulations governing prisons is admirably thorough, as she reminds the wardresses. It is thanks to her that we are now taken to the factory toilets every two hours, meaning four visits a day instead of two.

The other day, with an alacrity that was truly professional, someone stole my jacket. Rosette investigated the case, but naturally without success. I was guarding that jacket so jealously for the autumn . . . A Belgian woman who is supposed to be freed at the beginning of October promises me hers. She found it in the factory rubbish bins, and it is ripped, full of holes and has only one three-quarter-length sleeve; but I covet it just as it is, and she laughs as she promises to let me have it when she goes.

We've been wearing the same linen for six weeks now; we stink. A lot of the women, I learn, have crabs and lice. Sometimes we are able to take advantage of the freedom of the courtyard to wash our underclothes surreptitiously. All you have to do is steal a little soda; soap is such a distant memory that we can barely even remember what it looks like. My personal technique is to scrape off the dirt with a bit of brick that I pick up in the courtyard. Sand is quite effective, too – a tip for the laboratories where they make X and Y Beauty Products! There are nowhere near enough washbasins or toilets for us all. Everywhere there are long queues, women jostling each other, sharp words and thieving. Our sole possessions are a toothbrush and a comb, but if you take your eyes off them for a second they are likely to vanish mysteriously.

Searches are becoming more and more frequent. What on earth do they expect to find on us, for heaven's sake? We bury our most precious possessions, our most illicit treasures, in the sand in the courtyard, or stuff them down an old pipe that doesn't seem to serve any other purpose. A stub of pencil; a scrap of rayon that might be used to make a dressing or an improvised slipper; an aspirin procured in some unthinkable manner, which we squirrel away in case of flu, since when we ask for medication we are never given any, except sometimes a day later. The list of treasures also generally includes a sanitary towel. Having a period must be a shameful thing in Germany. When any of us asks for a sanitary towel, the wardress puts on a great show of disgust and says she hasn't got any.

Betty's bunk is next to mine; every evening we chat away together, making a little island for ourselves in this enormous dormitory. We don't get much sleep, as there are three different shifts coming and going much of the time. It's pitch black, with not a glimmer of light. As our food consists exclusively of soup, we all have to get up at least once in the night to go to the toilet, tiptoeing across the whole theatre and up to the first floor.

I am at a loss to know what kind of urge it is that drives women to perform their business on the stairs. Every night we encounter these trophies. Last night, Loulou slipped on one that had been deposited on the top step. When the others told her that it was a sign of good luck she didn't seem at all convinced, perhaps because her feet were bare. And this is only one of the nocturnal delights of Kölping Haus. There are also accounts to be settled between the lady boarders. The other night we were woken by a frightful shrieking. What was it about? We'll never know. After a few minutes the wardresses arrived with torches. There were at least two women involved in the fight, but who? A mystery. In the end, we decide that for safety's sake we will form a column to go to the toilets, so that we can leap to each other's defence if necessary.

I am extremely wary of a new inmate, a large red-haired woman with the physique of a man. She never undresses, and even sleeps with her shoes on (they must be less uncomfortable than mine). She will only eat if ordered to do so by one of us, and then her movements are like a robot. Her face is totally devoid of expression, as though carved from a block of wood, though her eyes are an extraordinary Veronese green. No one has heard her utter a word. She is here for having killed her son and her two nephews. She cut off their hands and let them bleed to death. Her sentence was only ten years' forced labour, as she was deemed not to be responsible for her actions. I can't say I relish rubbing shoulders with women like this, at night, in the dark, in a forced labour prison . . .

Just now in the courtyard a little ladybird flew on to my hand and crawled around on it for a while. It took me back to the ladybirds that we used to look at long ago in France. It reminded me so strongly of them that I asked it if, when it flew away, it would carry my tender affection to all those I love.

In the Rheika restaurant we see more and more groups of workers – Dutch, we hear – in a pitiful state. They are 'free' workers whose job is to make the rayon. Their prison overalls are in tatters, eaten away by the acid; their hands are bandaged; and they appear to be suffering terribly with their eyes, to the point where they often can't manage by themselves. A fellow worker will hold them by the arm, sit them down, put their spoon in their hand. They appear to be racked by excruciating pains. What sort of work can this be that causes such torments? I had no idea that the manufacture of rayon was such an agonizingly painful process.

By contrast, our eyes were gladdened a few days ago by a vision of grace and elegance. At our evening meal there appeared a young girl with blue eyes and brown hair in the regulation plaits. On her, the Anrath prison uniform took on a sort of comic-opera charm. She made the whole ensemble look like some kind of practical joke, and I went up to her with a smile, convinced that she must be French. No, I was wrong, Henriette Delatte is from Brussels. She is here for helping French prisoners to escape. Although she has been widowed for some years, she gives the impression of being very young. She has arrived from France, and brings with her the latest news, which does not give much cause for celebration. Our Russian allies have had to beat a major retreat; in Africa the British are suffering reverses; and the Americans are not yet ready to deal much of a blow. We'll just have to wait! We must resign ourselves to spending the winter here. By the spring the Americans and the Russians will be in a position to mobilize all their armour, and de Gaulle's forces will have gathered strength. Henriette assures us that the French people are beginning to understand the truth of what's happening, and are less willing to 'collaborate'. More and more people are being arrested, more and more people are being shot. The French people are in a serious state of mutiny. That's what really counts, until the Allies can muster sufficient might to crush the savage beast.

Krefeld, July 1942

Standing still at the machine will be terrible for Henriette, who has a heart condition. We know she is very brave, but at the end of an eight-hour shift silent tears stream down her cheeks. When we get back to Kölping Haus her legs are so swollen that she can't pull her drawers down, and we have to cut them off.

At last, a letter from Maman! She chooses her words with such care that she tells me almost nothing, just that 'everything's fine'. I'm disappointed. There are so many things that I would have liked to know. About the Cassous, the Duvals and all the others of whom I think with such affection each day she says nothing. It's more prudent that way.

Every fresh batch of letters unleashes more fits of hysterical grief. So many women discover that they have been divorced without their knowledge. One woman, whose divorce was pronounced just under a year ago, learns that her husband has married again, that her replacement has appropriated all her dresses, underwear and other possessions, and that to cap it all she is cruel to the children. The letters are full of deaths and houses destroyed. Perhaps I'm completely heartless, but I couldn't entirely suppress a smile when old Frau Zeloff cried: 'Everything in my house is burned to ashes, absolutely everything! All the lovely things my husband brought back from France – all gone!' One good turn deserves another, I couldn't help thinking. Poor little Annie shows me a letter from her mother. Clearly the poor woman has lost her wits: the handwriting and composition are proof enough. Annie's elder brother has killed himself, her other brother is in Africa and hasn't been heard from, her father is dead and now her mother is out of her mind, and Annie is here for sending love letters in Morse code to a French prisoner. She tells me that she craves only one thing: a merciful bomb to put an end to her misery.

Krefeld, July 1942

Nearly every night there's an air-raid alert. The wardresses lock us in carefully before making a noble dash to the nearest shelter with their bags. It's remarkable how these air raids lift our spirits and recharge our batteries. The noisier they are, the happier we are; we know it's childish, but it's as though the air crews are saying to us: 'Be patient, we're here, we haven't forgotten you . . .' Another firm belief to which most of us subscribe is that it is categorically out of the question that bombs dropped by friendly aeroplanes could possibly harm us.

Today the tram couldn't take us all the way to the Rheika, as a bomb had fallen on the rails and all the factory windows had been blown out. It only happened a few hours ago, and already they are replacing the panes with either glass or some ersatz imitation. Next time let's hope our friends will aim better, and that the Rheika factory itself will go up in smoke.

Kate heard the news in the kitchen. The British landed at Dieppe early this morning! There's fighting in Dieppe. That's it! They've landed! Everyone teases me because I didn't think it would happen this year. The German women pull faces, while we are delirious with happiness!

I am worn out, both by the heat and by the lack of adequate food. One could hardly accuse the Germans, on the other hand, of depriving themselves of anything. They are fat and greasy. The head chef at the Phrix factory creates prodigious *pièces montées*, spectacular desserts for the 'gentlemen' of the management. We are permitted to admire these mountainous sweetmeats through the glass walls of the kitchen.

People on the outside don't suffer as much as they like to tell us. They pillage, loot and pamper themselves while we prisoners starve. Our rations dwindle daily in both quality and quantity.

Fräulein Oberlack has been replaced for a few days by Fräulein Monia. She comes to find me at my machine and takes me off to clean out a cellar – me, who can only clean a room with a vacuum cleaner! She has clearly sniffed out my impressive flair for housework in all its forms. My feet are excruciatingly painful and my walking is slow; by way of encouragement, Monia rains down blows on my back. When I have cleaned out the cellar, she loads me down with an enormous bundle of dirty linen, which she orders me to take to the laundry.

One of the most melancholy sights in the courtyard comes at visiting time, when some of the German women are allowed the occasional visit from their families. Yesterday, a toddler caught sight of his mother through the bars. With all his heart and strength he was determined to get in. But it wasn't visiting time, and the wardress barred his way.

An elderly mother comes to see her daughter. The visit is so short that she doesn't have time to tell her everything she wants to. They push her outside. She can't see her daughter any longer, but out in the street, on the other side of the barred gate, she slips her hand under the central section of the gateway, where the step is worn. The hand waves a handkerchief, then suddenly the whole arm appears. The poor woman must be lying flat on her face on the pavement outside. Coming upon this scene unexpectedly, Rosette weeps silent tears. I had no idea that an arm pushed under a locked gate could be such a tragic sight.

Krefeld, July 1942

It's not just at night that the planes come over. Today there were no fewer than six air-raid warnings in broad daylight. One plane stayed overhead for some time, tracing figures of eight in the sky. Why figures of eight? What could it mean? August, the eighth month? Is there something planned for August? Whatever the case, some Belgian civilians assure us that the landings are continuing all over the place, and that the British are marching on Amiens. There's no confirmation of this from the Germans, and our guardian angels hardly seem panic-stricken. If all this were true, would they remain so unperturbed?

We are told there are to be major changes: the Russian women are now capable of spooling at a good rate, and there are too many prisoners working with them. Supplies of raw materials seem to be dwindling, moreover, to our great delight. So we might soon be out of a job. On the other hand, many of the Belgian and Dutch men, unable to bear any longer the indescribably harsh working conditions in the rayon mill, have escaped. There is talk of our being forced to replace these men in the gruelling work that they have fled.

It's a fait accompli. There has been a round-up of women for the *Spinnerei*, or rayon mill. Those selected are 'under thirty' and tall. Machines made for men need tall women to work them. The age of the women who have been selected gives me hope that I shall escape the next batch; but I fear for my dear young friend Henriette, who is already suffering such torments . . .

The factory top brass file past our machines and the head foreman picks out women at random. He puts my name and Henriette's on his list. This is alarming. But there's no point in asking questions: we'll find out soon enough.

8

At the Phrix Rayon Factory

Krefeld, July 1942
We are among the chosen ones, Henriette and I. Betty sobs
as she watches us go. When we arrive at what they call the
Spinnerei, or spinning shed, an overseer in blue overalls
approaches us. He looks us over like a slave trader, asks my
age, says that I don't look as old as I claim to be. I half expect
him to look at my teeth, like a horse dealer at a sale. After a
show of hesitation he finally agrees to take me – as though he
were doing me some kind of favour! Henriette passes the test
with flying colours. Then we are taken to the clothing store.
For eight hours each day we are allowed to cast off our slave
workers' rags and put on the factory uniform. Off with our
putrid, perpetually clammy underwear! Our uniforms are new:
khaki wool trousers and a white silk shirt with an enormous
'G' on the front and back. G = *Gefangene*: convict. A well-cut
khaki jacket, with the inevitable 'G' in the middle of the back,
a white silk headscarf, a thick black rubber apron and – oh
joy! – new clogs. Pretty little Belgian clogs with a butterfly
for decoration. So light are they to wear – so supple, I almost
catch myself thinking – that beside the monstrous Anrath
clodhoppers they seem like satin slippers.

The staff in the clothing store venture a little badinage with
us. It's strange talking to men who are neither jailers nor

soldiers. Certainly, life in the *Spinnerei* seems a bit less like prison. We are allowed to talk to civilians, we don't appear to have a wardress breathing down our necks all the time, and we enjoy the immense advantage of being able to go to the toilet by ourselves and to drink when we are thirsty. We are becoming human again! Perhaps life here will be tolerable after all. I turn my attention to the enormous machine hall around me, vast as a cathedral. The machines, twenty metres long and completely mysterious to me, are all protected by glass constructions like greenhouses. Everything inside seems to be in perpetual motion, twisting, turning, rising, falling. I am struck by the unfamiliarity of it all, the noise and the appalling stench of the acid.[14] We'll get used to it. The overseer places Henriette at one machine and me at another. Female prisoners like us are ordered to instruct us in the theory and practice of spinning. My tutor is called Lisa. She reassures me, saying that I will never have to work a machine on my own, as the work is much too hard. I will just be an assistant, as even the men can't be 'spinners' if they are over forty. Those who have entered their second childhood, like me, cannot match the physical and nervous stamina required.

The director of Anrath pays us a surprise visit at Kölping Haus. We are not there, but as he leaves he encounters us in the street. It appears that we do not march with absolute military precision – soon he'll be expecting us to goose-step. He snaps a curt reprimand, and we learn that we have earned four days in the punishment cells to teach us to march like soldiers of the Reich. Fortunately the weather is hot. We'll be sleeping on metal crossbars, a sort of hammock affair with our mattresses perched on top. We are allowed two blankets: a thoughtful touch.

On arriving at the factory I see a young woman stretched out flat on the floor beside her machine. She is all alone, and

14 Carbon disulphide.

no one is taking the slightest notice of her. I want to help her, but the others jostle me and tell me not to go near her. What on earth is wrong with her? Is anyone going to take care of her? Lisa tells me that it's nothing, she is just totally worn out, utterly exhausted.

As we come back from the restaurant after our break, we pass a column of Anrath prisoners. Looking even more wretched than we do, they are carrying one of their number, completely unconscious and stiff as a corpse. Bringing up the rear is a lad who is weeping bitterly; from the way he is walking, with his hand pressed against his leg, it looks as though he is suffering from an acute case of sciatica. It's so dreadful. We can't do anything or even say anything, not a single word of encouragement – all we can give them is looks.

Krefeld, August 1942

Before I go to sleep I put my beautiful prison dress at the foot of my bunk. Patched, mended and threadbare as it is, it's still a good deal better than some. I opened my eyes yesterday morning to find that someone had stolen it. The wardress says that there is 'nothing she can do about it' (what a surprise!). The thief must work on the afternoon shift, from two o'clock to ten, and tonight I am on the night shift, from ten to six in the morning. Fortunately it is hot. I am obliged to parade through the streets of Krefeld in a filthy white slip and a nightshirt. 'There's nothing I can do about it,' repeats the wardress with indifference. Three months ago I'd have found this humiliating, but now the humiliation (if humiliation there is) is for Hitler and not for me. My friend Martha, serving a sentence for theft and an expert in her field, promises me between two slices of bread that she will get my old rag back for me. How did she manage it? I don't want to know, but this morning my dress has reappeared.

I get back from the factory after a truly gruelling night, prostrated with exhaustion. I'm going to sleep like a log, I know. But then I see that my bunk is already occupied. I start to make a fuss, but a plaintive voice from beneath my blankets soon pulls me up short: 'Oh please, please, don't be angry, I haven't got lice and I haven't made your bunk dirty.'

I discover that this is the new regulation. For lack of space, the day shift and the night shift will take turns to sleep in the same bunks. From now on we will find our bunks already warmed for us. How delightful.

In the toilets, squatting in a corner, I discover a girl who is suffocating: unable to speak and gasping for air, she points at her throat in terror.

I call for Simone, the kind little Belgian social worker. She knows better than I what to do in such cases. Simone diagnoses a heart attack brought on by the acid; we lie the little patient down on the floor and put cold-water compresses over her heart. The overseer arrives. He clearly thinks the girl is dead. He pokes his grubby finger in her eyes, pulls back the lids and gives a low grunt. The girl is alive. He takes advantage of the opportunity to ogle her breast and make more or less obscene remarks to a colleague who has followed him in.

It's a funny thing how, during a night's work, old memories come flooding back with such clarity. Who can say why a conversation with Maman, a wholly unremarkable conversation, should swim up from the depths of my memory? Maman had been to the bank, and she said to me: 'I bought some shares in "Snia Viscosa" this morning as an investment. Artificial silk is becoming increasingly important in industry. It gives a good return.'

It gives a good return! Poor Maman, so good, so sensitive, how could she ever have imagined that this 'good return' was founded on human suffering? True, civilian workers in the artificial silk industries of civilized countries are treated very differently from the prisoners in the Phrix factory. They drink milk every day in order to ward off the stomach troubles and cramps brought on by the acid. We, on the other hand, are given soup with milk in it only during the night shift, which is to say one week in every three. When the eyes of civilian workers start to hurt they are given immediate treatment, whereas we prisoners are forced to stay at our machines until we are totally blind. To protect them from burns caused by the treacherous viscose, civilian workers are equipped with rubber fingerstalls and gloves; we prisoners work with our bare hands. And civilian workers can go for walks and fill their lungs with fresh air, and they have a better diet. Our food rations, meanwhile, are becoming increasingly meagre. Civilian workers in civilized countries are unionized and work a forty-hour week; we prisoners work sixty hours, and two Sundays out of three we are at our machines for a twelve-hour shift. In Hitler's Germany women political prisoners are slave workers, and their lives are held cheap.

Gradually I am starting to understand this work that seemed so mysterious to me – and so dangerous. The fear is still there as I circle the machine that I am learning to clean; I know that viscose, a substance that looks like buckwheat honey and has the consistency of glycerine, produces terrible burns. Like phosphorus, it sticks to the wounds it causes and is impossible to remove, eating the flesh away to the bone. Usually you do not realize you have been splashed with viscose until you feel the pain. By then it is too late. The damage takes its course and forms a sort of abscess. When this comes to a head, you squeeze the pus and the wound slowly heals up again. It is this viscose, which we all hate, that produces the artificial silk. It is piped to each machine from the viscose tank that lies deep in the bowels of the factory, and is passed through a pump, a filter and an inspection glass before it is finally extruded through a very fine spinneret made of gold or platinum. This spinneret is immersed in an acid bath containing carbon disulphide at a temperature of about forty-five degrees. As the viscose passes through it, it coagulates to form a white filament; this filament is then drawn up on to a glass wheel known as a 'pancake'. As the wheel turns it pulls up the filament, which then drops into a glass funnel with a very narrow neck. The funnel is immersed in a cast-iron vessel, hermetically sealed with two lids, which turns at a speed of two thousand revolutions per minute. The rotation pushes the filament to the walls of the vessel, filling it to produce a skein of white silk which, once unmoulded, looks like a hollow circular cake. The acid that solidifies the viscose burns the skin of our hands, arms, throats and faces. I'll never get used to it. If you have even the tiniest scratch, the acid eats into the wound, making it swell and blister and causing intolerable pain. Not everyone's skin suffers equally. Some of my companions can tolerate the acid on their skin quite well, but I just can't bear it, and yet my skin is so healthy. A spinner's work consists of extracting the fifty-two 'cakes' from the machine within the allotted time, then setting the cast-iron vessels rotating again and funnelling the filament for the next 'cake'.

First, she cuts the first four filaments on the machine, pushing with her foot on the pedal control attached to each pot to disengage and stop it. Then she unmoulds the 'cake' on to a metal tray set on a trolley behind her; this trolley is equipped with a lubricating device, a bucket of warm water, and a pot of coloured dye to indicate the quality of the rayon. She washes and greases the pot, puts it back in the machine and starts it up again. I can do all this: this is what an assistant does. After this the work becomes more skilled, the preserve of the factory hand. Once the four pots have been emptied, washed, greased, put back and set in motion, she grasps the filament in her left hand and, holding it between her index and middle fingers, takes it on to the glass wheel, follows it through and pulls it towards the funnel slightly. Still with her left hand, she tips acid on to the filament from a small lead tumbler; the acid draws the filament into the funnel and the pot starts to fill up again.

At this point, she uses a hook to remove a circle of rayon that is wound around the glass wheel before the funnelling process begins. This circle is set aside and gathered up with the other fifty-one by a specially designated factory hand. The funnelling process is quite a delicate job, requiring an apprenticeship of between one and three weeks.

When both trays on the trolley are full, the assistant carries them to a compartment situated at the far end of the machine, on the broad central corridor where the overseers stroll up and down, keeping an eye on production. The factory hand then turns her attention to running repairs, of which there are more and more with each passing day, caused by the poor quality of the equipment.

She changes any blocked spinnerets, an extremely dirty job and risky for the fingers, replaces any broken parts, and most importantly unblocks the extremely narrow necks of the funnels and checks that they are properly positioned. If the funnel is not absolutely upright or plumb in the centre of the pot, the filament will be 'frizzy' and practically unusable – so you have to watch out. At the end of the shift the machine must be left clean and in perfect working order for the next shift. This whole process usually has to be carried out six times on an eight-hour shift, and nine times on a twelve-hour shift.

I wonder – a worthy subject for meditation – what Descartes would have made of industrial machinery. What a subject for a philosopher! Not just the relationship between man and machine, and all the upheavals, material, moral and social that come in its wake, but simply the thoughts that sometimes come into your head when you are working at a machine. There's no tricking a machine; it's just not possible. A part out of alignment? Production immediately slows down. A loose screw? The whole machine seizes up. I like and admire the incorruptible integrity of the machine. With work done by hand there is always a little leeway, a margin of error, and any time lost can be made up with a little effort or improvisation; machinery, on the other hand, admits absolutely no possibility of inaccuracy or prevarication, is immune to all excuses, lies or flattery. Enduring, unswerving and fiercely tenacious, machines can teach men a marvellous lesson in integrity. The builders of the future, of our future, should take their inspiration from man's handiwork, the Blessed Machine!

Krefeld, August 1942

During the late shift on Sunday we were absolutely famished. We hope that the shortage of supplies is caused by military operations. For twelve hours' work we were given two paper-thin slices of sausage with our bread, and a watery soup in which I counted eight beans. The two other 'soups' were made according to the following recipe: water, sugar, synthetic redcurrant purée and a dessertspoon of semolina.

The consequences of my uncommon clumsiness have not been long in coming. My left hand sports six wounds caused by the viscose, my right hand three. Burned all over by the acid, the skin is grey and painful. And I am covered in splashes of Veronese green from the dye. Wash my hands, you say? With what? I have no soap, real or ersatz, just my bit of brick, and given the state of my hands a brisk rubbing down with a lump of brick doesn't seem quite the thing. Our friend Tonton, a doctor in civilian life, claims that a photograph of my hands alone would stand as a powerful indictment of the treatment inflicted on women prisoners. I seem to be losing a lot of weight, but I have taken to repeating a hundred times a day (in an updated version of the Coué method), 'They can have my fat, but they'll never have my skin.'

Suddenly and without warning, the wardress, a tall young woman who couldn't care less about us and leaves us alone, tells us that after work this evening we are going back not to Kölping Haus, but to new quarters.

We are not taken on the tram any more. No doubt our increasingly disreputable appearance does little credit to the civilizing race. Henceforth we are to be loaded up at the factory gate, on to either a bus or a windowless delivery truck. The bus is comfortable but much too small, and we end up in a heap on each other's laps. As for the truck, it is dark, airless and truly horrible.

Our new residence stands on Kölnerstrasse. Another commercial building doubtless belonging to Jews, it has been converted to house Belgian and Dutch 'free' workers. As we have seen, the latter were so keenly appreciative of the Phrix works that they made a run for it. So we have inherited their lodgings, which are quite acceptable: very clean and airy dormitories with beds, and a dining room and meeting room decorated with tolerable paintings of Dutch landscapes. The place appears to be run by a woman Party member whom we mistook at first for the concierge, and who is duly known by us as 'La Concon'. Here I am surrounded by young women and girls, many of them extremely pretty. What a consolation this is! Henriette and I are both admirers of a German girl whom we have nicknamed 'Minerva', a pure classical beauty, blonde and blue-eyed, with a creamy complexion, a profile of classical purity and a superb physique. If beauty really counted for anything her life should be extraordinary. But as it is she is an ordinary shop girl in a small grocer's, who was caught thieving and is now condemned to hard labour. Hermina sold dresses and coats on the black market and is now a slave at the Rheika; she too is ravishing to look at and so intelligent. With her halo of naturally platinum blonde hair, Ena should be a queen; instead she's a practised con artist. Erika looks like a Louis XV flower seller; it was armed robbery that brought her here. Lisa, my instructor, is a magnificent brunette with deep blue eyes. Leni has a splendid figure, but she is not as lovely as her friend Marlyse, who was brought here after a spot of looting following an air raid. Jeanne, on the other hand, is not pretty. Born in the French Flemish department of the Nord in 1917 to a German soldier father and a French mother, Jeanne has, as she puts it, 'done things the other way round'. She is in prison for having an affair with a French prisoner of war. As punishment she had her head shaved and was given two years' hard labour. Her hair has grown back thick and fast, because, she explained, 'I made lotions using my own pee.' As for her Frenchman, she is serenely confident that he will be faithful to her and even marry her. She can be sure of this because, unknown to him, he has drunk a love potion concocted by Jeanne: *café au lait* with a dash of menstrual blood. Macbeth's witches couldn't teach Jeanne a thing. And what, I wonder, did Yseult put in her love potion for Tristan?

Krefeld, August 1942

My dear little Henriette is completely blind. She is so brave that she never complains, but I know that she suffers from her head and her eyes, and that her entire nervous system is shattered. We lead her to the factory first-aid post, where the nurse, whom she says is very humane, puts ointment and drops in her eyes; this and aspirin are the only remedies available, it appears. Ill or not, we still have to go to the factory, even if it proves to be the death of us. Women who are completely blind like Henriette are taken down into a dark cellar, with boards and no mattress to lie on and a filthy blanket. Will Henriette survive this ordeal? I'm desperately worried about her health: last week she was doubled up with stomach pains caused by the acid, and her legs are terribly painful.

Contradictory news reaches us from outside. Nothing seems

to fire the interest of the Belgian workers. Between collections of 'cakes' we manage to exchange a few words with them. It seems that the landing at Dieppe led to nothing: the general view is that the British re-embarked. We have no idea what is happening. The street propaganda posters that we pass in the bus are uniformly optimistic in tone and flavour. But we are optimistic too!

Yesterday Sonni, the plump little German girl, suffered a violent epileptic fit at her machine, foaming at the mouth dreadfully while her body arched and jolted from one side of the central corridor to the other. The overseers and wardress found this highly amusing. I attempted to intervene, and as politely as possible begged one of the overseers not to try and stop her body jerking by sitting on her chest. Naturally he took no notice.

Half an hour later, Sonni was sent back to her machine, with no one to help her. She has a fit at least once a week, but receives no medication, no medical attention of any kind. What would be the point? She'll work for as long as she is able, and when she splits her head open against the machine we'll know soon enough. Funerals for slave workers must come pretty cheap. My thoughts turn to a *Register of the Galleys in the Time of Louis XIV* that I once looked at in the Bibliothèque Nationale. Out of every ten prisoners condemned to the galleys, two would be convicted thieves; the rest were 'heretics', in other words Protestants: anti-fascists like us. The dates when they died were noted in the margins: none of them survived the galleys for more than two years. How long will we slave workers survive at the Phrix works?

Krefeld, August 1942
Despite everything, this place sometimes throws up artistic visions of quite extraordinary power. It is hot, very hot. At night, when we women make our way to the restaurant for

soup in a long silent file, the effect is startling. The factory windows shed no light to pierce the inky blackness. We are illumined only by police lamps, shone very low. These throw the silhouettes of our column against the factory walls like an immense shadow play. Silhouetted against this backdrop, the procession is transformed into a surreal vision, a demented frieze. Beyond, the sky glows scarlet with the nightly air raids over Essen, Düren and Duisburg. Now and then it is criss-crossed with blazing trails of human manufacture, the brilliant flashes of anti-aircraft fire, and studded with explosive starbursts in a magical, barbaric extravaganza!

Krefeld, August 1942

Adrien, the young Dutch sailor turned prisoner of war, has had a bellyful of the Rheika; he can't take any more, he's fit to explode. Houben the overseer insults him at a slightly higher volume than usual. Losing all his self-control, Adrien grabs one of his cast-iron pots and flings it at Houben's head, felling him to the floor. Adrien then jumps on top of him and executes a wild dance on his body. He's taking his revenge, for himself and for all the women in the factory. Houben spends a week in hospital. And Adrien, how long will he spend in a punishment or reprisal camp?

At the end of every shift the same scene is always played out: we don't even find it repellent any more. We don't think about it; it's just part of our daily routine. We line up in three ranks in the central corridor, waiting for the order to leave. Taking advantage of the fact that our hands have been softened by eight hours of regular dunking in our water buckets, we 'squirt' our fingers, seeing who can shoot the pus highest or furthest. We all poke about in our wounds with pins that we have scavenged from somewhere or other, and that we keep jealously in our jacket lapels. We have noticed that if we tackle our hands as soon as we finish work they heal up more quickly. Today I have squeezed my fingers dry, but I am squeezed dry too, and before I change from my uniform into my prisoner's rags I slump down on the cloakroom bench. Collapsed in a heap opposite me is another exhausted woman. She's a 'new girl' and this is the first time we have spoken; angrily, she yells: 'Hey you, your job as a civilian – you don't work with your hands either, do you?'

I grunt in assent.

'What do you do? I work in a brothel, how about you?'

Despite the exhaustion, despite the bromide, the unexpectedness of this shakes me awake. Without waiting for a reply she goes on: 'A high-class brothel, you know, in Hamburg, behind the station. D'you know Hamburg? No. Well, it's the most exclusive brothel in town, full of mirrors and rugs and all that sort of thing . . .'

As we share further confidences, I ask her how she came to be living in a whorehouse in Hamburg. Drawing herself up with dignity, she replies: 'Well! I suppose you know other jobs where a woman can earn sixty marks a day? Here, look at this!' She shows me a massive brilliant set into one of her molars: 'You see that? Hitler'll never get that, will he?'

As I change my clothes, the subject of careers guidance as applied to women gives me pause for thought.

Krefeld, August 1942

After work I have one great pleasure: the prospect of the cloakroom, with its ingenious round basins, filled with lovely naked female bodies. How beautiful they are, these girls: Lisa, Marlyse, Kate, Amy, Sonni, Minerva and the rest of them. Our current wardress allows us to wash after work. She gives us a few minutes extra, so we have time, if not to wash properly, at least to scrape some of the dirt off. This revives me in both body and spirit. These pretty girls have no idea how beautiful they are, how exquisite their poses are, even though they pay no heed, *because* they pay no heed. It's just like Ingres' *Turkish Bath*.

Mimi, the French girl on the shift before us, has been left to operate a machine on her own for a fortnight now. It's too much for her. She is weak, and although she does not suffer acutely with her eyes, the pain of them is nagging and constant. Her nerves are completely shattered. To get her back on her feet, the overseer and the director, Herr Pils, together decide that she should do two shifts back to back, in other words sixteen hours at the machine. This will teach her once and for all how to spin, and above all how to spin straight!

I really do believe I am too old for this Folies-Bergère lark. The acid burns holes not only in our skin, but also, naturally, in our uniforms. Every drop makes a hole, and the little holes join up to make big holes. This is what has happened to the front of my shirt. So I turned it back to front, and for a while my back was exposed but at least my front was decent. Now the new front has had more splashes. I have shown the wardress how my left breast is now on view. She has refused to let me have a new shirt, a needle and thread, or a pin, declaring that I'll just have to work as I am. I beg to differ. As I pass an office doorway I screw up my courage and slip inside. A secretary is busy typing. I explain my problem to her, and ask if she has a safety pin. Very gently, she takes two beautiful safety pins out of her bag and holds them out to me, saying something kind about my 'humiliation'. It all happens so quickly that the wardress sees nothing of my act of unthinkable impertinence. By running I manage to catch up with the tail end of the kommando, as the women line up in three ranks to be counted before going to their machines.

Krefeld, September 1942

The director of Anrath carries out an inspection. We are not there. He picks another shift to search, and by a stroke of bad luck finds some chocolate in one of the bunks. As the prison authorities do not supply us with chocolate, Herr Direktor concludes that the girl with the chocolate must have outside contacts. To teach her to be more discreet, we are all treated to four days in the punishment cells, with no mattresses or blankets.

For a few days now we have had a new French comrade whom we call Maman-Gâteau or Maman Denise; she is sixty-five and in very poor health. Along with the rest of us, this poor woman will have to endure four long cold sleepless nights, as it's starting to get chilly at night. I wonder whether the British soldiers she hid will ever know how much this poor woman is suffering for their sakes?

Krefeld, September 1942

My companions have just found a new name for me: I am the Marquise de la Poubelle, or the Dustbin Duchess. There's always a reason behind a name. Mine comes from my daily habit of poking around with a stick in the factory waste bins. The treasures I unearth include rayon offcuts that we can cut up to make bandages for our burned fingers; bits of rubber to mend our aprons with; and once even a little scrap of woollen fabric. This will make a patch for the jacket that Loulou has said she will leave behind for me when she is freed on 9 October.

Krefeld, September 1942

Great excitement among the German women on the kommando: any day now the war will be over, Stalingrad will fall and we shall all be freed. Without wishing to lend too much credence to their cock-and-bull stories, we know that the war in the East is very, very hard. The other day we caught a distant glimpse of a map of the USSR, and even making allowances for undoubted exaggerations, it is certainly true that the Germans have penetrated deep into Russian territory.

On a more personal, mundane level we are experiencing our own misfortunes. There is not a drop of water to be had throughout the building. La Concon is to be heard bellowing on every floor. The toilets are blocked and unusable. Naturally there is water to be had outside the building, but we are prisoners. Dotted about in the corridors and on the stairs are three- or five-kilo jam pails, which are to serve our bodily needs. When these receptacles are full to overflowing or have already overflowed, the wardress stirs herself to accompany the prisoner whose job it is to empty them in a nearby yard. Naturally we have not washed for three days. And although we are in the middle of another heatwave, we are not allowed to open any of the windows (in case we communicate with people on the outside), so the building stinks to high heaven; the Germans tell us so.

Henriette is very ill and has been put in quarantine. With great difficulty, I manage to see her for a few minutes. I find her lying in a small room with Amy, who has an abscess on her throat. Henriette has a rash all over, is running a high fever and has acute heart problems. She has had a visit from a very young nurse; the doctor doesn't have the time. The nurse has prescribed some medicines, I gather, though I don't know what they are. With heart-rending, piteous urgency, Henriette begs me for a few drops of water. I can't do even that for her. Amy seems very bad: it's physically impossible for her to speak, and in any case she doesn't have the energy any more.

A third woman is suffering from what the Germans call 'the rose'. Her face is frozen into a terrifying mask, scarlet and bloated. Is it a case of erysipelas? All three are 'cared for' by

Gertrude, herself a prisoner who works the same shifts as we do at the factory. Devoted but bad-tempered, the poor thing is exhausted, and can do almost nothing for her three patients. Today she has brought them each a mountain of sauerkraut, and seems outraged that none of them has touched it.

The water is back on; Henriette is no better, but at least she can drink. Amy's abscess burst by itself; the other woman is still just as red and swollen. I pay a hasty visit to the sick room for a few minutes, while a comrade keeps an eye out for La Concon's comings and goings, so she can alert me to the slightest danger.

I share my fears with Henriette. The women are saying that Stalingrad has fallen, and on our way back from work this morning I saw masses of flags outside the station, and people preparing to hoist them. But if Stalingrad has been evacuated perhaps it's just to fool the Germans. In any case, we don't know anything, all we can do is wait; victory will just be a little longer in coming, that's all.

Henriette is better. What was wrong with her? Nobody knows. She is very weak, but as soon as the fever abated she and Amy were sent back to their machines. I keep an eye on them from a distance throughout the night. It's painful to watch them. Their heads are clearly swimming, and to stay upright they keep having to cling on to their machines.

The flags were not being got ready for the capture of Stalingrad, we hear, but for an agricultural show. The German women are much less convinced about our impending liberation. The war goes on, it seems, just as we thought. And despite all the premature claims of victory, Stalingrad has not fallen!

Oh, the nonsense spouted by philosophers – philosophers who know nothing of hunger, thirst or illness, with no medication, rest or even the most basic care; who don't know what it is to have to ask permission to go to the toilet, to not have enough water to wash, to be sticky with sweat, to have stinking breath because you can't brush your teeth, to be crawling with lice . . . Philosophers who know nothing of all this will assure you in their customary pedantic fashion that mental suffering is far worse than physical suffering. Here we suffer physical pain in all its manifestations, and we are not spared mental torture either. When we were reeling the thread today, old Annie was in so much pain that she was completely dazed; when the administration informed her that her son had died in Russia she just didn't react at all. She didn't even know which son it was, as she has three sons on the Eastern front.

Krefeld, 5 October 1942

Henriette is ill again. The work simply puts too much strain on her heart. We can all tell that our heartbeats are slowing down, and for those with heart conditions it's a real problem.

Yesterday, the British and American bombers missed the works yet again. Yet you'd think it's big enough for them to spot, and it's right by the Adolf-Hitler bridge, which also seems to have escaped the attentions of our allies. Although they missed the works buildings, they completely destroyed one of the shelters. Everyone inside was killed, German and foreign civilian workers alike.

Krefeld, October 1942

At last, after months of waiting, a letter from Maman. My family write to me every six weeks, but the letters are not passed on to me; it's much the same for all the other foreign prisoners. I didn't know that Jean and Monique were already expecting a baby; according to the letter the baby must even have arrived by now. What a strange feeling it is to be a grandmother! A feeling of pride and selfishness; a feeling of animal survival, of cheating oblivion; a feeling of absolute delight!

Krefeld, late October 1942

The wardress summons me to tell me that the director wishes kindly to inform me that I am a grandmother. I recognize Jean's handwriting on the postcard in her hand. Realizing that letters are not getting through to me, Jean has written to the director. Pinned to the card is a note written in German. I ask whether the baby is a boy or a girl. The surly wardress asks how I expect her to know. Peering at the note, I make out the name 'Yves'. So I have a grandson. Boldly, I ask if I may read the card from my son. She informs me this is quite out of the question. What a peculiar sort of woman I must be. Not satisfied with knowing that I am a grandmother, I also have to know the sex of my grandchild, his name, and whether my daughter-in-law is well. Doubtless German grandmothers are much less curious!

That same evening, I am ordered to push a trolley laden with spools. The trolley has not been oiled and will barely move. There are two of us trying to push it, but in vain. I push so hard that I fall flat on my face, my heart pounding. Furiously I say to myself: 'In fifty years' time my family will know how I was treated by the Germans. I have a grandson, Yves. He will tell his children how I was forced to work beyond the limits of human endurance.'

Why do I find such comfort in this thought? It's foolish, petty and self-centred!

I'll have much more to tell my grandson, and if things go on like this the register of complaints will make a very weighty volume. Today is even better. Siemens, the overseer, summons me and orders me to help him purge the pipe that brings the viscose. There is an airlock. The overseer opens the drainage tap, at the height of a man, making the viscose spurt out. The viscose is caught in a bucket and thrown into the waste duct. Two prisoners are always detailed off for this dirty, dangerous job. Siemens tells me to take a bucket and put it under the pump. When the bucket is full he orders me to empty it. It is full to overflowing. One false move, one clumsy mistake and the viscose will spill all over my feet. I can't do it on my own. I refuse to empty the bucket unless I have help. Siemens eyes me savagely and screams: 'You *will* empty that bucket, you lazy cow.' Looking him in the eye, the lazy cow calmly replies: 'No, I won't!'

I thought he'd have me arrested and beaten up. But no. Seeing my determination, Siemens calls another prisoner over and tells her to help me with the bucket. But five minutes later, as we continue the operation, Siemens turns the pump on just as I am putting the bucket under it. If there had not been so much air in the pipe, a torrent of viscose would have poured on to the back of my neck. As it was, a whistling in the pipe warned me to pull back out of the way quickly, to Siemens' great disappointment.

They are all in a foul mood. The Russian campaign is dragging on and on. The fall of Stalingrad was more or less a fait accompli, and yet somehow it still hasn't quite happened. Moscow and Leningrad, too, were both 'virtually' German. The air is full of wild rumours: according to some Adolf Hitler has been assassinated; others have it that he has fled to Italy; and others again that he is in Japan! Old Fatty Goering has been assassinated for the hundredth time, and to prove it the factory flag is flying at half-mast. On further investigation, however, it appears that if the Rheika swastika is hanging its head this is a mark of honour to its workers killed at the front.

The cold is starting to set in, especially when we get up for the morning shift, from six till two. We leave Kölnerstrasse at about half past four, sometimes earlier, depending on the whim of the bus driver. Thank goodness Loulou left me her jacket. Full of acid holes as it is, with a good third of one sleeve missing and the underarm of the other repaired by me, this pathetic rag of a thing is more precious to me than the finest fur could ever be.

We have to look after our clogs with care. There are no more to be had in the factory clothing store, although there are still rubber boots for the civilian workers. Seeing that some of the women were wearing clogs that were completely broken down and causing them agonies, the storeman thought he was doing the right thing in giving them some of the boots. Outraged by this demonstration of humanity, the director of Anrath ordered the factory police to retrieve the boots. The women had to leave barefoot, in the cold and rain.

Although we have heard talk of suicides and attempted suicides at the Phrix works, I have had no direct experience of any – until now. Now our kommando is affected too. Fingerling, the young Austrian girl, has set an example that others will doubtless follow. Overwhelmed by the savage treatment we receive, by the insults and the terrible eye problems, and above all demoralized, drugged and fuddled by the acid vapours, Fingerling hid behind her machine and swallowed a tumblerful of acid. Knowing what the acid does to our hands and faces, arms and throats, I can only imagine what it must be like to drink it. They gave her an antidote. She certainly can't be the first, as the antidote is kept ready at the first-aid post. She was taken to hospital, where she spent a few days; and now here she is, back again at her old machine, a little paler, a little more exhausted.

Next it's the turn of Martha, the pretty Spanish-looking girl. Ditched by her husband, battered by the overseer, overcome by the excruciating pain of her eyes, she had reached the end of her tether. She too swallowed acid. She wasn't just seeking attention, I'm convinced. No, she couldn't endure any more suffering, and she couldn't see any future for herself once she was freed. Better to finish it all. She was twenty-five years old, gentle and beautiful.

The scene was truly worthy of the Third Reich. The women in another kommando at Kölnerstrasse are infested with vermin: head lice, body lice, crabs. La Concon announces that we will get less sleep tonight and be up earlier than usual tomorrow as we are going to be disinfected. So it is that at daybreak we are conducted to a building like a large garage. There, a woman in a white coat inspects our hair; just as Charlemagne used to visit schools and place the good pupils on his right and the bad ones on his left, so the nit nurse divides us into two groups, the lousy and the louse-free. I fall in the latter camp, though there is no honour to this, just sheer fluke. Witnesses to this scene include not only our wardress, Fräulein Herold, but also a handful of factory policemen and an SS man.

Watching women being deloused makes for great entertainment. Evidently, healthy distractions are currently rather thin on the ground at Krefeld. From the delousing room we are sent to the steam room, one hundred and six of us in all. As luck would have it, I am the first in. Fräulein Herold orders me to take off all my clothes and tie them up in a bundle. I reply that I will do so once the SS man, the policemen and another individual of indeterminate occupation have left the room. Herold tells me that 'these gentlemen' are police officers like her, and as such have the right to be present at the disinfecting process. So I undress and make a bundle of my rags.

The bundle is taken by the individual whose role I couldn't work out. He is none other than the boilerman in charge of the steam room. My comrades are forced to follow my example. We are sent into the showers. As we wash, the men watch us. One of them points out a German girl whom we call 'Michel Simon' after the actor, as she looks uncannily like him. The lice are dropping down her back from her magnificent mane of blonde hair. Immediately, the SS man demands a pair of scissors, calls over 'Michel Simon', who is in tears, and with an expansive gesture shears off all her hair. For a moment he stands there beside this tall naked woman, holding her glorious golden tresses in his hand; he hesitates, then tosses the hair into the furnace that heats the steam room.

The women range in age from seventeen to seventy, and are from all social classes. Simone, our young Belgian comrade, has turned scarlet; I try to make her feel better by telling her that the humiliation is theirs, not hers. After an hour of waiting, the 'gentlemen' decide that it is insufferably hot, and open the windows to create a nice cool draught. One minute we are melting with the heat, the next we are frozen by the cold December air on our damp bodies. Our teeth chattering, we rub each other down for warmth. This goes on for five interminable hours, during which the men stand there watching us, never tiring of the melancholy spectacle. At last the steam room is opened up. The attendant climbs up, grabs one bundle after another and hurls them at the throng of gesticulating, screaming, jostling women. How repulsive it is to feel their naked bodies pressed against mine! And the prostitutes among us are outraged: it's a swindle, men ogling them naked without paying; well really, it's daylight robbery!

Krefeld, December 1942

For a long time now, one of the factory policemen has been eyeing me with a sympathetic air. The other day he slipped beside me and said a few words in French, sentences that he must have prepared laboriously in advance. He worked at the Paris Exposition Universelle of 1937, and he says he pities us with all his heart. A few days later he tells me that a fellow inmate of Kölping Haus has died for lack of medical care.

Finally, he whispers that the news from the eastern front is very much in Russia's favour. I divine which persuasion my new friend belongs to. When we manage by a deft manoeuvre to find ourselves alone on the storeroom stairs, I silently clench my fist; he responds with the same salute, and we shake hands. Sometimes actions speak louder than words. I spend the whole shift singing, a weight lifted from my heart.

Achille Cordez, one of the last Belgian spinners on our shift, has had enough; he can't take any more. He has decided instead to enlist in the German army and go to Russia to kill our allies, or perhaps be killed by them.

The overseer called Daum, better known to us as 'Big Nose', ordered me to take charge of a new machine that I had not yet seen in action. I told him that I wasn't familiar with the machine, but that if he would show me how it worked I would willingly take over. He replied with a volley of blows that left me sprawled on the ground. It turns out that he himself knows nothing at all about how the new machine works, and that this was his ingenious method of instructing me.

Krefeld, December 1942

There's one tragedy after another. Francesca, despite her pretty Italian name, is German. She has three children and is married to a farmer who has been in the Air Force for six years. She last saw him two years ago. Working on their farm was a French prisoner of war, willing, kind to the children and good-looking. Francesca became pregnant by him. She was denounced, and here she is doing hard labour: her swelling belly earns her no dispensation. Within a few days she was expected to work a machine by herself. Her back aches, her legs hurt, and it is only a matter of time before she is afflicted with the full gamut of Rheika woes. At the house yesterday, I encountered a sobbing Francesca on the stairs up from La Concon's office. Down below, with La Concon, was an airman, a big stocky country lad. His implausibly red ears protruded from under his grey-blue forage cap, the ears of a naughty schoolboy. It was Francesca's husband. What can their feelings possibly have been at this meeting, when they have three children already and haven't seen each other for two years? Their interview lasted fifteen minutes, with a prison wardress positioned between them. The husband has returned to the eastern front. He has forgiven Francesca: if he comes back, he will bring up the fourth child along with the other three.

How I curse my hopeless memory for literature; how I wish I could remember a poem. Often a line will swim up from the depths of my memory and float on the surface, but then the next one refuses to come. And yet for someone like me, who used to live too much through books, it would be such a huge comfort to be able to distract myself during my long shifts by reciting verses by Ronsard or Villon. Imagine: never to see a book, or a photograph of a painting or sculpture. I like to conjure up images of my bookshelves, with all my beloved books: shall I ever see them again?

> Et la garde qui veille aux barrières du Louvre
> N'en defend point nos rois . . .

> (And the guard that watches the gates of the Louvre
> Cannot shield our kings at all [from Death] . . .)

Why have I dredged this couplet up from my memory? Why these particular lines?

So this time that's really it: Houben, the head overseer, has come to my machine to tell me that I have to learn to spin, to operate a machine by myself. Apparently it is intolerable that I should be merely an assistant. I don't argue with him.

My docility surprises him, it seems, and he tries to make a scene, hurling insults at me in his Cologne dialect. I don't catch all that he says, and I decide to play on this: 'Herr Meister, please speak more slowly, my German is not good enough to follow you . . .'

'Oh, well, if you don't understand German, you old sow, I'll say it in French: *baise mon cul*.'

Kiss my arse. I know it's stupid, but that night in my bunk I break down completely. Not to be able to answer back, not to be able to say anything at all, to be forced to accept everything! Henriette is outraged, and tells the German women in our room about it. They too are full of indignation. But this won't be the last insult I'll hear, not by any means. Sticks and stones may break my bones but words will never hurt me; my body may buckle, my spirit never.

Leni Kramer is a supervisor selected from among the prisoners, with responsibility for the group of machines that includes mine. When she hears that I am to start my apprenticeship as a spinner, she wonders if the management has gone completely mad. But Emilie is to join me in this apprenticeship. Emilie is about the same age as me, though more solidly built. Even with her glasses on she can't see much. Leni counsels me urgently to be as clumsy as I possibly can, something that I can manage perfectly well without even trying. But where my sight is concerned there is nothing to be done: I've got eyes like a hawk and there's no hiding the fact.

For hours – eight hours – I fling acid on the blasted filament as it obstinately refuses to go into the glass funnel, which bobs up and down as though mocking my hopelessness. My hands are drenched with acid, my wounds are shockingly painful despite being bound up with rags, and my whole face stings. Before this I have never had to spend a whole shift with the acid right under my nose. In all good faith, Emilie meanwhile can't see a thing. She flings her acid in all directions, and the wardress comes and gives her a volley of slaps round the face. There's no doubt about it, I am the most craven of cowards. Their revolvers didn't frighten me, but I simply cannot bear the thought of their dirty hands touching me. By hook or by crook I will learn to get that filament into the funnel. I am driven by a feeling for which I have only contempt: fear.

Henriette's advice and that of various other comrades has borne fruit, and now I can get the filament into the funnel passably well. Sometimes I allow it all to get on my nerves, which wastes time as it all goes wrong. But all in all I'm not doing too badly. And after all, everyone says that I won't be alone at the machine, that I'll always have an assistant. If so, life will be difficult but possible — if only it weren't for my poor hands.

As I am changing the filaments, a job that I loathe, a drop of viscose falls on my bare foot. Our clogs barely cover our feet and give them little protection. As usual, by the time I notice the problem it is too late. When we get back I ask La Concon for some ointment to put on it, whereupon she retorts that she won't let me have any for 'such a small thing'. For she it is who holds the key to the medicine cabinet, dispensing its contents when and how she sees fit. The cabinet 'serves us well': we must take the greatest care not to deplete its stocks.

Now I know what it is to have sore eyes! First you are plunged into a dense fog, then the pain starts: streaming eyes and nose, followed by stabbing pains in the eyes, a splitting headache and excruciating pains in the back of the neck. You can't keep your eyes open, and you find yourself bowing your head to ease the pain. Your nose, throat and ears hurt too.

I am taken to see Houben, the head overseer and eye specialist. He prods around inside my eyelids with his filthy fingers, declares me unfit for work, and allows me to be led over to a group of women who are in the same pitiful state. Later on we will be taken to the first-aid station, the virtually blind leading the totally blind. Then the nurse will put drops or ointment in our eyes; an aspirin will complete our treatment, and we will go down to the cellar. The cellar! There we have bare boards for beds, while the most enterprising among us manage to procure a dirty blanket. In a corner stands a foul-smelling bucket. Yet despite the cold and damp we are grateful to be there. My hands have been reduced to a pulp, and are useless when it comes to feeling my way. The nurse has bandaged them, after removing the viscose from my wounds and applying a soothing ointment. But despite it all the pain is still agonizing. All around me I hear nothing but moans of pain. I don't know how many of us there are. We all say our names: Erika, Maria, Sonni, Lisel, Annalisa, Kate. We try to work out who is in the most pain. They decide that it must be me, as my hands are well and truly pulverized.

In the morning the wardress comes to fetch us. My eyes are a bit better. But I am completely empty-headed: I have lost all sense of direction and go crashing into the walls. I hear the wardress say, 'The Frenchwoman will empty the bucket'; and so, reeling like a drunk, the Frenchwoman duly totters off to perform the communal slopping out.

I am reminded of the old Irish tradition of St Dunstan's Cave, mentioned often in Breton chronicles. The monastery of St Dunstan stood on an ancient Druidic site, and the monks continued a number of Druid traditions, including, notably, their initiation ceremony. Only the prior received the full initiation rites. The final ordeal involved descending into the depths of St Dunstan's Cave and spending a certain number of days there, alone and without food. Whatever the prior saw at the bottom of the deep pit was believed to be so horrifying that he was prohibited from speaking of it to a living soul. He alone was to keep his terrible secret. On his return to the land of the living, the prior would be utterly changed in appearance and expression. He would never laugh again, and he would often be found staring fixedly into space.

We prisoners, likewise, have plumbed the depths of our own abyss. When we return to the land of the living we too must speak to no one of what we have seen, for who could understand what we have suffered? Only those who, like us, have descended into the murderous depths of the Nazi abyss.

My dear little Henriette possesses only a cotton dress, with an unlined, short-sleeved cotton camisole serving as an apology for a jacket. The cold is bitter, and our feet in our clogs are bare. Just now we were trying to decide which was more unbearable on our bare legs and feet, rain or snow. We both agreed that the rain feels colder, chilling us to the marrow. The viscose burn on my foot has got worse: it keeps me awake at night; my foot is swollen, and my clog hurts. La Concon was quite happy to give me some ointment, but I fear it's a bit late now. It worries me. I'm in no fit state to bear any more physical pain than it is absolutely necessary to endure in this place.

It's my lucky day: I am put on a machine with an altogether delightful German woman called Gerda Vossing. She is here for some trifling offence; actually she's a communist, but she keeps quiet about that. We get on well. Yesterday she offered me a definition of Germans that appeals very much to me: 'Germans are born either to beat or to be beaten, but not to be free.' How right she is! She tells me about a Nazi anthem that boils down to something along the lines of:

> Today Germany is ours,
> Tomorrow the world . . .

To get the bad taste out of our mouths after that we sing the 'Internationale', she in German and me in French, while a Belgian mechanic joins in in Flemish. It doesn't take much to raise the spirits of a couple of women prisoners. Gerda is the same age as me, and we think that we will always be able to work together: the thought of the empathy between us makes the harshness of the work easier to bear.

A week ago I noticed a 'new girl', a pretty young woman who explained to me that she had been a *souris grise* with the occupying *Wehrmacht* forces in Etampes. She did something stupid, and now here she is. She was already spinning by herself and finding the work appallingly hard when she was literally overwhelmed by agonizing pains in her eyes. Did the prisoner beside her not guide her? Whatever the case, she tripped on the stairs, crashing her head against the concrete steps. She remained unconscious for two hours. The next day she had a slight squint and couldn't tell who I was. They put her in a tiny stinking room known pompously as the 'quarantine ward', and then they took her away.

Oh! What's the point? Why bother to write all this down? It's all too much. When we arrive at the factory we ask the women on the previous shift, 'Who have they beaten?', and they reply Hilda, or Annalisa, or Gerda. One day recently Gerda had been so badly beaten by the overseer that her top was a mass of bloodstains.

Meekly, the women whose eyes are worst line up in the appointed spot; a pitiful sight, each leading the next. Dressed in a grotesque collection of rags, their hair all over the place, they hold a cloth in front of their eyes to protect them from the light, or else they simply shield them with a bent arm. There they await the overseer's verdict. Only those who are totally blind get sent down to the cellar. Not long ago I was there when he uttered the following pearls of wisdom: 'There are already six Frenchwomen in the cellar, so we won't send any more down.' The seventh and in great pain, I had to work an eight-hour shift in order to ensure that the percentage of Frenchwomen off sick wasn't too high.

Krefeld, 20 December 1942

My companions don't spare my feelings: I look appalling.
The flesh is falling off me at a frightening rate. When a 'new
girl' arrives, the great amusement is to make me strip off to
show her what the Phrix factory can do to a woman in six
months. When I am naked, my nickname changes from the
Dustbin Duchess to Gandhi, and not without reason. I've
lost count of the number of times I've passed out recently.
On the way from the house to the bus the other day, I came
round to find myself sprawled on the pavement in Henriette's
arms. The wardress ordered the others to haul me on to the
bus, just as I was, declaring that the journey would bring
me back to my senses. Once we got to the factory it was
work as usual.

The wardress tells us that a pastor is to visit us, bringing
us festive wishes for Christmas. He appears as we are eating.
Evidently he has had to make determined efforts in order to
penetrate our strictly guarded quarters. An elderly man with
a beaming face, he wishes us a cheery '*Bon appétit*', adding, 'I
see that all is well here.' Martha, who cannot get over her
failed suicide bid, shouts angrily, 'Only because they make us
pretend it is.' He pushes the door shut. Following in Martha's
wake, the girls take turns to talk to the pastor, telling him
rapidly and nervously about all that we are made to suffer.
Clearly their stories bear each other out. After using up all the
incredibles, inconceivables, abominables and other similar
adjectives in his vocabulary, the pastor is lost for words. Finally,
one of the girls asks him not to be angry, but would he grant
forgiveness to all the women who have committed suicide or
attempted it. He replies, 'The sufferings they have had to bear
are beyond the endurance of any woman; I give them all
absolution.'

Krefeld, 31 December 1942

Christmas has come and gone without our even noticing. On Christmas Day we worked an eight-hour shift. At the express demand of the director of Anrath no concessions whatever were made in our daily routine, and he refused to allow a prisoners' charity to give us a few little treats. This evening I was working at the machine with my good friend Gerda Vossing. We were being cheerful, as we wanted the year to end well. My friendly factory policeman came over to us and said to me very quickly: 'It can't go on much longer; try to escape, find a way! If you do, my name is Erb and I live at Spinnereistrasse 29. No one will look for you there.'

I am so moved, so stunned by such kindness, such generosity, that I can't speak. Our young friend Daniel, the last of the Belgian civilian spinners, observes the scene from a distance; the minute my friend is gone Daniel swoops down on me: 'What did that swine want? Making a nuisance of himself, I bet.'

Daniel always tries to protect us, even though the dear kind boy knows only too well that all he can offer us are his charming smile and a helping hand when no one is looking.

I reassure him. The policeman was just wishing me a happy new year. Yes indeed, a happy new year. Never has a man offered me such a precious new year's gift! Erb knows as well as I do that if he hides me he will be putting his own life in danger.

Henriette and I talk and talk about Erb's proposition. Escape is not impossible. Three German women got away last week, as a result of which we have been stripped of our factory jackets in the bitter cold, as our white tops are easier to spot in the dark. Now, in January, we go out for our midnight soup soaked through with sweat and naked beneath our thin rayon shirts. Henriette has a racking cough, and I fear it may be something serious.

We consider the enigma of Erb. Since we have been in German hands we have encountered so many traps that we wonder whether this isn't another one. No, I dismiss the idea;

I don't want to sully this man's extraordinary generosity with such unworthy thoughts. But I won't accept his offer all the same. I am too ill to make the effort to escape, and if I were to escape, Pierre might be taken in my place. No, the die is cast and there's no going back. 'After the rain comes the sunshine', as we used to sing in the Revolutionary song 'La Jeune Garde': yes, soon the sunshine will come. As Armand Schmidt said in the prison van from Düsseldorf, we must just grit our teeth and get on with it. I only hope that my imprisonment will not outlive my strength!

It's stupid, but this wound on my foot is affecting my whole body. I can hardly sleep any more, and my foot and ankle are all swollen. Fräulein Dross, the wardress, does not see any point in taking me to the first-aid post.

Krefeld, 15 January 1943
There are definitely changes afoot in the outside world, as overnight there has been a crackdown on discipline. The factory police are now armed with guns. My poor Erb looks as if he wouldn't have the faintest idea what to do with his. The police who fetch us for work every day now have an SS escort. I find him rather disconcerting, as he is the image of the actor Louis Jouvet in SS uniform: not an encouraging sight! The SS man counts us as we leave the house. To do this with maximum efficiency he pinches our arms as we pass, preferably twisting the flesh as he does so.

In the middle of the machine hall they have erected a reinforced concrete guard post, a sort of mini-blockhouse with loopholes, through which a single sub-machine gun can command respect and obedience throughout the machine hall. There is a similar construction in the courtyard, and in all the factory departments. I am delighted at the sight of these first signs of a potential uprising, and there is talk of rioting.

Agnès Humbert in 1921, with her son Jean at Ploumanac'h, the little Breton fishing port where she and Georges Sabbagh brought up their two sons.

Agnès Humbert, 1930s.

Georges-Hanna Sabbagh, *Les Devoirs de Vacances* (Holiday Homework), 1924.

The curved and colonnaded white wings of the Palais de Chaillot housed the Musée de l'Homme and its sister institution, the Musée des Arts et Traditions Populaires.

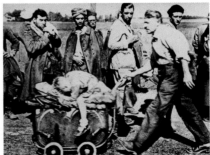

Under the scorching sun of June 1940 the terrified people of Paris fled in unspeakable confusion, watched helplessly by their own defeated soldiers.

Paris, 24 June 1940: Adolf Hitler and his party stroll in triumph from the Eiffel Tower towards the Musée de l'Homme.

Civilians have their papers scrutinized before crossing the demarcation line between Occupied and unoccupied France (here at Moulins).

Boris Vildé, linguist, ethnographer and specialist in polar civilizations.

Anatole Lewitsky, head of the European-Asiatic department at the Musée de l'Homme and world authority on Siberian shamanism.

Pierre Walter, society photographer and debonair man-about-town.

Léon-Maurice Nordmann, prominent Jewish lawyer and associate of Jewish socialist former prime minister Léon Blum.

René Sénéchal, an eighteen-year-old accountant at the outbreak of war.

Pierre Brossolette, prominent left-wing journalist and broadcaster.

Yvonne Oddon, highly respected chief librarian at the Musée de l'Homme.

Jean Cassou, distinguished writer, art critic and poet.

Simone Martin-Chauffier, writer and translator.

Jacqueline Bordelet, a young secretary at the Musée de l'Homme.

Sylvette Leleu, garage owner in the northern town of Béthune.

Honoré d'Estienne d'Orves, aristocratic Free French naval officer.

The Prison du Cherche-Midi, the notoriously insalubrious French military prison run by the German authorities throughout the Occupation.

Captain Ernst Roskothen, lawyer, Wehrmacht officer and presiding judge at the trial of the 'Vildé affair'.

One of the prison huts in which slave workers were held at Krefeld, 8 March 1945. The capture of Krefeld on 1 March was the culmination of 'Operation Grenade', the US Ninth Army's spectacular advance across the Rhineland.

'We were battle-tired and combat-wise medics,' wrote one soldier of that day, 'and we thought there was nothing left in the books we didn't know. Yet in a short period of two days [we] saw and lived a story we shall never forget.' (Sergeant Ragene Farris of the 329th Medical Battalion, 104th Infantry Division)

Mutual puzzlement as a spearhead detachment of the advancing US Army, its brief to impose order and American military rule, deals with German civilians, Rhineland, March/April 1945.

Agnès Humbert and other members of the Association France-Yougoslavie with President Tito during his official visit to France, 7–11 May 1956.

'A woman deserving of the highest admiration, unassailable in her strength of character and will, unflinching in her absolute integrity.' (Pierre Sabbagh). Agnès Humbert, 12 October 1894–19 September 1963.

Maria B., a young German communist on another shift, has been put in solitary confinement at Anrath. What fun she must be having there! This is her punishment for announcing the glorious news that the German armies in Russia have been encircled. Where? No one knows exactly, but everyone's talking about it. I'm dancing with joy, and we dash from one machine to another; some people have heard that ten divisions are involved, others a hundred, but since none of us knows what a division is anyway we are none the wiser. Then we hear that a clandestine German source is saying that this is the beginning of the end. This sets me off again, twirling pirouettes like a lunatic despite the mounting pain in my foot. Houben sees me and calls over one of his deputies, and together they watch my ballet solo. Henriette yells at me to stop, but it's too late. They've seen me. Too bad!

Too bad indeed. Houben tells me that since I am young enough to dance I am young enough to operate a machine on my own. Gerda Vossing will also have to work by herself, even though she didn't dance. This is alarming news for both of us.

It's a fortnight now since I started operating my machine on my own, and my hands and arms are covered with acid and viscose burns. The pain in my foot is remorseless; the trolleys are so hard to push, the trays of rayon so heavy to lift. Every component on the machine seems to be breaking or cracking, and my nerves are more frayed than words can describe. Before this I never used to cry; now I'm learning fast. The tears stream down my cheeks as we leave the factory every day after work, and I have no shame; I'm not even embarrassed enough to hide them. Henriette acts as my guide, tying and untying my bundle of civilian rags in the cloakroom for me, as my fingers are in such a state that I am incapable of untying a piece of string. Henriette's devotion is remarkable. I have only one consolation: my attempts at sabotage. Whenever I produce a particularly fine 'cake', I rub it hard against the tray. While the rayon is still damp no one can tell if it has any imperfections. When it dries, the filaments will be matted together and impossible to unwind. I've also developed a good trick which, when deployed with sufficient skill, breaks the cogwheels under the machine and puts some of the pots out of use for a good day at least, as the mechanic is an extremely busy man and happily is often unavailable. After every successful act of sabotage my heart feels lighter. It's a sort of rite of atonement for me, between me and my conscience. I am all too well aware that the rayon we spin goes to help the German war effort: the waste to make explosives, and the rayon to be used for uniforms, underwear and parachutes. I swore that I would never do war work: where are all my fine resolutions now? But how to resist? I know that the soldiers of every country – Russia, France, Yugoslavia or wherever – are all in the business, directly or indirectly, of slaughter and carnage. For whom, for what, do workers in France toil? There are millions of us, tens of millions of slaves . . .

My foot is more and more excruciating, the swelling is spreading; it's a sinister colour and the stench is appalling. At last I am allowed to go to the first-aid post. Herr Scherer, the nurse and a thoroughly decent chap, looks concerned and insists on seeing me on a daily basis.

The 'first-aid orderly' on the other shift declares that my foot is at risk and that he can do no more for it without a doctor's opinion. My weakness is extreme, and if I am quite truthful I am shocked by what has happened to my good friend Gerda Vossing. Unable to operate a machine by herself, she has been pushed to breaking point. One day she was so strong and cheerful; the next she wept incessantly, the burns on her hands and arms forming one continuous wound. Several times each day she passed out cold, and yesterday she suffered a stroke that left her paralysed down her right side. Because of this she was useless. They took her away, and she was sent to hospital on a stretcher. Did they have to push her to such extremes of suffering? I hear the German women saying that it will be my turn next, and that it won't be long either. The age-old lamentations of the Old Testament spring unbidden to our lips: 'How long, O Lord, how long?' The same suffering, the same words. Shamefully, my thoughts turn with a twinge of envy to my comrades now laid to eternal rest in the cemetery at Ivry. Vildé, Lewitsky, Nordmann, Walter, young René, Ithier, Andrieu ... For you the struggle is over, you have earned your slumber, you are at peace.

And today I received a letter from home. Friedmann's child has had whooping cough, my grandson has two teeth, Jean and Monique have been on a skiing holiday in Haute-Savoie: all these things seem so remote that I can only feel them through a thick fog. A fog of indifference? Quite possibly, I fear.

Yesterday as we left for work I passed out again, but apparently the SS man had me loaded on to the bus, declaring that the journey would bring me round. In the end he was proved right, as I still managed to work my eight hours. As you enter the factory you are struck by an extraordinary atmosphere: the noise of the machines, rows of women working like robots, hundreds of wheels spinning and whirring and funnels slowly rising and falling, all combining to create a rhythm that destroys your soul. You are sucked into this surreal vision, working like a whirling dervish, possessed by the stench and power of the machine.

I was still half asleep this morning when Tonton walked past my bunk and noticed my hands; she is a doctor, and they caught her professional eye.

'When they put the ointment on yesterday they certainly didn't do it by halves,' she remarks.

'Idiot,' I reply drowsily. 'Take a closer look. It's not ointment, it's pus.'

The Czech woman, Maria Dopsch, started to stack her 'cakes'

two minutes before her allotted time. Seeing this, the
'Controller' grabbed a cast-iron pot and hit her over the head
with it, twice: the first blow smashed her temple, the second
made a ten-centimetre gash on the back of her neck. Maria
was taken to see a doctor. The 'Controller' was moved to another
shift, so that other women may benefit from his rigorous
notions of punctuality.

Every night now the late shift has a loud musical accompaniment. From the landing window we can see the sky glowing
red and criss-crossed with exploding shells and searchlight
beams. Now it's Duisburg going up in flames, we tell ourselves;
now Essen, now Düren. Everywhere has been going up in
flames for so long that we wonder how there can be anything
left to burn. There is? Why of course, the Phrix factory! Don't
they know how to aim their bombs, these British and American
airmen? Surely the factory's big enough! The other night they
dropped an incendiary bomb on a building housing Russian
girls. The poor children were terrified. While all this was going
on I was completely blind, and the wardress had parked me
all alone in a corner of the factory. The smell of burning was
nightmarish. Not a single soul knew where I was, not Henriette
nor anyone else, and it was all but impossible for me to find
my way without help. If the factory were to catch fire around
me I had no idea how I would manage to get out of there.
Just my luck! If my hands had been just that bit better I could
perhaps have felt my way out . . .

A week of hell. On Monday I am unable to lift my head.
Henriette leads me, eyes streaming, to the machine. Siemens
tells me to go and count the spinnerets (we always have to
count them when we arrive, in case our predecessor on the
machine has stolen them for the gold or platinum they contain).

   'Count the spinnerets?' I splutter. 'But I can't! You can see
the state of my eyes.'

'Count your spinnerets!' he roars, following this up with a hefty blow to my back. For a moment I lose my grip: the pain of it all is too much, and I yell at him that he must be a swine to hit a woman who's almost blind. In response he gives me another shove and tells me that 'to teach me a lesson' he'll make me work all night. He allots me a factory worker to do the funnelling, and I am to be her assistant. I can't see the girl I'm working with, who must be new as I don't recognize her voice. Throughout the shift my pain is unbearable, and I howl like a dog at the moon. After we have stacked our 'cakes' the wardress, who is fairly decent, stuffs me with aspirin. Back at the house I collapse into my bunk, where I drift in and out of consciousness for five days and nights. The doctor happens to be passing, and by some miracle La Concon asks her to examine me. She explains my case, pointing out that two of the factory nurses have asked for an urgent consultation for me, fearing that I might lose my foot. Drawing to a halt a couple of metres from my bunk, the doctor says, 'You will be given a tablet.' I uncover my foot, but clearly it is of little interest to our devoted physician, who stalks off, slamming the door behind her. The promised tablet never materializes, needless to say.

Nature, the great healer, gives me the strength to get up and go back to work. The rest has made my poor foot feel better.

Every day the new wardress, Fräulein Jansen, takes me to see the nurse, a really decent fellow. Yesterday he gave me a sandwich. Neither he nor his two colleagues bother to hide their feelings regarding the treatment meted out to us. At last my foot is getting much better.

I don't dare look at my reflection in the little mirror in the toilets any more: I look about seventy. I stoop, my skin is yellow (like all my companions), my eyes are hollow and every day I seem to get thinner. Operating the machine seems to get harder and harder. The factory receives streams of visitors, some of them military, others civilian.

Houben escorts a respectably dressed individual past my machine. In a mocking tone, he sneers: 'Yes, this one's French. And she can spin, even though she's a grandmother! I've had my work cut out with her, I don't mind saying, but she got there in the end. It's some feat to get a grandmother to spin, you've got to admit!'

I hum the old seventeenth-century pacifist song to myself:

> Qui parle de la guerre
> Et ne sait ce que c'est
> Je vous jure mon âme
> Que c'est un piteux fait . . .

> (A stranger to war,
> Of great deeds you sing:
> But I swear on my soul
> 'Tis a piteous thing . . .)

And so it goes on, and on and on. I spend the night licking my burned fingers like a dog. It's the only remedy I have. The warmth of my saliva seems to soothe the pain. When we reach the factory I am sent to the first-aid post. There at last I receive proper treatment. They dig out the viscose, apply ointment and bandage each finger, one by one. Now I look as though I'm sporting smart white gloves like the ones soldiers used to wear on Sundays when I was a child.

Herr Scherer tells the wardress that I shouldn't be allowed to work. I am hardly back in the machine hall before I am sent to operate 'number thirty-two', a pig of a machine that's always going wrong. Naturally the wardress says not a word. As there's nothing else for it, I start stacking the 'cakes'. I work slowly, keeping my thoughts to myself. Siemens keeps his eye on me.

Doubtless he concludes that I won't finish my work in time, so by way of encouragement he comes up behind me, grasps my wrists firmly with both hands and plunges my hands into the acid bath. I take comfort from the thought that he could have done the same to me as Herr Lenartz, another overseer, did to a Polish woman on Madeleine's shift. Her eyes had been bad for a fortnight and she really couldn't work any more, but Lenartz didn't want to let her go down to the cellar, so he decided to try out a new remedy. He pushed the poor woman's face into the acid bath, then made her spin on her own for eight hours. As for me, it's just my hands, and my eyes are fine at the moment. There are always compensations in life . . .

Our emotional life here is rich and varied. Olga, the Viennese woman, had a terrible nightmare, crying out in the night in the strange voice of people who talk in their sleep: 'She's going to die, she's dying!' Olga has maintained up to now that she is a 'political'. Following her nightmare, however, further investigation on our part reveals that she is here for poisoning her lover's wife. And now guilt stalks her in her dreams . . .

A month ago I sent a message in a bottle. A kind Belgian civilian worker gave me some paper and an envelope, and put my letter in the post. Now he has brought me the reply. A letter from Jean and Colette Duval with a photograph of Yves. Although my eyes do not hurt terribly they are not much good. I can't manage to decipher the news that I have waited so long for. I can make out the shape of my grandson's head, but not his features. In the hope of receiving a letter I have made a little pouch in black material inside my dress. I shall hide my precious letter there; if anyone finds it, it will mean four weeks in the punishment cell at Anrath. I have known several women who have been punished for receiving clandestine letters. The punishment cell is on the ground floor and is streaming with damp. The inmates are stripped of their underwear and jacket. At night they have no mattress, and by day they are on a diet of bread and water, with two rations of soup per week. They nearly all come back with rheumatism in their joints and a high fever. In my present state, four weeks in the punishment cell would amount to a death sentence. In this certain knowledge, I take special care in concealing my precious letter and the picture of my unknown grandson . . .

I have managed to read my news from Paris: I know the contents of my letter by heart, and I repeat them over and over to myself as I work at the machine. Pierre Brossolette has managed to get to England with his wife and children.[15] Jean Cassou is in a French concentration camp.[16] His wife and young daughter are living near Toulouse. Claude Aveline and Marcel Abraham are still more or less in hiding, as is Friedmann. All of them are in danger, it seems. What a jolly time they must be having in France! But they are alive, and soon our ordeal

15 Pierre Brossolette reached London by plane in late April 1942. Parachuted back into France in June of that year, he organized (among other things) the departure of his family. Gilberte Brossolette and the couple's son and daughter reached England after a perilous journey. Pierre returned to France on two further occasions, carrying out important missions and laying the foundations for the Conseil National de la Résistance (CNR). In February 1944 the boat taking him back to England sank off the Ile de Sein. Forced ashore, he was arrested by the Gestapo at Audierne. They did not manage to identify him until March, when he was immediately taken to Paris. After three days of torture, realizing that physically he was at the end of his tether, he threw himself out of a window on the fifth floor of 82 avenue Foch. He died without uttering a word that could have compromised his comrades or the cause for which they were fighting.

16 Jean Cassou was arrested in Toulouse in December 1941 and sentenced to a year's imprisonment for 'offences against national security'. He served his sentence at the camp at Mauzac in the Dordogne, and was then made to spend a further month in the internment camp at Saint-Sulpice in the Tarn. As soon as he was released he returned to active work in the Resistance, adopting the names Alain and Fournier in memory of our early exploits. He became inspector of the southern zone for the governing council of the Mouvements Unis de Résistance (MUR); finally, in early 1944, the Algerian government appointed him Commissaire de la République for the Toulouse region. Taking up his duties immediately, he travelled between different Maquis groups to organize for the Liberation. On the night of 19 August 1944, in a street in Toulouse, Jean Cassou and three comrades came under attack from a German patrol. Two of the men were killed, and Cassou was left for dead. He spent three weeks in a coma, and was not yet off the danger list in late September, when General de Gaulle came to his hospital bedside to present him with the Croix de la Libération.

will be over: the letter gives off a heady air of optimism. Colette mentions people who are interested in me but whom I don't know. How strange it all is! She makes a number of veiled allusions that I don't understand. I'm so out of touch. I still remember so clearly that first night at Cherche-Midi: *Here lies Agnès Humbert, died 15 April 1941*. It's not so daft after all: that epitaph that floated over me as I lay between sleeping and waking contains a grain of truth. There is a part of me – all that is romantic, gentle or kind in me – that died that day. I shall never be the same again.

On her first day here I was struck by the noble character and resplendent beauty of Elsa Mauwinkle. She reminded me of Rubens' Mary Magdalene at the foot of the Cross, with the same voluptuous, creamy skin and lavish profusion of wavy blonde hair. When I think about her, I see her as she was when she arrived here. But who would recognize her now? At twenty-nine, she has gone grey at the temples, she is truly frighteningly thin, her eyes are always bad, and we have noticed that she is constantly scratching her head. Simone, our little Belgian social worker, well versed in all the woes of the human condition, has a good idea what that means. She inspects Elsa's hair. It's not just infested with lice; it's heaving with them. Her scalp is covered with scabs, and when you pick them off there are lice swarming about underneath. A few days later they decide to treat her. They shave her head and slather ointment all over her scalp. But is anyone remotely concerned about the general state of her health?

The director of Anrath has been to carry out an inspection. This is always a great drama. Someone in room thirty-five had stolen the gold from a spinneret. How they know these things is always a mystery. None the less, all the women in room thirty-five were to be punished. For five days they were to be deprived of mattresses and blankets, while their daily food ration was reduced to just three hundred grams of bread and nothing else. They had to be present at our meals, naturally, and they were expected to do the same work as us. And if any of us tried to help them in any way we would be subject to the same treatment. Henriette and I took some of them under our wing, passing them slices of bread and contriving to give them a blanket. By the end of the fifth day, over a third of the women were so weak that they were collapsing like ninepins. What productive workers they must have been.

My eyes are bad again, and the pain is more excruciating than ever. This does not escape the notice of my good friend Siemens. To attract my attention, he deals me a hefty kick on the ankle, his way of telling me that the wardress has permission to take me down to the cellar. My hands are as agonizing as my eyes; finding myself alone in the cellar, I understand the true significance of the phrase 'banging your head against a brick wall'. Yes, I bang my head against the wall. Then I pull myself together. I tell myself that even alone and untreated in a cellar there must be something I can do. An air raid is in full swing outside, and its muffled pounding keeps me company. What I need for my hands is damp dressings, but there is no water. So let's try something else. I urinate on my wretched hands, soaking the rags that serve as dressings. Say what you like, five minutes later the pain starts to ease, and ten minutes later I am asleep. The following day my wounds start to heal. Someone should tell the Academy of Medicine.

Krefeld, 8 May 1943

Great and marvellous news, and what's more it's true! The Allies have captured Tunis! Now they will move up from Tunis to Sicily and then up through Italy. We know exactly how much Mussolini's army is worth. Before long the Allies will be pushing into southern Germany. We are delirious with joy. We think and talk of nothing but Tunis.

Air raids always provide background music to the night shifts now. Thoughtfully, the management has perched an ack-ack battery on the roof of one of the factory buildings, so our nights are lively. Last night, shrapnel from an anti-aircraft shell fell right beside my machine. One of the prisoners was wounded, though fortunately it was nothing very serious. The overseers scream at us to stay at our machines no matter what; only the 'civilians' are allowed in the shelter. This suits me perfectly, as I can't bear shelters. At midnight soup I see Erb, looking very hot; he makes a great show of mopping his brow, holding his helmet in his hand. As I file past he whispers in my ear: 'There's an egg for you in my helmet, take it.'

We shared that egg, Henriette and I, in our bunks after lights out. How can we ever forget gestures such as Erb's? And to think that there are people who have lost their faith in human nature!

Krefeld, 21 June 1943

Tomorrow it is the feast of Saint Jean. The weather is warm and mellow. We are still on the night shift. Flowers cascade from the window boxes on all the houses we pass, and the gardens are glorious. The air that we breathe so greedily is heavy with perfume, and we gulp it in from the bus door. My thoughts turn to France, to the traditional bonfires of Saint Jean when I was a child in Lorraine, and dancing round them with the other village children. I mull over our traditions: the folk remedies and herbs of Saint Jean, and the dances. And then in the cloak-room I am brought down to earth with a bump. I put my top back on, and it is still soaked with yesterday's sweat. It's incredible how sweat from the day before feels cold and clammy on your skin sixteen hours later. Since midnight the anti-aircraft guns have been pounding away incessantly. It feels like being on board ship in a heavy storm. The overseers pace to and fro anxiously in front of us. If the factory siren sounds tonight, we have been ordered to slide under our machines. By a quarter past midnight nothing has happened, but nearly all the lights are out. We can't carry on with stacking the 'cakes'. Too bad! The pots will overflow, and what fun that will be! The siren sounds. I run to join Henriette, and together we hide in the channel under her machine. It's dark, streaming with water and thoroughly unpleasant. Still, we make a little discovery, or rather a great one, in the form of a comb. What a joy, as our combs have just been stolen! After ten minutes we creep out of our hiding place, of which we have had quite enough. The bombs are falling thick and fast. At two o'clock we start work again, attempting to repair the damage as best we can, while the overseers yell at us as though that will make it all better. We hear a rumour that Krefeld is in flames. Why the hell did they have to stop at Krefeld? Why couldn't they have pushed on into the suburbs, as far as us? Perhaps tomorrow?

A rumour reaches us that Kölping Haus has been destroyed. We are worried about our comrades who were still there. Shall we ever know what has happened to them? At six o'clock there is no sign of the next shift. At nine o'clock for the first time they bring us bread to eat at our machines. It seems certain that part of Krefeld has been destroyed. We are dropping with exhaustion by the time the next shift arrives at midday. No sooner have we formed ranks than the overseers come back to select fifteen women to work with the day shift. Henriette and Marie volunteer without a moment's hesitation, as the women who have just arrived are in a tragic state. Kölping Haus is completely destroyed. Amazingly, all the prisoners were in the shelter and are safe.

The atmosphere in the courtyard is strange. We can feel that the day is fine, but the sun is hidden behind a dense fog: the dust of what used to be the town of Krefeld. The bus arrives to collect us. Busloads of dazed-looking children are brought to the village of Linn. Linn does not appear to have suffered, but as soon as we leave the village we see the flames. The bus negotiates a path between two infernos. The fire engines can't do anything; the fire hoses lie on the ground, useless for lack of water. Little knots of people wander about, their dusty white faces making them look like clowns, adding a touch of burlesque to the tragedy. This is one of the effects of phosphorus bombs, it seems.

I see a very aged couple setting off on foot, leaving behind them what used to be their home. Each of them carries a few possessions wrapped up in a towel. Their old faces are black with smoke, and they have enormous scarlet rings round their eyes. Tears course down their powdery cheeks, but do nothing to wash them clean. In a square stands a random collection of broken furniture: a sideboard, a settee, a sewing machine, a cooker. Perched above this hotchpotch, in pride of place, is an immense faux-bronze bust of Adolf Hitler. A ruined house, its timber staircase shooting great tongues of flame, forms the backdrop to this vision of the god Moloch himself. No question about it: this bust, filched from some Party organization, is an anti-fascist gesture: silent propaganda, the image and quintessence of destruction. No one will be sent to a concentration camp for creating this striking tableau. Now and then the detonation of an unexploded bomb ruptures the deathly, clotted silence that lies over everything like a thick blanket. Last night I admired a great horse-chestnut tree in bloom; today all that remains of it is a charred skeleton. Beside the tree stood a home for elderly Protestant ladies, its doorway decorated with a bas-relief of a dove holding an olive branch in its beak. Many times I had watched those old women, so peaceful and dignified, slowly living out their last years in the shade of ancient trees and under the dove's protective wings. This morning nothing remains of their home, only this section of wall with its mocking image promising peace unto death. Where are the old women?

Boys in brown shirts are everywhere, spruce and smart, with neatly parted hair. They move from group to group, listening in silence. These are Hitler's informers, their job to report back to the Party on what the victims of the bombing are saying and to denounce any dissenting voices. This is the sum total of their contribution to society.

Watching all this, I feel my heart and mind split in two. One half of my heart aches for all this misery, weeps for all this destruction. But then I tell myself for the hundredth, perhaps the thousandth time, that this is the only way that we can destroy the monster. Who started all this butchery, who kindled these infernos throughout the world, who torched London, Rotterdam, Dunkirk? The monster was all-powerful, all-powerful though cowardly even then. But now his enemies are strong, and they must kill, kill, kill to live. In the struggle between barbarism and civilization killing is a necessary and unavoidable evil. Civilization has to use the weapons of barbarism in order to prevail. That is the great tragedy.

Krefeld burned for three days and nights. We went for a week without washing. Our excellent food rations are supplied by field kitchens; troops are stationed in the town in force, doubtless because of fears of an uprising. An uprising? These people are not capable of it. Where I used to count on a revolution at least as much as on the Allies, if not more, I now begin to think that they will never rise in revolt. They are supine, supine to the point of abject stupidity.

On one occasion we are given white bread in the factory refectory, and the German women chuckle and say, 'Thanks, Tommy,' as (they explain) it is to the Tommies that they owe this favour, this surprise treat. For the Germans, food comes before everything else.

I write home. My letter is disjointed, and I try to inject a little cheerfulness into it by explaining my lack of coherence thus: 'My companions are laughing and talking all around me, and I can't concentrate on what I'm writing.' At that moment, we hear terrified screams coming from upstairs. The director of Anrath is up there. With his cosh, he is battering the women who can't see or are ill, and who, with the wardress's permission, have stayed in their bunks this morning. With him in pursuit, they stagger down the stairs, crashing into the walls as they go.

A week ago he came into the toilets while we were washing, and – in his usual bullying way – made me turn my pocket inside out so that he could check that it contained only the regulation handkerchief. It was empty, as someone stole my regulation handkerchief three months ago. Since then I have had to blow my nose in my fingers.

When we are working the day shift we now have to go down into the cellar during air-raid alerts, sometimes three times a night, for prolonged periods. Naturally we are not allowed an extra ten minutes in bed to make up for this. Punctuality is all. We are worn out by it. I'm getting thinner and thinner. Two new Frenchwomen have arrived on our kommando. Henriette explains to them what our lives are like, and makes me strip to show them what the Germans can do to a woman who until quite recently was relatively presentable.

I manage to weigh myself. Even wearing heavy factory trousers I weigh forty-nine kilos: not much for a woman measuring one metre sixty-eight tall with a normal weight in Paris of sixty-five kilos. I decide to make the 'new girls' laugh by clowning about a bit, and to justify my new nickname of Gandhi I put on a pair of glasses and wrap a cloth round my loins. The Frenchwomen promptly burst into tears, from which I take it that my little entertainment is not an unqualified success.

Ruth is a lovely girl, and very sound. Four years ago, in another life, she belonged to a sports club. She disliked Hitler and said so. Which cost her four years in a concentration camp outside Hamburg. There, for twelve hours a day, she had to shovel coal on to ships. But that hard, filthy work was better than her life at the Phrix factory. What brought her here? A raincoat, quite simply, a handsome raincoat that she bought in Holland. One of her friends admired it and wanted one the same. Ruth had one sent from Amsterdam, adding a few marks to the price for her trouble. 'Black market,' said her lover, a fine young man who was in the Gestapo and had grown bored with her.

The management has become aware that too many women receive letters from their families that have dual meanings. Some are obviously written in code, while others contain obscure hidden meanings. So, to make sure that we do not have time to decode them, we are allowed to keep our letters for one hour only, and even that varies between kommandos. The women of Kölping Haus, currently under the tender care of Fräulein Gaeta, have to read their letters in front of her and give them straight back. We are allowed an hour, sometimes two. Amy is blind and in excruciating pain. She has just had a letter from her husband, who is fighting in Russia. She has been waiting for news from him for months. One of her companions reads the letter to her, but she would like to read it herself, to see the handwriting of the man she loves and whose last letter this may be. She begs the wardress to let her keep it. But rules are rules, and no exceptions can be made for the accidents suffered by the women forced to work at the Phrix factory. Amy will never see her husband's letter.

Krefeld, June 1943
Is it the intense heat that has caused our eyes to get bad again? Whatever the reason, at breakfast yesterday morning most of us were wearing dark glasses. The sunlight flooding the refectory

was simply unbearable. Then La Concon swept into the room in a fury, declaring that the sight of all these women in dark glasses was depressing. On the strength of which she confiscated our glasses; we're not convinced this made us any less depressing.

Certain notions of elementary hygiene are clearly in need of updating. Scabies is supposed to be contagious, for instance. An old wives' tale! Marguerite, the young apprentice to whom I am now teaching our job, has scabies. Her arms are covered with more or less oozing sores, which she scratches assiduously. For eight hours every day and twelve hours on Sundays we plunge our hands and arms into the same bucket of water. But I haven't caught scabies yet.

Krefeld, June 1943

You can always find something to laugh about. Gerda, the fat, red-headed butcher, comes to find me at my machine. She is very downcast: 'The war's not over yet, you know! You said that things were going badly for us in France, that we were recalling our troops to send them to the Russian front, and that the British and Americans would take advantage of this soon to land in France. But they can't now. The Japanese have sent us reinforcements, and hundreds of thousands of them are landing in France. It's true, you know; I saw a photograph in the paper, and it's a disaster as it means the war will go on . . .' Keeping a straight face I reply, 'They must have come through the tunnel from Yokohama to Marseille.' She ponders this, then declares, 'I don't know about that, it didn't say where exactly in the paper, but it was definitely in France . . . *Herr Gott*, it's so sad!' My, how I laughed.

Kate Dreimuller, the one with the large brilliant set between two of her teeth, complained to Houben that her trolley's wheels had completely seized up for lack of lubrication, making the work even more exhausting. He slapped her twice in the face, so hard that she fell to the ground, whereupon he gave her a good kicking. She was only a couple of metres away from me, and there was nothing I could do. You just have to clench your teeth, dig your fingernails into the palms of your hands, and wait till it's over.

Today Kate was still aching all over and completely drained. To make the work easier she stopped her pots with a cloth, which is against the rules. Herr Pils, the director, happened to walk past and noticed this. He threw a bucketful of cold water over her, soaking her to the skin. 'Thank you, Herr Direktor,' was Kate's response, 'my shirt was in need of a wash.'

Krefeld, June 1943

Erika, who looks like a Louis XV flower girl, and Ena, who is a natural platinum blonde, were caught making love with some Belgian factory workers under their machine. They all do it. Some do it to get more to eat, others for a bit of soap, others again so that the Belgians who oversee our work are not too mean, and a few just because, despite the bromide, they want to make love. But they were a bit too obvious about it, and things looked bad for them. Houben and Siemens were fairly lenient, however, giving them extremely heavy trolleys to push, insulting them and laughing at them. They got off lightly.

The numbers of women who are sick are impressive. Gertrude has a prolapsed womb, and old Madame Reversay a terrible leg ulcer. Marguerite is still plagued by scabies, and lots of us are suffering from boils, abscesses and other suppurating wounds of mysterious origins. They say that these wounds are caused by the acid vapour that is poisoning us, as we are given soup with milk only one week in every three, with not a drop of milk in between. But the news that's causing a sensation today is that the factory doctor, a fat woman with glasses, is in the house, having come to visit La Concon. The sick women cluster together on the landing at the top of the stairs, where she will have to pass them on her way out. They take off their rag dressings to expose their wounds, and they wait. A veritable court of miracles! At length Frau Doktor appears. She raises her arms to heaven, and with a little pout of distaste cries '*Ach lieber Gott!*' Then, waving her right hand as though she were swatting flies, she makes a funny little noise, '*Pfui, pfui, pfui,*' three times and, pushing the sick women aside with a sweeping gesture, makes her way down the stairs and leaves.

Krefeld, late June 1943

Henriette has had her most severe attack of eye trouble yet. To look at her you would have thought she had goitres on her eyes. The swelling was so bad that when viewed from the side her eyes projected further forward than her forehead. Her heart seizures were becoming more frequent, too, and to make matters even worse she was barely over all this when Hermann, who is in charge of her group of machines, decided to beat her until he drew blood. Hermann is Dutch. A new recruit to the SS who feels the need to prove his true Nazi credentials, he never misses an opportunity. He failed to understand a phrase that Henriette used when she was interpreting some rebuke he had aimed at Marie-Jeanne. Because he didn't understand, he fell upon Henriette and cut her breast. The good Scherer dressed the wound for her, and sent a report that will go the way of all the other reports; that is to say, it will be wilfully overlooked. To think of it, an SS man! That was all poor dear Henriette needed to finish her off. So there she was, completely prostrated and with a temperature of over forty degrees. But still she had to go to work.

Today there was neither aspirin nor quinine to be had at the first-aid post. Daniel, the kind little Belgian spinner, managed – heaven knows how – to get hold of some aspirin.

He gave her a whole tube. To crown it all Houben put her on machine fifty-eight, which has just been converted, is unreliable and spins silk thread so fine that it is barely visible with the naked eye. In the middle of the night, Henriette came to my machine and embraced me. This little demonstration of affection surprised me a little, but I was too busy to really think about it. I was in the middle of changing my spinnerets; it was hard and going badly, my fingers were burning terribly, and on top of all that I was having heart problems. So I just said: 'Not now, love, I'll come and see you at your machine later on.' Ten minutes later I heard screams and saw women running. Wearily I asked, 'What is it now?'

'She cut her wrist with some glass,' I heard someone say, 'but one of the Belgians saw her do it and stopped her from killing herself.'

Another one! But who was it this time? It was Henriette, they told me, my dear Henriette, who had been like a mother, a sister and a daughter to me, and better than that, a friend . . . And I was so worn down by exhaustion, revulsion and suffering that I couldn't even react.

Krefeld, July 1943
The air raids are becoming more and more intense. The women are at the end of their tether and can endure no more. Another woman in the shift after us has just thrown herself out of the clothing-store window. Apparently she only broke her leg. And another has thrown herself down the stairwell.

Krefeld, July 1943
Occasionally, I catch a glimpse of the little Russian girls who do the spooling. The change in a year is startling. It's not that they are physically abused, as their work is quite bearable. But

the promiscuity in which the wretched girls are forced to live, the shameful existence reserved for them here, has degraded most of them utterly and killed their spirit. Where have they gone, those pretty girls with their fresh, innocent faces framed by their traditional headscarves or headbands? Most of them have abandoned their national headdress, and with it all the human dignity they had brought with them from their home-lands. Now they all curl their hair and wear heavy make-up, shout and yell all the time and sleep with the lowest of the low from among the Belgian and Dutch workers. Many of them have been infected with diseases, and twenty-five are pregnant. Those who make it back to Ukraine will have a handsome souvenir of 'western civilization' to take with them.

Krefeld, August 1943

I often distract myself by thinking of things I have left behind me at home. Shall I ever see them again, or will Paris be destroyed before I get back? I might think that I feel quite detached about the inanimate objects waiting for me there, but no, I am more attached to them than ever. I think about my books, especially: which one shall I open first when I get back? I can see my book-shelves, and the rows of my beloved books. By the time I get back I shall have quite forgotten how to read, and I'll have to start all over again by looking at picture books like a child. I try to conjure up images of the paintings in my bedroom, the Renoir drawing above my bed, the little Fragonard, and Max Lingner's exquisite *Youth*. I stand before them all again, contem-plating at length the Chinese ceramic Buddha on the mantelpiece, so serene on his plinth of theology books, beautiful seventeenth-century volumes with faded gold tooling, and my little Louis-Philippe pieces; will they survive? Come now, of course they will; if I'm going to survive (and I will) then so will they.

We have just had an inspection. All the French and Belgian

women are lined up on the landing. The director of Anrath, a fat general, the director of slave-labour camps in Germany and another individual all scrutinize us. We are not a pretty sight in our rags, but today of all days not a single one of us has bad eyes. What rotten luck! I decide to speak out (in the state I'm in, what have I got to lose?). Declaring that I am in the last stages of exhaustion, I demand work that is appropriate to my physical capacities and state of health. By some miracle, they do not abuse me. The general asks me my father's profession, and my son's if I have one. Gravely they take note. Then the director proposes that they should sign a plea for clemency. I refuse politely, declaring that I would prefer to serve out my sentence. They appear surprised. Clemency? Appeal to them for clemency? I'd rather die!

Krefeld, 20 August 1943

We are certain now that 'something' is about to happen. We have been waiting so long now for the Allies to come and destroy the factory that we are beginning to lose patience. We can't believe that this hideous building is still standing – after all, it's big enough! Some of the women claim that Phrix shares are to be found in too many British portfolios, and that this is the reason why this lousy dump has been spared. But at last we think that things are coming to a head, as every day the bombing gets more intense. One shift of prisoners out of the three will inevitably be sacrificed, as we are not allowed in the shelter. The overseers seem worried, and huddle together in corners for whispered exchanges.

As we file past the massive portrait of Hitler in the restaurant today I am suddenly reminded of gladiators in a Roman arena and intone, 'Those who are about to die salute thee, O Adolf!' Henriette, who is gradually recovering her spirits, thinks this is terribly funny.

Krefeld, 22 August 1943

It was incredible how everything shook tonight. If it goes on like this, the ack-ack alone will destroy the factory building! 'It's tonight or never,' said Daniel. He is allowed out, and he brings back all the news. The sky was very clear, and our friends were circling over the factory. For the fiftieth time I told Henriette that I would meet her beside the entrance and to the left of it, the only spot where there didn't appear to be any electric cables and where a corner probably offered a degree of structural resistance, with the entrance close by. My twelve-thirty 'cake' stacking was finished, and I was cleaning my machine while waiting for the next one at one forty-five, when at one thirty-six a bomb finally fell. It fell precisely on the spot where I had arranged to meet Henriette, beside the entrance and to the left of it. That whole section of the factory building collapsed like a house of cards, and instantly immense flames shot into the sky. I just hoped that Henriette hadn't had time to run that far. I headed for another little doorway that I know, attempting on the way to calm down some women who were screaming, which didn't help anything and got on everyone's nerves.

The far door was already smashed open, so we got through easily. I was holding Mickey by the hand. I always liked her, and now I liked her even more. I could feel that she was shaking, but that she was battling bravely with her fear. Her expression was strained, her eyes staring, but she was very calm. In front of us lay a vista of open country, lit by the glow of fires on all sides. All the factories around us were in flames. Everything was red. What a magnificent job! We were free. Some Germans standing on the doorstep of a house shouted at us that we were mad to stay there and invited us into their shelter. But no, we wanted to see it all, to relish the joy, the wild jubilation we felt at this scene of destruction. Suddenly a Dutchman barred my way. He recognized my uniform and thought I was escaping. Threatening me with his revolver, he told me to go back into the factory, into the viscose cellar, which was still intact. I refused, as I wanted to see; I wanted to savour the pleasure of watching it all burn, of hearing the explosions. Then I saw my friend Erb the policeman. He was looking for me and we went off together, thumbing our noses at the zealous Dutchman.

Once more, Erb offers to save me. Too frightened of reprisals for Pierre, I refuse, and we go to look for Henriette, whom we find carrying a wounded prisoner known as 'La Chèvre Morte', or 'Dead Nanny Goat'; she has a minor leg wound and as usual is pretending to be at death's door. At the first-aid post Mickey (a doctor in civilian life) offers her services. She is told that it is not up to a prisoner to take such an initiative, and we are all sent back into the factory to unscrew the spinnerets on the machines that are not buried under the rubble. The ruins are still smoking and there is a very strong danger of collapse, as every now and then large sections of ceiling come crashing down with a great roar, but we must still save the gold and platinum in the spinnerets.

We survive the night, as it turns out, to return to our bunks with happy hearts. Phrix is not completely destroyed, sadly, but all the same it will take six months to get it working again. Oh joy!

The Fall of the Third Reich

Krefeld–Anrath (25 August–19 October 1943)

At the Rheika we were working in a nationalized factory. For political prisoners such as ourselves, this arrangement had a certain logic to it. We had done injury to Nazi Germany, and Nazi Germany took its revenge by working us to death. But now it's all very different. Nazi Germany has hired us out (at rock-bottom rates no doubt) to a slave-driver who will duly line his pockets off the sweat of our brows. There are sixty of us, all women – French, Belgian and Dutch – and we are the property of Herr Joseph Scheuring, who, although German, a Party member and necessarily a pure Aryan, looks like a prosperous white slaver from Syria. Swarthy complexion, black curly hair, Panama hat, pale jacket, yellow-and-white co-respondent shoes, massive gold ring set with lapis-lazuli and – of course – red tie: it's all too good to be true. You really couldn't make him up. No one knows what stone this shameless crook has crawled out from under, though we know him to be an intimate associate of the director of the prison at Anrath. From five o'clock every afternoon he is pretty much sodden with drink. His factory was largely destroyed in the recent bombing. It is our job to demolish the tottering walls and clean up the bricks so they can be used again. It is our privilege, all sixty of us women, to erect a new factory so that Herr

Scheuring can continue to swell his coffers. In addition to us, his workforce also includes Adolphe and Georges, two French prisoners of war, and two German convicts.

Naturally, we have to do all the hardest jobs, and the men are forbidden to help us. We shoulder iron girders, mix cement and mortar, and unload lorries laden with building materials and merchandise. The men erect the scaffolding and build the walls. Clambering up the scaffolding with only clogs on their bare feet gives some of the women vertigo. It doesn't bother me, and I'm quite happy to take the place of anyone who doesn't like working on ladders or rickety platforms. But I categorically refuse – no matter how much Scheuring shouts at me – to carry sacks of cement. Like the overseers at the Phrix factory, Scheuring maintains that because I am tall I must be strong. In the end he has to admit that no matter how hard I try I simply can't carry heavy weights. My shoulders are black and blue from heaving around bolts of paper fabric to be used to make sacks. Stuffed with straw, these sacks will serve as mattresses for soldiers, prisoners and refugees. Gradually I worm my way into the good graces of the female supervisor, so I get to spend most of my time in the workshop where the sacks are made. The 'workshop' is in fact a cellar in which the sacks are turned, counted and parcelled up.

It is the bombed-out workshop that we are currently rebuilding. Several times a day the slave-driver persists in calling me out to do heavy work. The fate reserved for the women who aren't either sewing sacks or turning them has to be seen to be believed. They do all the excavation work, dig the trenches for high-tension electricity cables, lay the cables, mix cement and mortar and heave it to the building site and up the scaffolding. As a result, Marthe Ferret has no skin left on the palms of her hands, which are nothing but two large raw wounds. One day, when the slope leading up to the factory was particularly muddy, Herr Scheuring was concerned that his heavily laden horses might slip and lose their footing. The solution he hit upon was to have them unyoked and to use us instead.

The food is pathetically inadequate: boiled red cabbage for lunch one day, boiled white cabbage the next, and for supper unpeeled potatoes alternating with a watery broth containing unspeakable lumpy bits. Scheuring spends his entire day directing the work. In addition to our female supervisor, we are also overseen by Scheuring's two children, aged eleven and twelve. They are admirable little Nazi informers who never take their eyes off us. The girl is worse than the boy. Scheuring has us put in the punishment cells for the slightest thing, for by a stroke of luck we are billeted at Anrath once more. The prison hasn't changed since I was there in April 1942 – except for one new feature. The main entrance now sports a splendid printed notice bearing the following announcement:

In case of bombardment by aeroplanes, each person must keep absolute calm, whosoever makes noise or attempts escape will be shooted [sic].
   Signed: Dr Combrinck, Director of Prison for men and Forced Labour for women.

Our director prides himself on being quite a linguist. This notice was posted on the door in the aftermath of a terrible panic in the prison. During a particularly heavy air raid the wretched inmates were all double-locked in their cells, when a bomb fell close by and the adjacent buildings caught fire. The terrified women made frantic attempts to break down the doors of their cells: hence this picturesque appeal for calm.

Thankfully, Henriette and I have not been split up. We are in a dormitory for forty, equipped with sixteen sets of bunk beds. Eight women have to sleep on mattresses on the floor, which in the ordinary way is not so terrible. Here, however, it's a different matter. We have two latrines. One of them leaks, and, naturally, it is quite beyond those in authority to do anything about it. Thus it is that, since we are not creatures of spirit alone, every night the mattresses of the women sleeping on the floor get soaked. To make matters worse, the room is so cramped that we are obliged to trample over them more or less continuously throughout the night on our way to the latrines and back. When it comes to our ablutions, the forty of us share four bowls and six jugs of water. Try as we might, we cannot get them to give us more. Our Saturday showers have been virtually abolished, and Henriette has appointed herself water monitor. Only the women who work on the building site are allowed a daily wash, with Henriette distributing carefully measured rations of water in a food bowl. When they have finished, Henriette lets the rest of us have a bit of a wash on a rota basis. Not surprisingly, there is an outbreak of lice, and once again Henriette Delatte is to the fore in ridding us of them, aided by Marie-Jeanne.

We were overjoyed to see Betty Spriet when she returned, though the state she was in was truly shocking. She must have lost at least twenty kilos. For weeks she had been in the grip of a raging fever, abandoned in a building on her own with no medical attention. Our friend Mickey, who is a doctor, says it must have been typhoid. But Betty's spirits are as high as ever.

Italy has surrendered! We heard the news from the French prisoners, and we are ecstatic! The minor inconveniences of our daily life pale into insignificance, and we can hardly contain our joy. We owe a lot to the two French prisoners who work with us: every day they bring us a newspaper, and back in the Stalag their fellow prisoners club together to send us all sorts of delicacies to eat, along with even more vital provisions: medicines for the sick, vitamins and tonics. Whenever I pass Adolphe, he mutters at me (or rather to himself) with his delightful Toulousain twang: '*Pôvre femme, pôvre femme* (poor woman, poor woman).' Yellow and cadaverous as I am, it cannot be denied that I am not a pretty sight. I'm so thin that I don't dare sit down in the lorry that brings us to work from the prison, as I'm afraid my bones will poke through my skin. But all in all I feel much better since we have been freed from the Rheika.

The four of us are inseparable: Henriette, Betty, Mickey (Doctor Florence Penning in civilian life) and me. Mickey is English,[17] and her husband is Dutch. Mickey 'worked' in Amsterdam, rather too efficiently for the Germans' liking, which is what brought her here. Once at Anrath she was systematically abused, needless to say. At the Phrix factory she had more trouble with her eyes than any of us, and invariably displayed the most remarkable courage. She too is gradually getting back on her feet, and the four of us make great plans for the future. It's so wonderful to talk about the future and to believe that we'll really be here to see it. One Sunday morning the four of us were busy building castles in Spain (or rather France and Holland) when the door was suddenly flung open to reveal a wardress. She barked out a list of a dozen names, mine included.

We are to be transferred somewhere else, to a concentration camp on the French border, we are told. Henriette, Mickey and Betty are not included in the convoy. We got on too well together; it was too good to last! Just time for quick hugs, then more shouts from the wardress, we have to go *now*. Where are they taking us? We'll find out soon enough.

Hövelhof, 19 October 1943–30 August 1944

I feel as though I have sleepwalked through ten months here. Sometimes this long sleep was disturbed by nightmares, at others it was peaceful and uneventful. And just occasionally

17 In December 1945, Mickey returned to Krefeld with the British Army, which she had rejoined. On finding that our friend Joseph Scheuring was still at large, she immediately had him arrested by the occupying authorities.

there was a magnificent awakening. The first of these came on 7 June, when a Russian prisoner broke all the rules to come and tell me that the Allies had landed in France. This time it was the real thing; a French prisoner told the women who unload railway wagons at the station that Paris was liberated! Then a few days later we heard that Toulouse and Lyon were free!

They had told us we were going to a concentration camp on the French border. Of course they were lying: we were billeted in relative comfort at Hövelhof in Westphalia. There we had to spend ten hours a day making wooden crates. I used to hammer in my nails and then snap off the shafts so that the crates would rapidly disintegrate. The supervisors were decent; the wardresses were only doing their job. We were constantly starving, except on days when the director came to visit. He was a good man, that director, a livestock dealer whose four grandparents can't all have been of pure Aryan blood. On the days when he carried out his inspections the soup was thick and the portions reasonable. The rest of the time our rations went to the wardresses' families or to refugees who had lost everything and had been given temporary shelter at Hövelhof. They needed to eat, and as long as we weren't actually dying of hunger we couldn't object. In any case, they weighed us every two months. Every time this happened we had lost a bit more weight, and the woman in charge would solemnly note it all down in her register. On days when we were more starved than usual, my dear friend Chagnoux would pretend to have a stomach ache and give me half her soup and one of the four thin slices of bread that made up our daily ration. On Sundays they gave us potatoes in their skins, and we would peel them with meticulous care. First we ate the potatoes, then we ate the skins. I preferred to eat my skins first, followed by those of our more fastidious companions – the 'little rich kids', we called them – who were too delicate to consume potato skins.

The Red Army soldiers at the factory were generally not too badly treated; whenever the news was good they would sing, in that inimitable Russian way, and we would understand. When they sang the Komintern song it was so beautiful that I wanted to cry. One day, we were sent to a different workshop. I had a brand-new workbench, on which someone had written a few words in Russian. I carefully transcribed them, as though copying a drawing, and Vera, the Russian girl in our group, translated the message for me: 'Welcome to our French comrades'.

Nothing ever happened except for a few distant air raids, we didn't know where. Very often at night we would hear hundreds of aircraft heading for Berlin, or so everyone said.

Our only way of measuring the passage of time was by the illnesses of our companions, in the same way that respectable families refer to 'the year that Gustave had measles', or 'the year that Riquet had his operation'. We used to place events according to whether they happened before or after Jeanne died for lack of medical treatment, of what we never knew; no one thought to bother the doctor, in any case; she just gave up the ghost one day because she couldn't bear the waiting any longer. And then there was Raymonde, the little communist from Brest, who went berserk. She absolutely insisted that her daughter Michelle had to be locked up in the cupboard, and we were at a loss as to how to calm her down.

I had a letter from Jean, the first of my son's letters that I had been allowed to read. He wrote to tell me that Maman died in November. She didn't suffer. She just fell asleep. The endless waiting was too much for her. This was a brutal awakening; then I subsided once more into a blessed torpor. However hard I tried, I simply couldn't imagine my life, my future, without the warm presence of Maman, and yet . . . As I hammered in my nails I reflected wanly on what my existence would be like without her, but it was cold (it was January when I got the news) and I felt numb; I remained frozen like that until the spring, or more particularly until the day the Russian told me the Allies had landed . . .

Schwelm, 30 August 1944–February 1945

At Schwelm I spent another six months sleepwalking, but now my sleep was less deep. If I slept more lightly now, it was thanks to the French prisoners whose goodness drew me a little closer to consciousness with each passing day. I had a duty, after all, to thank them for their unfailing kindness.

Schwelm was still in Westphalia, but on the border with the Rhineland, fifty-five kilometres from Cologne. Our life there was lived to the perpetual din of gunfire, with the exception of December's tragic interlude. At Schwelm we got news every day, but even without the news we would have been able to follow the progress of the war simply by the cacophony of artillery fire, ever louder and ever closer.

We worked at the Rondo munitions factory. I was put on an automatic milling machine, a brainless job that – despite my best efforts – proved almost impervious to sabotage. As at Hövelhof, the wardresses were decent, likewise the factory overseer and supervisors. Nearly all the factory workers were foreigners, including two Greeks. There were about forty French and Belgian women, but most of the Rondo workforce was made up of little Ukrainain girls. Who could ever put into words the tragedy of these young Russian deportees? All of them were just fifteen when the Germans brutally uprooted them, for no reason other than to flaunt their triumphant power and barbaric supremacy. I managed to exchange a few words with them when the wardress's back was turned. I spoke to Nina. She still wore her black bandeau, and I sensed that she longed desperately, against all odds, to preserve the traditions of her homeland. Her spirits were high, and she was looking forward to returning soon to her farm outside Kiev, with its wide-open plains and the rural way of life she loved so much. She detested the factory, Germany and the Germans.

I liked Anna, who was from Smolensk. She had her heart set on going to university after finishing her compulsory schooling. The Germans had deprived her of this pleasure, another thing for her to hold against them. Brought up as a communist, she kept up her companions' spirits. 'Smolensk has been destroyed,' she said, 'but we will build a new Smolensk, even more beautiful than the last. As beautiful as Moscow. Do you know Moscow? Have you visited Lenin's mausoleum?'

But it was Raya, above all, who became my friend, my heart-rending friend. At first I couldn't understand why this lovely girl was made to do the sweeping. Her beauty was of such purity, and she always looked after her appearance and arranged her hair with care. She was from Kiev.

'I lived there back then, with my parents and my little sisters. Papa worked in an office, Mama stayed at home with the little ones. Papa joined the army and went away. Then Kiev was destroyed. The Germans took Mama and my little sisters away, I don't know where; and they brought me here . . . I'll never see them again, Papa, Mama or my little sisters.' She would recite this like a litany, with a trance-like, faraway look in her eyes. 'Russia is too big, I'll never find them again.' Over and over again she would tell me this story, simply and softly, always using the same words, as though it were a prayer she had learned by heart. At first I didn't understand why Raya had been set to do the sweeping. But the Germans knew that by tearing this child from her family they had also ripped out her spirit. She was as gentle as her lovely face, and she was good at sweeping. I often used to see another Ukrainian, a tall blond boy called Franz, talking to her, slowly and gently; I would see him nodding his head, encouraging her. Although I couldn't understand their musical language, I knew that he was telling her, as I used to, that soon she would be back with her Papa, her Mama and her little sisters . . . that the guns of our American friends were getting closer.

It takes a prisoner to understand the sufferings of a fellow prisoner. No one told the prisoners of war at Schwelm that our feet hurt; they just knew, and they cut up the hems of their greatcoats to make us slippers, and when our shoes started leaking they repaired them for us. They sent us food, medicines, delightful letters and more. I was 'adopted' by one of them who called himself 'le Cheval' (the Horse), who contrived somehow or other to produce some biscuits for me. With them was a note: 'Don't worry about the cost, they're only stolen goods!' Another prisoner, a native of Montmartre, signed his letters 'Poulbot' (Street Urchin); they were long and interesting and I looked forward to them. I shall always be convinced that around Christmas Poulbot must have killed someone. On Christmas Day he sent me a parcel containing a large piece of roast goose, sausage and bread; we had a feast on my bunk, Chagnoux, Madeleine and I. Eating anything rich and oily was unbelievable, impossible, inconceivable except in our dreams! When I later met Poulbot, I never did ask him just exactly what he had done, so that on Christmas Day 1944 'Delphine' and her friends could feast on goose, in Germany, in prison . . .

All these letters, parcels and tokens of affection slipped right under the noses of our wardresses, through a hole in the window of the Rondo factory toilets. This is where the postal deliveries we dubbed 'Air France' touched down. Generally, the pilot would also give a kiss to the young postmistress who received the mail. Then one day the pilot brought a friend with him and, as there were too many parcels for one person to conceal, the postmistress also enlisted a friend to help. Before long the toilets had become known as the 'kissodrome', as it was there that we made the acquaintance of our protectors and exchanged hurried kisses through the hole. It didn't seem to matter how often I tried to persuade them that I had all the allure of an old witch got up as Puss in Boots, their affection never faltered – quite the opposite, it seemed!

And then one day we heard that Pétain and all his gang had fled to Germany and put themselves under the protection of Hitler, their great leader. Sacha, the little Soviet prisoner who had only a rudimentary command of German, rose to the occasion with admirable succinctness: 'Pétain *kaput*, de Gaulle *gut gut*.' These were the words that rang in our ears as we prepared to leave. The growing intensity of the air raids and the American advance combined to put our precious lives at risk, and on 19 February the powers that be decided to evacuate us. And so we left Schwelm, and with it our cherished protectors. We also had to leave behind the old SS uniforms in which we used to look so ridiculous but which offered two great advantages: they kept us warm and they made us laugh. As always, we left Schwelm behind us with no idea where our next destination might be.

Allendorf, 20 February 1945

We travelled all day in the railway wagon, and then it stopped and we spent all night in it too. Locomotives passed by at frequent intervals, driven by women. All around us we could hear the dull thud of bombs. The rails were severed, and our guardian angels appeared at a loss to know what to do with us. At daybreak they made us get out and walk for some distance through the open countryside. To our right and left we could see long columns of prisoners toiling along the roads and paths on their way to work, looking as though they were in the last extremities of physical and mental exhaustion. The silence lay heavy like a blanket. We intersected a column of Soviet prisoners of war. One of them asked us in a whisper who we were and where we came from; hearing him, the guard struck him with the butt of his rifle – a mechanical gesture born of habit.

At length we see some buildings surrounded by barbed wire. For some time we stand outside the camp entrance, waiting as a kommando of women emerges. One of them whispers that she is from Luxembourg, that we will be working in a powder magazine and that it is hard, very hard. A fat wardress stands at the entrance, surveying the prisoners as they pass. In among all these women wearing grimy cloths on their heads is one very young girl who is bareheaded. The wardress grabs hold of her by the hair and jerks her roughly backwards, giving the order for her head to be shaved, *now*. Another wardress leads the girl off towards one of the buildings. Taking Chagnoux's hand, I murmur, 'Well, little one, it doesn't look much fun here!' Eventually we are all herded into a hut that is completely devoid of furniture. A wardress comes to warn us not to go near the windows, which in any case are blocked by tangles of barbed wire, as the guards will open fire at the slightest infringement of the rules. Large police dogs patrol the paths between the huts.

With a few of the other women I ask to be taken to the toilets, and a wardress escorts us to a neighbouring hut. On the way she hisses, 'Chin up, it's nearly over for you!'

'How far are the Russians from Berlin?' I venture.

She replies with visible relief, 'Yesterday fifty kilometres; today they're even closer!'

We walk along a corridor lined with cell doors. Inside one of them someone is banging, but the wardress seems not to hear. I tell her someone wants her. Wearily, she pushes open the spyhole. The ensuing dialogue is clearly audible:

'What is it?'

'There are two dead in here!'

With a despairing gesture the wardress retorts, '*Ach, mein Gott*, what am I supposed to do about it?' And she walks away.

'So there are two dead women in there?' I ask.

'No, not women . . . vermin,' she counters with a bitter, sarcastic laugh.

The name of this camp is Allendorf. It is a place where, if you don't have a filthy rag to cover your head, they shave your hair off. Where they abandon you in the cells to die. Where the food is inedible. You never know what you're going to find in the soup: bits of wood, paper, filth of every description. This is what we learn during our long day of waiting. The other women are full of questions. Do you think we're going to stay here? Do you think we're going to die here? Do you think the Americans will arrive in time? We try to keep the youngest ones calm. As long as they allow us to keep our clothes all hope is not lost; we can still go a little further.

As night fell they came to take us to the station, where the tracks had been repaired. The rain was sheeting down. Allendorf remains the most desolate memory of my life.[18]

Ziegenhain, 21 February 1945

We are in the main prison at Ziegenhain. They have allowed us to keep our belongings. For the first time since we arrived in Germany we can touch and look at the small treasures that we brought with us from France. I have a few books, a stub of pencil, paper, clean underwear, eau de cologne and a mirror. We hold fragments of our homes in our hands, we can see them with our eyes and feel them with our fingers, and they help to take our minds off the way we live here. We are in an attic room with sloping ceilings. I have a tape measure in

18 After I had been liberated I learned that the camp at Allendorf had been completely evacuated in March and totally destroyed by bombing. When I questioned a former wardress she assured me that there had been no gas chambers or crematoria at Allendorf, but she conceded that the regime there was hellish in every respect.

my sewing bag, so I can measure our garret. It measures two metres seventy-five at its highest point, five metres sixty long and five metres twenty wide. The window is not large. Twenty-seven of us live and sleep in here, with our belongings piled in the middle of the room beside the bucket, which mercifully has a well-fitting lid and doesn't leak. The floor is strewn with a thin layer of straw, and we have been given blankets. The women sit on the floor all day with their backs against the wall, shoulder to shoulder – all of them, that is, except Chagnoux and myself, as we were the last to arrive and there was no wall space left for us. So we have chosen a spot by the door. During the day we make a divan for ourselves by rolling up our straw in a couple of blankets. 'Madame de Pompadour's chaise longue', as we christen it, is not too uncomfortable, especially when we think about those poor wretches in the camp at Allendorf. Just as at Anrath, we have only three wash-bowls for the twenty-seven of us to wash in, naturally, and hardly any water. The food seems decent enough, but there's so little of it that even without working we all suffer excruciating hunger pangs. We never leave this room, except when there is a particularly heavy air raid. The gunfire is definitely getting closer, and they are still trying to keep us as far away from it as possible. We joke that they are so keen to 'save' us from the Americans that they are on the point of thrusting us into the arms of the Russians, who are also drawing closer with every passing day . . .

Wanfried, 5 March 1945

After a fortnight at the 'Ziegenhain Palace Hotel' we were ordered to pack our things again, as they were evacuating us to Wanfried. For the first time we knew the name of our destination, though it didn't enlighten us much. The journey was torture. We had to walk part of the way. Not only were we not used to walking, but our feet had also become deformed from so much standing at our work and wearing clogs, so that wearing our own shoes was agony. And modest though they were, our bundles of belongings soon felt like lead weights. At last we reached Wanfried, which turned out to be not far from Kassel. Prostrated with exhaustion though I was, I couldn't help but be moved by the beauty of the streets and buildings that we saw on the way from the station to the prison. Wanfried is so improbably picturesque that it simply has to be the original setting for every single German fairy tale. The houses, all dating from the seventeenth or eighteenth century, jostle each other along the narrow winding streets, festooned with flowers already, and all is neat and gay. We are billeted in a fortified farmhouse dating from the eighteenth century. Some sixty or so German women prisoners are there already. They tell us that 'Schloss Wasserburg' was a local headquarters of the Hitler Youth, recently converted into a prison. The food is tolerable but scarce. For the rest, we don't have much to complain about. The woman director and the wardresses are kind; the work isn't too bad. We have to make camping equipment: tents, sleeping bags, rucksacks and the like. For the most part it is the German women who go out to the factory, while the foreigners stay at Wasserburg, working in the great hall which doubles as the refectory. What heaven compared with the hell of Allendorf! And we know that the Americans are not far off, and everyone, Germans included, is longing for them to arrive. A Russian woman, the prison's unchallenged fount of all wisdom and general repository of all the latest 'news', has announced that they will be here for Easter. Easter falls on 1 April. Although it smacks a little of an April Fool's joke, her prophecy gains credence. The Americans will be here for Easter!

Wanfried, 29 March 1945

We have the compelling feeling that we are entering our final hours of captivity. They must have doubled our dose of bromide, as despite all our excitement we keep dozing off, heads on the table. Nobody tells us anything; they just warn us to keep quiet. There's no question of work any more, and we please ourselves how we spend our time. From the dormitory window we can see endless columns of refugees, both civilians and military; they are too far away for us to be able to make out their uniforms. Some groups carry a white flag. From the snail's pace at which they walk we can tell that they are utterly drained and exhausted. Our hearts and thoughts go out to all those poor, suffering boys. If only we could do something for them! Perhaps our protectors from Schwelm are out there somewhere, trudging along half-dead with exhaustion.

Wanfried, 30 March 1945

The women are growing increasingly agitated. The food is woefully inadequate. Even without working it's impossible to survive on such meagre and inadequate rations.

Wanfried, 31 March 1945

There certainly don't seem to be any food shortages in the town. All day long, we see women parading beneath our windows bearing aloft enormous tarts to cook in the baker's oven. Easter cakes, no doubt. We wonder whether we might be given a little extra to eat tomorrow, as our hunger is intolerable. The artillery fire now comes in bursts; often we can even distinctly make out the stutter of machine guns. Will they be here tomorrow, as the Russian woman prophesied?

Wanfried, 1 April 1945

The time hangs heavy on our hands. I ask the director for our belongings, and she agrees to give them to us tomorrow. This evening, they let us go up to bed earlier than usual. As soon as we reach the dormitory we smell smoke. What's going on? Craning our necks out of the window as far as the barbed wire will let us, we see that they are in the courtyard, making a bonfire of our files. It lights up the darkness all around. Do the air-raid precautions people raise any objections? No, they do not.

Wanfried, 2 April 1945

Our clothes and our personal belongings are returned to us. I have a lump in my throat and my knees go weak; I can hardly believe that it's all over! As darkness falls we hear a series of explosions: they're blowing up the bridges. Clearly the Americans can only be a few hours away. Frau Herpès, our wardress, comes into the dormitory, her face streaming with tears. Barely able to speak, she manages to convey to us that we are free, that we should leave the prison immediately. On behalf of us all, I tell her that we have decided to wait for the Americans in the prison, where we are in relative safety. Then I go down to the director's office, where I find the wardresses terrified out of their wits in case of reprisals. I give them my word of honour that since they have treated us with great humanity and courtesy no one will lay a hand on them, neither us nor the Americans. I also try to impress on them and the German women prisoners the dangers of going out in the streets. The cacophony that accompanies my little speech lends further weight to my argument. The wardresses decide to stay. Only the most unreliable of the German prisoners decide to leave – doubly overwrought with the fear of being killed on top of the exultation of freedom – amid the most unimaginable pandemonium.

Wanfried, 3 April 1945

We are told that the Americans are at Eschwege, twelve kilometres away, and that they'll be here before the day is over.
Even so, we are treated to a visit from a hectoring bully of a
stormtrooper. The director and wardresses are all trembling
and deathly pale. I can hardly make out what he's saying,
except that he's threatening to have us shot. What immaculate
timing! I have great difficulty keeping a straight face. Has
this charming individual never heard of such a thing as
reprisals? The wardresses know that their skins have been saved
by their decent treatment of us. But does this swaggering Nazi
in his khaki uniform and his scarlet swastika armband really
think we are about to throw him some kind of lifeline? What
a cretinous, loutish idiot! A few minutes after he leaves, the
local constable rings his bell and announces to the people of
Wanfried that life is to continue as normal and the shops are
to remain open. Which means that the town intends to surrender without resistance. A crescendo of bombing sends us all
flying down to the cellar, where we stay for several hours.
Then, weary of this enforced idleness, I emerge to see German
soldiers shuffling past the building in groups of two or three.
Filthy and exhausted, they have thrown away their weapons
and walk with their backs hunched and heads bowed. Oh what
joy! What glorious *schadenfreude* at the sight of Germans looking
like the French soldiers I saw on the roads in June 1940!

My thoughts turn to Vildé, Lewitsky, Walter and all the
others. This is what they died for, so that Nazism should
perish. And now, before my very eyes, the beast is slowly
dying . . .

Darkness falls, and Chagnoux, Madeleine, myself and three
other women leave the rest of the prisoners and the wardresses
in the cellar and go up to the great hall. There we turn off
the lights and open a window. On our knees, so as not to be
seen from outside, we wait and watch as events unfold. The

tremendous din we hear must be the noise of armoured cars in the streets of Wanfried, firing in all directions and in every corner, we suppose, in order to impress the population. On the German side there seems to be silence, with no return fire. At last the town is completely shrouded in silence, and nothing moves. Then a car arrives in a neighbouring street, and I hear an unmistakably American shout of, 'Harry, come here!' I shout and yell for joy, but sadly Harry can't hear me! In silent accord we head for the kitchen, where we help ourselves to the wardresses' dinner. Exultantly, we go upstairs to the dormitory (followed by the other Frenchwomen, who have also helped themselves from the kitchen) to savour our victory banquet.

10

Hunting the Nazis

Wanfried, 4 April 1945

You have to have been locked up for four years to know how strange it feels to walk downstairs freely, push open your prison door and walk outside, in order to do something that nothing and nobody can stop you from doing any more. Outside the door is a young soldier in a khaki uniform. Madeleine[19] and I stop for a moment to take in this unfamiliar figure. Then we walk up to him, hands outstretched and broad grins on our faces.

'Hello, we are French political prisoners and you have just liberated us; we are so glad . . .'

'French! French?' the American replies. 'Are you quite sure about that? Because if you're German I'm not allowed to talk to you. I can't afford to lose three months' pay for talking to some German women, no thank *you*!'

We are completely taken aback, and this lends unexpected force to the arguments we muster to allay the little American's fears. The cross of Lorraine with which we have decorated our jackets means nothing to him, but the tricolor flag, combined with our talkativeness, at last convinces him. Slowly he draws off his gloves and shakes our hands; whereupon he declares that he's starving and some eggs would be great.

19 Madeleine Commont.

At this point, with impeccable timing, the farm steward appears. With lofty hauteur I order him to fetch a dozen eggs for 'Herr Offizier amerikanisch'. When he sees the way the steward scuttles off to obey my orders, the little American squaddie can't be left in much doubt as to my Frenchness.

Erring on the side of caution, the steward reappears with a basket of eggs in one hand and a two-litre jug of milk in the other. Had there been a roast chicken to hand, no doubt he would have brought that too.

At our request, the soldier leads us to a house where a young officer is just waking up. His hair is all over the place, and so are his thoughts. Our friend with the eggs explains our position to him. Still fuddled with sleep, the officer looks us up and down: 'So who are those two women again?' His tone is more suspicious than friendly. Undeterred, the two women explain that, as they can speak both English and German, they would be happy to put their services at the disposal of the American forces, and that they are billeted at the Schloss that was their prison. To which the officer retorts, 'If we need you we'll come and find you in your prison.' As there is still a good deal of shooting in the streets, and the liberating army doesn't seem over-eager to take advantage of our offer, we return to our cage a rather sorry and disappointed pair.

From the window on the stairs I can see the Polish prisoners, busily settling old scores. The steward has been badly mauled about and they have taken away his shoes. Another man, older than the steward, has come off even worse. His head is split open, his face covered in blood. Relaxed, their rifles slung over their shoulders, the Americans let them get on with it. Then they decide that enough's enough, and lead them all a little way off. A few minutes later, the man with the head wound has been shot. Now the frenzy begins. Within less than half an hour, the Polish prisoners have completely ransacked the Schloss. I have seen documentary films of trees being stripped and devoured by locusts. This is the same, except it is more wanton. Everything is destroyed, defiled, smashed beyond use. I don't even attempt to raise a hand to stop this senseless vandalism. These are primitive people, I tell myself, venting their primitive instincts. As I turn away from the window and its unedifying prospect, I see the director coming up the stairs with a large key in her hand. She greets me formally and explains, 'Here is the key to my toilet facilities, madame; they are more comfortable than your own facilities, so it is only right that you and "these ladies" should have the use of them now.' Oh Burghers of Calais, would that you were here to see this day!

By this point Wanfried has suddenly and miraculously become festooned with white cloths. It looks as though the entire town has hung out its washing to dry. We order the woman we still call the director to hang a white sheet from one of the windows at the front of the building. With due German solemnity, she asks me whether the sheet should be hung lengthways or widthways; with due French solemnity, I reply that we really couldn't care less, just as long as there is some white rag or other hanging in a prominent position.

The wardresses are terrified out of their wits; they are convinced the Poles are going to run amok in our wing of the Schloss and plunder their belongings, all that they managed to save from the bombing of Aix-la-Chapelle, where they come from. I tell them to put all their possessions in one room, then to lock it and give me the key. If the Polacks come they'll have me to deal with, and then we'll see.

The Poles don't come. By contrast an American NCO, a sergeant, does, climbing slowly up the stairs. He examines the barbed wire-filled windows with an air of concentration. Seeing me, he asks, 'This was a prison, wasn't it?' I reply that it was, and explain that I am a French political prisoner. 'Political?' he queries. 'Of what persuasion?' I tell him. There is a long silence as he looks into my eyes. His eyes are impossibly blue. Then slowly, very softly, he says: 'I've been looking for you, comrade. I knew I would find you. You don't need to worry any more. I'm here to help you.'

He asks me if after lunch I would give them a hand in the town, where there is so much to do. I tell him about Madeleine, who speaks good German, whereas I can only speak the cosmopolitan pidgin, the strange Esperanto that twenty million deportees must have had to learn. He is very tall and looks so strong; his smile is charming, and when he takes off his helmet to reveal his hair I swear it is pure gold! His name? I'm convinced he doesn't have a name, or in any case not an American name with two or three initials attached. He is not like other Americans: he is St George, our very own knight in shining armour come to rescue us!

St George comes to fetch us after lunch, Madeleine and me. We are to go with him to the town hall to see what is going on. The town hall, or *Rathaus*, would make a perfect backdrop for the sufferings of young Werther. The mayor, on the other hand, is not at all like something out of Goethe. Standing stiffly to attention, his lower lip trembling, he is manifestly terrified. With ceremonious courtesy, St George invites us to be seated and says a few words; then, turning to the still-rigid mayor, he permits him too to sit down. Visibly relieved, the *Bürgermeister* perches on a hard, upright chair, while the three of us sink into the armchairs . . .

A young woman we had noticed earlier scuttles up to St George to offer him a large box of cigars, more or less on bended knee. Pushing the cigars away firmly and silently, St George turns to us and for a few minutes expounds on his personal thoughts regarding the repulsive obsequiousness of the Germans and their craven lack of human dignity. That said, he asks Madeleine to enquire where the concentration camps are in this region. The mayor replies that there aren't any; St George warns him that if the Americans find any he will regret it, but the mayor stands by his assertion. St George then demands to know what has happened to the Jews of Wanfried, and the mayor assures him that those who were not forced tò leave in '38 are still here, in good health; he even adds that he protected them, at the risk of his own life. This little speech is cut short by a roar of laughter from St George, who, still chuckling, points out in reply that the whole world knows only too well what a paradise the Third Reich was for the Jews. Undeterred, the mayor asks for permission to go and find the Jews in question there and then. We postpone the introductions until later.

Moving on to more immediate matters, St George specifies that we are to be fed, and fed well, at the town's expense; that Madeleine and I are to be responsible for the welfare of all prisoners in Wanfried; and that our wishes are to be considered as orders. Since the mayor has no choice but to accept this arrangement, Madeleine wastes no time in issuing him with our initial orders for eggs, butter, meat and other provisions.

As we leave the town hall, St George asks us to take him to the camp where Russian prisoners are held. We have seen young Russian girls from our window, and we know that their camp can't be far out of Wanfried as we could hear their singing. So the three of us set off in the direction from which the singing came. It doesn't take us long to find a small hut, cramped and squalid, beside a stinking swamp. Sixty people live here, men, women and children, in conditions of the most appalling over-crowding. The poor creatures have done their best to divide it up into small spaces, but in these few square metres how can sixty of them even breathe? Three years they have spent here, and during that time there have been many deaths, and a few births. They are slave workers, mostly from the Crimea. Is this the first Russian camp St George has seen? It must be. He is shattered at the sight of such misery, such unimaginable, unspeakable misery. Tears fill his blue eyes and roll slowly down his cheeks. He has been to Russia and speaks a few words of Russian, about as much as I do. Fortunately, the Russians speak German. St George tells them that their suffering is over, that they will be decently lodged, fed and clothed, that they are no longer slaves, and that if they encounter any difficulties with the Germans they are to bring them to Madeleine and me. Then he asks if there are any communists among them. As there aren't, he addresses himself to the men. Whatever happens, he is count- ing on them to protect the French women prisoners. They pledge their word eagerly. When they saw us arrive these brave people were alarmed; now that they understand why we are here they erupt with spontaneous, unaffected joy.

On our return, we find Wasserburg in a complete and unbelievable shambles. It was only to be expected. I explain the situation to St George. Most of the German women prisoners still at the Schloss are young and not exactly shrinking violets. Since the Americans' arrival this morning they have been leading them on, invariably pretending, needless to say, to be French, Luxembourger, Czech, and I don't know what else − anything except German. Wasserburg is now nothing more nor less than a brothel. We have to get all the soldiers out of here before they get completely drunk and out of hand. St George accom- plishes this with rare tact and diplomacy. I ask him to give us guards for the night as, like everywhere else, Wasserburg has to leave its door unlocked, and I'm a little afraid. St George promises to do his best for us, but there aren't many American troops and they are still busy fighting.

Wanfried, 5 April 1945
All night we heard gunfire, while the farm cows lowed incessantly. It turns out that they haven't been milked since the day before yesterday. At six o'clock, three of the Frenchwomen

and a Russian set out to milk them. Martinière, one of the
Frenchwomen, says that she was never frightened of the Gestapo
but is terrified of the cows; but she overcomes her fear and is
learning to milk them.

The Poles who are supposed to be looking after the cows
didn't turn up all day yesterday. At last one of them appears,
then another. I am told that shortly the farm will be pillaged,
and the fifty-four cows stolen and slaughtered. In my pocket
I have a toy, a child's toy revolver that I picked up at the
town hall yesterday, where the townspeople have handed in
their weapons. I need to act, and act quickly. There are many
children in Wanfried. They are not responsible for Hitler; if
I don't do something immediately there will be no more
milk for the children. For the sake of the three or four Poles
in the cowshed I start to scream and shout like a German,
the only way of dealing with them. Discreetly I brandish my
'revolver' at them. I make the oldest of them responsible for
the cows, on pain of immediate execution. Also on pain of
immediate execution (naturally), I order that the cows should
be attended to forthwith and that life on the farm should continue
as before.

At this juncture the German deputy steward arrives, shaking
like a leaf. I repeat my orders to him, and there and then start
distributing milk to the women who are queuing outside the
cowshed with their children. Then I make arrangements for
tomorrow's distribution, which will take place as it used to,
at the dairy in town. The milk will be handed out on presen-
tation of a ticket, with priority going to children, the elderly
and the sick. If there is any left over from supplies brought
in from other farms, it will be distributed afterwards to those
with ration cards. Then I add my own little rousing flourish,
as though delivering an election speech: 'The Americans will
not countenance the fine ladies here washing their faces in
milk while there are children who have to go without.' This

ludicrous declaration causes quite a sensation. Two days ago I was told I was going to be shot, and now it's me making the death threats, me giving the orders, and − most priceless of all − me being listened to with respect. St George, arriving in time to hear the end of my speech, takes a childish delight in the whole proceedings. He reiterates my death threats to the Poles, repeats my orders regarding the life and well-being of the cows, and then it's back to headquarters.

On the way, we stop to look at the town hall, looted last night. The portrait of Hitler has been slashed and now presides over what remains of the official furniture. Ripped Nazi flags and uniforms have been trampled underfoot. The sight reminds me of similar scenes, photographs that I helped to pin up in Paris as part of our anti-Fascist exhibitions. But those were photographs of synagogues and churches that had been defiled, not Nazi town halls: so now they've got their just deserts! St George's headquarters are installed in a charming villa, though only very briefly, as sadly our friends expect to leave us in a few hours. Madeleine and I are offered wine, then in the kitchen that serves as the communal dining room we lunch on veal with peas, washed down with cherry brandy served in tumblers. The window on to the street is open; now and then one of our friends shoulders his rifle and takes aim at a passing plane.

That night we held a banquet at Wasserburg. St George presided over the festivities, aided by his good friend Politzer, a young musician, very serious, very charming. The table was spread with a white cloth, and there were masses of flowers − pink azaleas. We listened to the news on our newly acquired radio: the Russians were fighting in Vienna. Then we listened to Paris . . . the news from Paris! After that there was dance music, and we danced . . . we danced, while a stone's throw away the killing went on. Gunfire rang out in the nearby woods. We danced, and I reminded St George of the ball on the eve of the Battle of Waterloo. Yes, tomorrow would be Hitler's Waterloo! St George had a bottle of champagne tucked inside his jacket, and we sang the old Revolutionary song:

> Dansons la Carmagnole
> Et vive le son, vive le son,
> Dansons la Carmagnole
> Et vive le son du canon!

Words cannot describe the extraordinary atmosphere, the childish exultation, the harrowing pain, the animal delight in satisfying our hunger, the embraces . . . *C'est la guerre!*

Wanfried, 6 April 1945

We don't get much sleep that night, what with the incessant rumbling of nearby artillery, punctuated by frequent bursts of machine-gun fire. We have set up a guardroom inside the Schloss, in what used to be the wardresses' dining room, and I have installed our MP boys in there. We make sure they have comfortable mattresses and good food: Chagnoux manages to rustle up mouth-watering cakes and pancakes for them, and they tuck into these with relish. Thanks to our MPs, all is now quiet at Wasserburg. A few French prisoners of war have come to live here too, and we enjoy a life of luxury! The bursar having decided that it was more prudent to make herself scarce, her room has now become mine. Cheerful and well furnished, it serves as our office during the day. From its three windows, with no barbed wire, we enjoy a view over a beautiful landscape of wooded hills – hills in which so many tragedies are even now unfolding.

Since many of the women didn't hear my instructions yesterday concerning the distribution of milk, there is a queue outside the cowshed. For today I decide to distribute the milk on the spot. One of the women catches my eye: very young, pretty and elegant, she holds a small aluminium jug and asks for a litre of milk for her child. This is Baroness von Scharfenberg, I learn. The Schloss, the cows and half the town all belong to her. And here she is, waiting patiently until a foreigner and former prisoner is generous enough to allow her a litre of milk from her own cows. Recent events have not completely hardened my heart, and I cannot help but find this touching. Endeavouring not to show my feelings, naturally, I converse with the Baroness about the latest news and – as she says she speaks little English – urge her to come to me if she should encounter any difficulties with the occupying forces. I give her a scrap of paper on which I've scribbled my name, but she looks flustered and protests, 'But I can't keep your name on me, it could cost me my life.' Laughing, I ask her if she really thinks the Americans would execute her for such a trifling thing. 'No,' she replies, 'not the Americans, the others.' Assuming that she means the SS, I reassure her, adding loftily, 'The Americans will get rid of those vermin for you.' It's not the SS she's worried about, though, it's 'the men in the woods, the ones who give orders by radio'. And she adds, 'I'm so frightened of them!' My heart skips a beat. Trying to stay calm, I tell her that she has only to give me any information about these mysterious men and the Americans will make short work of them. With the utmost dignity, the Baroness replies that as a German woman she cannot denounce her fellow Germans. I know enough already, so I leave the frightened Baroness as an American soldier comes to ask me to go with him into the town, where I am supposed to find him some crates of munitions. Once this is done, I go back to the Schloss to write a note, which Madeleine hastily types up. I dash off to take it to the commanding officer of Wanfried. Clearly some sort of secret society has sprung up in the woods and forests around the town; we're plumb in the middle of an adventure story.

I bump into Politzer, who confirms that there is indeed a secret society, the *Wehrewolf*, or Werewolves. Outside the commanding officer's villa, I find St George. It's obvious that he's hardly slept and is very worried. Assault troops don't usually spend more than a few hours in any one place, but at Wanfried they seem to have ground to a halt. Something serious is going on. They shouldn't have to wait this long for their orders to advance. I show him my note and explain what I intend to do with it. He reads it, then quite calmly folds it up and tears it into tiny pieces, as I look on in amazement. 'You don't understand the way our officers think,' he tells me. 'They don't know the first thing about politics; they're just soldiers, and that's all. If you tell them about this they'll be suspicious of you. You'll get into hot water because you're getting mixed up in something they know nothing about, and nothing will be done to combat the Werewolves. It would take another war to make them understand,' he adds with a rueful smile.

Wanfried, 7 April 1945

St George is still here. He is a worried man. I don't ask questions, as I know he can't tell me anything; all the same, I can see that the situation is bad. There are now three Red Cross stations at Wanfried, and I know that the chief medical officer has just been seriously injured in both legs. Four gun emplacements have been set up in the field opposite the Schloss. St George says that the looting is worse than ever. The Poles are flooding into Wanfried from all around. They are becoming increasingly difficult to tolerate, playing football with the bread in front of the baker's shop, threatening the local people and killing any livestock they come across, not so that they can eat the carcasses — which would be understandable — but just to leave them to rot where they lie. Now that the initial exultation of liberation is over, the Poles have to understand that they must conduct themselves like civilized human beings.

A fat American sergeant whom I call 'Fatty', though I could equally well have called him 'Babbitt', asks me to go with him to see a baker who is refusing to sell his bread to certain German refugees. There is a queue outside the shop and the atmosphere is volatile. After five minutes of discussion, everything is sorted out to the satisfaction of both the baker and the customers. Climbing up some low steps, I address the crowd of mutinous housewives. How I long to hear someone, just one voice, asking what earthly business it is of mine; but these people are so supine, they accept anything, whatever you tell them, just as long as you say it loudly enough. There is chaos everywhere. St George sends us his captain, who, though utterly bereft of any political understanding, is a good man of considerable intelligence. We find him most impressive. He tells us that he is overwhelmed, and asks us if we can give him any advice as to how to restore some degree of order in the town, where the Poles are now practically in control. The number of refugees is growing and the looting is getting worse. Not content with ransacking and plundering, they are now threatening to burn down the whole town.

I suggest three stopgap measures. The first is to plaster all the houses with posters warning in several languages that looters will be shot, and if necessary to shoot a few of the most troublesome Poles in the foot in order to calm down the rest. The second is to requisition a cinema, cover the floor with straw and turn it into a temporary shelter for refugees, with a soup kitchen twice a day. The third is to requisition a hotel and convert it immediately into a hospital for sick or injured refugees and deportees. The Germans will provide the manpower for these projects, and the town council will provide the soup. The captain approves all three schemes and gives me carte blanche. So off we set, Madeleine and I, to requisition a hotel and a cinema. It's all we can do not to dissolve into giggles. A few days ago we were slave labourers, and today here we are requisitioning buildings in the face of total apathy from the Germans; it's a complete farce. Then we go to the town hall to inform the mayor of what we have done, and to order him to be at Wasserburg at nine o'clock tomorrow morning, bringing with him social workers and nurses, so that they can all receive my instructions.

The mayor is just about at breaking point. His position is certainly not an enviable one. He is an excellent administrator, of that there can be no doubt, and if he joined the Party it was only as a pragmatic move dictated by political necessity. A doctor of philosophy and lover of art, as is clear to see in his private office at the town hall, Dr Braun appears to me to be a man of great honesty, possibly a little prosaic, a touch lacking in gumption in that typically German way, but with a strong social conscience that impels him to do all he can, whatever the cost, for the town to which he is so clearly devoted.

We have it on official authority that the SS have recaptured the village of Frieda, four kilometres from Wanfried. The Americans are cut off from their supply base, and we are currently surrounded. On our way back to the Schloss, Madeleine and I discuss the fate that lies in store for us should the SS make a temporary return to Wanfried. What I love about Madeleine is the way she devotes herself single-mindedly to the job in hand, whatever it may be, turning a persistently blind eye to any risks or drawbacks that it might entail. It is at this point in our conversation that we hear a strange whistling sound, followed by an explosion a little way off. We look up, but there are no planes; where the devil can the bomb have come from? A couple of American soldiers flattened against a house at the end of the street yell at us: 'Eighty-eight!' We gaze at them in blank incomprehension: eighty-eight? Another whistling noise, the Americans press themselves harder against the house wall, and we realize that we are under fire from artillery shells. I don't like this one bit. You can't tell where they're coming from, or where they're going to land. With a plane, at least you can hear it, even if you can't see it, and you can work out what's going on, but this artillery fire I don't like at all.

Back at Wasserburg, the soldiers on guard have made everyone go down to the cellar. An engineer, tall and fair, looks worried: we are in the sights of one of the dreaded 'eighty-eights', he explains. At this juncture two enemy aeroplanes appear above the Schloss: evidently they have taken exception to the gun emplacements in the field opposite. Now the show really begins. The boys all rush out into the garden while I cheer them on from the window, shouting inanities as I can't take this seriously. Sheltering behind the wall, they take shots at the planes amid shouts of laughter. I can see my sons Jean and Pierre laughing just like that when they were ten or eleven and playing at soldiers! At last one of the planes is hit and limps off somewhere to crash or land, and the other escapes. The show is over. All evening we hear explosions. St George arrives to give us two revolvers and a few cartridges. He is supposed to come back and eat with us, but doesn't appear. He is weary and a little sad.

Wanfried, 8 April 1945

Pleased as punch with her new radio, Madeleine tunes in for the news first thing in the morning. We are tuned into Paris, I think, when we hear an announcement that advance units of the American Third Army which have pushed beyond Kassel, and which yesterday found themselves cut off and in serious difficulties, have now been relieved on all sides! These 'advance units of the Third Army' are none other than our very own Americans; it is we who have been 'relieved' and we've seen the last of the SS! What a huge relief!

I dash over to the Russian hut to find people to help me draft the poster that is supposed to be printed later on. After we draw up the text in all manner of languages, I head back to Wasserburg for my meeting with the mayor. There I find him surrounded by a bevy of good ladies, all decked out to a greater or lesser degree with red crosses and all weeping bitterly. I tell them that it's no use crying over spilt milk and give them a quarter of an hour to pull themselves together. Meanwhile, Madeleine and I take a stroll round the gardens, like the true ladies of the manor that we have become. When we return, our nurses have regained their composure. I explain what we expect of them: that the fate of their town lies in their hands; that if they treat the sick refugees and deportees well the town may be spared; that if they don't, the trouble-makers, spurred on by hunger and exhaustion, will loot everything that remains to be looted, torch the town and string up three-quarters of the population. They all nod in agreement and thank me effusively for giving them the opportunity to be of service. In reply I assure them that I know that the work will be well done, that it is not an area in which I have any special competence and that consequently I shall leave the organization up to them. I insist on one thing and one thing only: that *all* the sick and dispossessed, of whatever nationality, should be treated and fed with the same irreproachable care. Madeleine and I will make daily inspections, I tell them.

Today, while we are waiting for the refuge and soup kitchen to be set up, Madeleine and I serve good nourishing soup to all passers-by on the porch at Wasserburg. Our many guests include Dutch, German and Russian refugees and deportees, happily washing and eating. I know what it is to be on the road, on foot and . . . my thoughts are flooded with memories of June 1940.

By three o'clock in the afternoon posters have been put up on all the houses in Wanfried. The mayor takes heart. After long discussions, I manage to persuade him to withdraw the resignation that he tendered last night. There's no doubt about it, this is a man of good faith who sincerely wants to serve, and to serve well; he was only ever a Nazi on paper, I'd stake my life on it.

Wanfried, 9 April 1945

St George is still here, but we almost certainly won't see him again. He sends us an affectionate little note via a friend who collects the quilted jacket we have had made for him by our ex-wardresses. They all work for the Americans without being asked. Since the day Wanfried was liberated they have been assiduous in looking after our every need, applying themselves diligently to the housework, the dishes and the laundry. And they sew for the Americans from morning till night.

A terrific commotion in town, followed by total silence. Our friends are all gone, with the exception of fifty cooks who have been left behind in Wanfried, though no one knows why. The tall soldier we called 'the Sioux' is still here, as he is a baker. He alerts two other bakers, so now here we are at Wasserburg guarded by three bakers who have elected to spend their nights in the guardroom.

As we go to bed, Madeleine and I chat about the extraordinary little Russian boy we met yesterday. 'Russki', as they call him, is eleven years old and one of the Third Army's favourite mascots. He was deported with his mother, who died. The Americans picked him up somewhere – no one knows where now – starving and dressed in rags. Our friends dressed him in leather from head to toe, and since this made him look like a motorcyclist they also gave him a motorbike, which he took to straight away. And so he embarked on a career as a liaison officer of outstanding courage. The Americans talk about Russki the way we talk about Bara or Viala. When I

saw Russki he was playing a plaintive tune on an accordion
that he had just found; it was a melancholy air from 'back
home', and he had his eyes half-closed and was smoking a fat
cigar. As 'the Sioux' introduced us he remarked, 'Great habits
he's picking up from us, that kid.' But I said that given the
symptoms of tuberculosis that he displayed the unfortunate
Russki might as well pick up all the bad habits he pleased.
The poor child will never go back to the home whose music
he plays so well without even knowing it.[20]

St George has left; I'm sad, and I fear for him. It's always
men like him who get killed. But soon I take heart: nothing
can happen to St George, as he is not a man like other men!
To be honest, I don't mind if I don't see him again. There are
some memories that are so precious that they are best treasured
intact and untainted for ever. I want always to keep that vision
of him trudging slowly up the stairs at Wasserburg, moving
wearily and heavily, his helmet dented and his battledress crumpled and stained; he was magnificent! But what if he were to
come to see me in Paris? I'd be told that Mr Elmer G. Handcher
(he does after all have an American name) was there to see me,
and I would see before me a tall, heavily built fellow, probably
rather ordinary, in a tweed jacket from Chicago. Thrust back
into the workaday world, we would feel embarrassed, a little
awkward, and we wouldn't know what to say to each other.
No, better not to see each other, to keep our memories. And
anyway, in Paris I wear make-up and dresses and colour my
hair. Here I am *au naturel*, got up in an old pair of trousers
and a factory overseer's jacket on which I have sewn the French
flag . . . It was war, and we were on the front line.

20 My prognosis for Russki turned out to be unduly pessimistic. I have recently
heard that he is in good health and at college 'somewhere or other' in the United
States. As he categorically refused to leave his 'adoptive fathers' at any price, they
clubbed together to give him a good education. They got him back to America
without much difficulty as he was still so small. On embarkation and disembarkation
they hid him in a mail sack, which one of his 'fathers' then slung over his shoulder.

Wanfried, 13 April 1945

Madeleine has got to know a French prisoner of war of whom she speaks very highly. Pierre Dupont has spent four years at Wanfried, and during that time he has made a study of local Nazis and their families. He speaks perfect German, and has made friends with anti-Nazis all over the area. As he doesn't know much English, I think we could work together, and later, if ever we succeed in gaining the ear of an American who is prepared to take action, we could form a team. For the moment, the Americans have all left. We are all alone, and doubtless not particularly popular with the Nazi sympathizers of Wanfried; we'll just have to hope that we won't be left alone for long. Anyway, there's no time to sit twiddling our thumbs. People are perpetually coming to fetch us to arbitrate a dispute, give an opinion or advice, or make a translation. Just now a Russian had given a thrashing to a German who was taunting him, so we had to calm down the Russian and give the German a telling off. Yesterday we were fetched from table in the middle of eating because some Poles were threatening to kill an inoffensive German burgher. We have to explain to the Poles that it is not they who make the laws here (thank heavens!) but the Americans, and that if they have grievances they have to talk to me about them, and I will translate them and pass them on.

Wanfried, 14 April 1945

I pay a visit to the wing of the Schloss that was so comprehensively ransacked by the Poles on the first day. It is now home to the Russians. Everywhere is clean and tidy, the courtyard is carefully swept, and there is a family living in each room, with whatever they have found to furnish their makeshift accommodation. Today it is Easter in Russia. There is great revelling, with laughter, singing and dancing to the accordion.

I am greeted with cries of 'Christ is risen', and I feel as though I have been transported back into the pages of a novel by Maxim Gorky. They kiss me on the mouth. How delightful!

Wanfried, 15 April 1945

We are still on our own. Strange rumours are circulating. The mayor is to be 'sorted out'. He has received so many death threats that he no longer sleeps in his house, which is too close to the woods. He tells us about a group of twenty or so Italians, soldiers of Mussolini employed in a local factory, who demand improbable quantities of supplies which they then pass on to men who are hiding in the woods. This story is corroborated by several witnesses.

Since I had to accompany a poor Russian boy who was dying of tuberculosis to the neighbouring town and local administrative centre, Eschwege, I took advantage of the opportunity to see the 'town major' and tell him about events in Wanfried. I came up against a blank wall of total incomprehension. All soldiers must be as dim as each other, whatever their nationality! I told them that I was perfectly well aware that whether or not we were murdered was a matter of no concern to him whatever, but that the fate of the American soldiers in the region was surely not a matter of complete indifference to him. He knows as well as I do that there are reports of attacks on all sides. Last night I was told that a couple of SS men in uniform were seen calmly strolling through the streets of Wanfried. 'Yup, we have SS swanning around here too,' he replies with a laugh. He finds this highly amusing, but it's a type of joke that neither we nor the German anti-Nazis can see. For most Americans, war is an abstract, theoretical activity. They are waging this war and doing so extremely well – they are winning it, after all – but in their hearts and souls they haven't suffered its pain. They haven't seen their young girls carried off by the tens of thousands, their hostages shot, their wives imprisoned, their houses destroyed, their possessions looted. They've heard about it all, but it's happened to other people, not to them.

Wanfried, 16 April 1945

Our daily visit to the 'Stadtpark Hotel' is always a pleasure. Our little hospital functions well, and our 'clients' at the refuge are happy with their soup and with the care the nurses give their battered feet. We have hundreds of boxes of cigars at our disposal from a local cigar factory. We are generous with them, but our largesse extends only to foreigners, to the exclusion of the Germans. This makes them very cross and also perplexes them. The other day, however, when I gave a fine box of cigars to a young German Jew, their stupefaction scaled new heights. Since these people have to have everything explained to them, I delivered a little speech, to the recipient's satisfaction, in which I explained why he had the right to cigars and they didn't. No one ever dares to poke fun at my terrible German, not a soul ever sniggers at it. Whereas if we were in France, and the boot were on the other foot . . .

Wanfried, 17 April 1945

The mayor has sent for us to interpret the orders of two new American soldiers. Gosh! Still, at least they're here. Will these Americans understand the importance of making sure the Nazis can't re-form behind their advance? After an hour's meeting at most at the town hall, they accept our invitation to lunch at the Schloss. They seem to have no difficulty in grasping our point, and agree that it reflects badly on American prestige if Nazis of the likes of Gottlob Gries and Arthur Kalden are allowed to roam free, when everyone in Wanfried knows that they were responsible for torturing a Canadian parachutist who landed here in August 1944. The unfortunate Mac Lee (we know his name even) was defended by Georg Pressler, a German anti-Nazi who arranged for him to be taken to the hospital at Eschwege. Having risked so much to protect Lee, Pressler is bitter at the thought of the Nazi murderers swanning around scot-free. It is to Pierre Dupont that we owe all these details. We now have quite a collection of records of this sort, all typed up and waiting for an American who understands their significance and is up to the task of acting on them.

We have drawn up a list of the Nazis of Wanfried, the fanatics who joined the Party before 1933; and we also have a list of German anti-Nazis who are just waiting for the opportunity to act as guides to the Americans in the woods. Pierre has known these men for four years now, and can vouch for their integrity. Two French prisoners of war who have worked in the woods, Martin and Peugniez, have also volunteered, and can also guarantee the good faith of the German guides. In addition, we have a respectable number of records documenting events in communities within a twenty-kilometre radius of Wanfried: not gossip or tittle-tattle, but unimpeachable testimonies that have the Americans shaking their heads. Tomorrow, they tell us, a new detachment might arrive, and they will at last be able to start the work of flushing out the Nazis. Today's pair of Americans are full of praise for our work, and say that they will draw it to the attention of their headquarters at Mühlhausen, thirty kilometres beyond Wanfried. They even suggest that we should go and work there, but we turn down the idea, saying that there is too much to do here. And indeed, Wanfried turns out to have been the mustering point of numerous Nazi organizations in retreat. On 1 April, Dr Ley in person dined at the Wanfriedhof. Martin Bormann, celebrated friend of Hitler, has relations in the region. The Air Ministry made its final retreat here; this is where the ruins of the War Ministry eventually crumbled; and the last broadcasts of German Radio were made from a disguised studio in the cigar factory at Waldkappel, near Wanfried.

During the evening Glick, our new American friend, comes to see us. From the Wasserburg terrace I show him the flares shooting up from the woods, manifestly not launched by the Americans. Highly alarmed, Glick says that he will send an armoured car through the streets of Wanfried tonight, all lights blazing, with the sole aim of making sure that the SS don't feel they are free to come into town with such brazen impunity.

Wanfried, 19 April 1945

This time it is a captain who comes all the way from Mühlhausen especially to see us. This one certainly takes us seriously! A little too seriously, perhaps, as he announces that he has requisitioned an apartment for us at Mühlhausen, where we will be working in future. He offers us an officer's pay, which I refuse on the grounds that however wealthy the American government may be, all the riches in its possession could never equal the pleasure that we derive from tracking down the Nazis. The question of pay being settled, we allow ourselves to be persuaded to go and work in Mühlhausen, on condition that we are driven back here every Sunday. We are determined to keep our office at Wanfried, as well as our contact with Pierre Dupont, who will carry on working here. I'm also reluctant to lose touch with the Russians, who now make daily trips into the forest, bringing back with them not merely excellent intelligence but also abandoned weapons and sometimes even prisoners, who don't appear to put up much of a struggle.

Wanfried, 20 April 1945

It's Charley who comes to fetch us in a jeep. We know Charley, as he was present at one of our hilarious searches in the grand style. He's already our friend, and he's gloriously funny, every inch a clown. He takes full advantage of his exaggeratedly Jewish looks to needle the Germans, though without any malice. 'If I didn't look like this it wouldn't be funny,' he says, 'but as it is, it's fun to shake them up a bit.' On the slightest pretext he flings his arm up in a Nazi salute and barks '*Heil Hitler!*' He is terribly homesick in Germany, he says, and has only one thought and hope: to get back to his wife. To judge from her photo she is ravishing; but then they are all lovely, the wives, fiancées and girlfriends of our American friends, with their dazzling smiles and eyes to tempt a saint in heaven.

So here we are in the jeep with Charley, heading for Mühlhausen. Thirty kilometres through the forest in the fresh air: what bliss! Charley drives like a maniac; we're not so much driving as flying. I suggest quietly that I wouldn't mind slowing down a little so as to enjoy the spring air and sunlight, and Charley retorts that it's precisely because he wants to be able to go on enjoying those things a little longer that he's going so fast. I don't understand what he means. So he spells it out. The day before yesterday, one of his friends got a bullet through the shoulder on this same route, so he's pretty keen to get out of the forest and into town.

At first sight Mühlhausen is not a picturesque place: a large, unfriendly town, not too badly bombed. Here and there we catch a glimpse of a pretty house, but on the whole we don't much like what we see. The Americans have set up their headquarters in a secondary school. Thirty or so kids are milling round the soldier on guard duty, pestering him in English for 'chewing gum, chocolate'. The soldier is lavish in his generosity, adding the odd lesson in English as a bonus. The playground is strewn with an eclectic array of objects, clearly thrown from the windows. The pandemonium that reigns inside the building is truly indescribable. Somewhere in this building – amid hundreds of soldiers singing and playing the banjo, ocarina or accordion, the 'music' they produce being constantly interrupted by howls that are positively inhuman – we assume we are to find our office. Our arrival appears to cause something of a stir. The stairs can't have been swept since the Americans arrived: it is literally impossible to find anywhere to put your feet amid the litter of weapons, rags and all manner of curious objects.

After this visit to our future 'office', the captain takes us to the Kaiserhof restaurant for dinner. We set off in a car that he has just requisitioned, and that he drives himself, successfully stalling the engine. Immediately, we are surrounded by laughing soldiers who openly mock their 'old man' who can't drive a Jerry car. The captain seems to tolerate their cheek as though it were the most natural thing in the world. Madeleine and I look on in growing amazement, though our astonishment is set to reach new heights at the Kaiserhof restaurant. There we are seated gravely to either side of the colonel in command of the region. There is practically nothing to eat, as the rations haven't yet arrived. Neither of us dares to ask why the colonel hasn't requisitioned some food, since he and his officers are positively famished. While at table they talk loudly and openly about matters that are no business of the Germans. Serving at table is the hotel proprietor, who is all ears. I point this out to the colonel, who assures me that the fine fellow doesn't understand a word of English, let alone American. In addition to this, large numbers of German policemen keep trooping in and out, listening all the while. I take the liberty of casting doubt on their honesty, suggesting that it is their nosiness that is making them rather too zealous. The colonel blithely reassures me that these good men have all given him their word of honour that they were never Nazis.

Throughout this extraordinary meal, German children stare at us through the windows, tapping on the glass and running off screaming with laughter. Every now and then, Madeleine and I exchange eloquent looks: it is clear to both of us that we should not stay here in this bedlam, where we cannot feasibly achieve anything of use. So I inform the colonel quite candidly that since we don't know a soul in Mühlhausen we run the risk of wasting our time there until we can establish useful contacts and create an intelligence network. Since these systems are up and running at Wanfried, we feel we would be better advised to go back there. I don't have much difficulty in convincing the colonel, who seems a little vague. He promises us a jeep for the following morning. We go to bed fortified by the prospect of leaving Mühlhausen at the very earliest opportunity.

Wanfried, 25 April 1945

Since our excursion to Mühlhausen we have not seen a single American soldier. Our young friend Dimitri Lestroyé's reconnaissance trips into the woods are becoming more and more interesting. Alone and unarmed, he has already arrested a number of Germans and has also supplied information to the Americans about guns that have been abandoned in perfect working order. Of all the Russians, Dimitri is my favourite. Handsome as a young god with his suntanned face, blue eyes and white-blond hair, he invariably wears a Russian shirt of dazzling whiteness. On his daily visits to our office to share his latest discoveries with us, he has the air of a hunting dog on the scent of a quarry he detests.

Wanfried, 26 April 1945

Today Dimitri outlines a plan to me. It is highly elaborate, involving first the road to the forest, then a path leading to a house that stands beside the entrance to an underground lair, and close to all this an abandoned car. It's all a bit far-fetched, and I suspect that Dimitri's head must be stuffed with Ukrainian crime thrillers. So it is with considerable reservations that I show his plan to the sergeant on duty at Wanfried today. So intrigued is the sergeant by my young friend's tale, however, that he decides to set off immediately to investigate. I yearn to go with him but say nothing: I know he won't take me. In a few minutes the expedition is ready, and they head off in a truck with six men and a machine gun. Dimitri sits next to the driver, laughing and in seventh heaven. Standing beside me, Chagnoux watches him go in despair: 'Poor kid,' she sighs, 'he's going to get killed.' But the 'poor kid' doesn't get killed, or even wounded. An hour later the entire party is back in Wasserburg. The sergeant tells me that Dimitri's plan was absolutely sound in every respect, but that sadly the house, though showing signs of recent occupation, was empty.

In Wanfried's main square, a military vehicle draws up in front of me. Painted on its door is the tricolor, with a cross of Lorraine drawn on the white section. This is my first sight of a Gaullist flag. I go up to the truck, joyful and smiling. A lieutenant-colonel leans out. Without giving me any form of greeting he shouts, 'How many kilometres from here to . . . ?' There follows the name of a place I've never heard of. He speaks to me in French, and like all the Frenchwomen here I sport (with a degree of defiance) the tricolor on my lapel. I say that I'm sorry I can't help them, but that I'm a political prisoner only recently freed and I don't yet know the topography of the region. The colonel's response is a muffled groan: 'So you're telling me you don't know, is that it?', and curtly orders the driver to carry on. This is the first free Frenchman I've seen; I've been waiting for this moment for four years . . .

At last we have Lieutenant Jones based at Wanfried for a few days, with ten men. He too studies my notes, and we pass on to him what Pierre has told us: the Nazis who fled when the American forces arrived are now quietly returning to resume their former occupations. Jones goes off to Eschwege, where he promises to press the request I lodged many days ago now. Poor Jones reappears, looking crestfallen. What should he find at Eschwege, our administrative headquarters? One single officer, with four men to guard the bridges. We are beginning to lose hope.

We hear an unaccustomed commotion coming from the Russians' quarters. Fearing something sinister, I dash over there, and to my utter stupefaction see a line of trucks driven by Germans under the orders of an American soldier. They have come without warning to collect the Russians, to take them away and group them all together in one camp. The Russians have been given an hour to pack their belongings. The Germans' way of doing things is clearly contagious! I negotiate with the soldier. I have become attached to my Russian friends, and it distresses me to see them leave, and especially to witness them being rounded up like slave workers. The American, who speaks a little Polish, explains to them very slowly – as though they were children – that when they are at the camp big Russian planes will come and fetch them to take them home. As if they could possibly be repatriated before the end of hostilities! Here they enjoyed peace and quiet, they could recuperate in the fresh air, and they had as much food as they wanted. I beg, scream and shout; there's nothing the unfortunate soldier can do, he's only carrying out his orders. All I can do is hurry to the Stadtpark to warn the Russian convalescents of their imminent departure. Who will take care of them now? I'm so disgusted that I declare to Madeleine (for the tenth time, no doubt) that we might just as well spend our time sunbathing. After all, the weather is glorious just now.

We have hardly listened to the radio recently. We know that the Russians and Americans are advancing rapidly, and we are sure that victory is not far off. But today I heard a broadcast that shattered me, made me sick to my stomach. A young political deportee was speaking. Very simply and with no rhetorical flourishes, she related the horrors of the concentration camp in which she had been incarcerated. The prisoners weren't merely tortured; when they could no longer work they were sent to the gas chamber, and from there to the crematorium. When the liberating armies arrived, it appears that the Germans killed thousands upon thousands of prisoners. I am haunted by this woman's voice, by her palpable sincerity. And then, since we always come back to ourselves in the end, I reflect selfishly, 'You've got off lightly.' I think back to the threats of that stormtrooper on the day the Americans arrived. At the time I found his threats to have us shot puerile and laughable. Now I realize we were lucky to escape with our lives. I am desperately worried about the fate of my friends. Where are they? What have the Germans done with them? Shall I ever see them again? Betty who was in such poor health, Yvonne Oddon, Mickey and all the others? I had pictured them lounging in the sun somewhere as they waited to return to France. Are they still alive even?

Wanfried, 29 April 1945

This morning we hear from Pierre that a new American captain has occupied the castle of Kalkoff, two kilometres from here, with two hundred men. Pierre has seen him: his name is Captain Blumenthal, he speaks German and Pierre thinks he is intelligent and sympathetic. I declare roundly that I'm prepared to try one last approach to this new captain, but that this will be absolutely and definitively my final attempt.

Captain Blumenthal does not appear as receptive as Pierre had led me to hope. Nevertheless, he promises us a jeep to take us to Eschwege, where he says things are finally getting organized. There we will be seen by Captain Landes, commanding officer of the Eschwege *Kreis* or sector, who will doubtless know how to make the best use of our information.

Wanfried, 29 April 1945 (evening)

The reception we receive from Captain Landes comes as a huge surprise. An exuberant man with flashing dark eyes, he speaks with an ease and fluency of which he is not unaware and which he uses to great effect. He welcomes us with these words: 'Are you the two Frenchwomen who have put together these remarkable records?' And with that he flourishes a fistful of our little slips of paper, with which his office seems to be covered! We modestly acknowledge our role, aided by information from Pierre Dupont. Apparently the captain has been looking for us for some days in order to put us in contact with the Counter-Intelligence Corps at Eschwege. Never in my life have I heard such extravagant praise. He speaks of our 'inestimable' help and of the 'professionalism' with which we have carried out our work. In short, this time we have before us an officer who has not only the will but also the means to take every possible measure to combat the Nazis.

I raise the matter of the arbitrary round-up of the Russians. He bangs on his desk with his fists and says that the Russians were moved following complaints from the local population. I assure him that any such complaints were completely unfounded, that the Russians never behaved like the Poles, but on the contrary were tremendously helpful to us. Too late, the true reason why the Germans demanded the ruthless removal of the Russians (and not on his orders) dawns on Captain Landes. He promises to take great care of our own safety, which he feels is precarious; he will provide us with a car and a police driver for our sole use. The plans that he outlines to us demonstrate a reassuring robustness of vision: his understanding of the occupation of Germany is absolutely sound in every respect. I am fascinated by his facial expressions. When he is talking about matters close to his heart, his dark eyes flash with an extraordinary brilliance.

Wanfried, 1 May 1945

We have thrown ourselves heart and soul into our work, Pierre, Madeleine and I, following up leads, talking, asking questions, taking notes – in short, having a wonderful time.

Madeleine and I find ourselves by chance at Sontra, another picturesque little town straight out of a fairy tale, rather like Wanfried. I have heard that the local chief of police is a remarkable man, a German who has just been freed after five years in a concentration camp. We can be pretty confident of his anti-Nazi credentials. Herr Schellhase has only just taken up his post, and the work he is embarking upon promises to be of great importance. He has information that all the Nazi documentation regarding Sontra has been hidden at the bottom of a mineshaft. When he has recovered this, as he plans to do shortly, he will be able to work objectively and dispassionately, on the basis of irrefutable evidence. Herr Schellhase is still extremely emaciated, with fine, translucent features that remind me of certain seventeenth-century mystics. The hair has not yet had time to grow back on his shaven head. He looks older than his fifty years, but he is in good heart. He tells me that he fully expects to spend another quarter of a century fighting fascism.

As we talk, my eyes wander to a pretty little house on the other side of the square, one of those charming old houses where one imagines people must once have lived contented lives. 'Pretty, isn't it, that house opposite?' observes Herr Schellhase, following my gaze. 'Some Jewish friends of mine used to live there. They had a little boy, and in about '34 they managed to send him abroad. Yesterday I saw a handsome young American soldier come into town: it was my friends' son. He had come back to Sontra to find his family. When he asked me where they were I said I didn't know, I'd lost touch with them. Let someone else tell that poor boy how his parents were murdered, and the circumstances of their deaths . . .'

He moves on to his five years in the concentration camp, where intellectuals were chained up like dogs and forced to live on their hands and knees. To obtain their rations they had to bark like dogs, otherwise they starved to death. He relates other similar events. Then, controlling his emotions with difficulty, he says, 'There are things that a man cannot say to a woman face to face.' He stands up and walks over to the open window, his gaze skimming over the vista of picturesque houses. But he doesn't see them; he sees only the appalling scene that he describes to me in short, staccato bursts: 'It was what we anti-Nazis used to call their *Kultur* sessions; there was always something new, some theme conjured up from the monstrous imaginations of the SS. One day they ordered us to fetch five Jews. There were two doctors, two professors from Berlin and a lawyer. They were all prominent men, two of them much celebrated in Germany. We wondered what new horror lay in store. The SS guards had five cows brought in. They put a stool behind each cow. Then they forced the Jews to couple with them.' Meanwhile the SS guards stood around laughing. 'I had to hold one of the cows. I can still hear the SS laughing,' adds Herr Schellhase. 'I shall hear them for ever.'

But they have not broken his spirit, and he is full of hope. Nevertheless, this is the dungheap on which he and his friends will have to build a new Germany. 'We can do it, yes, we can do it, if we get help, and if we find that the occupying forces have a real understanding combined with a cold and absolute determination to root out the evil and punish the guilty.'

Every morning at nine o'clock the car comes to collect us, Pierre, Madeleine and me, and we set off on our investigations. First we pick a village. Then Pierre goes off alone to see the men who are his contacts there. Madeleine and I, meanwhile, generally tackle the women. When we don't have any specific information to act on, we head straight for the presbytery and ask to see the pastor's wife. Nine times out of ten the pastor is not there. Sometimes he is in the army, but usually he is a prisoner, or a former prisoner. These are circles in which Hitler's name commands little respect. The houses have a handsome charm, cool and dignified. Frau Frankenheimer, for instance, receives us in a room with polished floorboards, two armchairs, three dining chairs, two stools and a little desk. In the middle of the room stands a small table draped with a heavy white lace tablecloth, on which lies a Bible. This magnificently bound volume is the room's sole ornament. The cream-painted walls are bare except for a reproduction of the portrait of Luther by Cranach. Frau Frankenhausen notices that I can't take my eyes off it. 'The only portrait we have ever had in the house,' she explains with pride.

We always begin by introducing ourselves and explaining how we come to be in Germany. Then we explain that we have been sent by the Americans to draw up an inventory of anti-Nazis, and we add that it is difficult, if not impossible, for the occupying forces to sort out the wheat from the chaff. Good and upright citizens therefore run the risk of being mistaken for the wicked, and of paying the price for them. This simplistic preamble is designed to inspire their confidence. Then I ask who in the village has suffered the most at the hands of the Nazis. This instantly provides us with a list of those with a grievance, who should make good informants.

After this we try to obtain the names of people who have helped the persecuted, and little by little, slowly but surely, we arrive at the names of the persecutors themselves. Leaving the presbytery with this store of information, we then set off on a tour of the surrounding countryside, where one tip leads to another, one confidence prompts another. Naturally, we have to disregard the personal vendettas, petty grudges, idle gossip and interminable tales of the parish pump that try our patience so sorely, but once we have jettisoned 50 per cent of all that we have gleaned and gone through the rest with a fine-tooth comb, we are left with a handful of reasonably firm leads.

At about four o'clock, exhausted and with our heads ringing with grievances, we meet up with Pierre, and we have a quick bite to eat in the car with Herr Traub, our driver, before heading back to the Schloss. In our office there, the three of us then compare notes and write our reports, and Madeleine types them up. At about eight o'clock, she and I present the finished reports to Captain Lampp, who is at last installed as commander of Wanfried and with luck will be here for several months. It is he who ensures that our reports are transmitted to the CIC in Eschwege on a daily basis.

Our enquiries take us into a great many German homes. Many of them are very modest, but everywhere we are struck by how superior the German standard of living is to the French. The peasant dwellings and small farmhouses are cleaner and more harmonious than our own, and generally better and more tastefully furnished. Catholic country-dwellers do not seem to favour the hideous pious images sadly to be found in French homes, preferring images of distinctly superior artistic merit.

I have been in contact with members of a sect that appears quite widespread in Germany, known as the *Bibelforscher*, or Jehovah's Witnesses. Those whom I have met conduct themselves with outstanding dignity. Today our investigations led us to the home of Herr Mengel, recently freed from the concentration camp where he had been held since 1937. While the *Bibelforscher* are greatly to be respected, they have never been of the slightest practical help to us. Infinitely discreet, they refuse to denounce their persecutors, trusting in God to avenge them. I have tried in vain to suggest discreetly that perhaps we have been sent by God to help them, but they obstinately refuse to view us as archangels in disguise, and keep their lips firmly sealed.

Wanfried, 8 May 1945

It's all over, Hitler is defeated! At three o'clock we heard General de Gaulle's speech, so brief and moving; then we heard the bells of Notre Dame de Paris! As a lively American soldier called Al points out without a hint of sentimentality, we absolutely cannot let the evening pass without toasting our victory: some things really do deserve a drink, after all.

The assault troops have left precious little wine in their wake at Wanfried, and it is with some difficulty that Madeleine and Al contrive to 'requisition' four or five bottles. Marie Fromond and Fidéline Legrand are excellent pastry cooks and swiftly rustle up choux buns and tarts, and the seven of us set off to spend the evening at Schloss Kalden, where the Americans who have occupied the building are waiting for us. In the great dining hall, bristling with hunting trophies, the table is laid with a glittering profusion of glorious flowers, fine crystal, silver and porcelain. We take our places, seven French women political deportees and seven American soldiers. At first we are all very subdued. It all seems so unreal: the party, the ponderous luxury, the lights. Slave workers that we were until so recently, we find all this happiness oppressive. After our little dinner we move into the drawing room. A globe catches my eye, and I pick it up and start to play ball with it. It's up to us now to handle the world as we see fit, and we toss the whole world from one to another, joking all the while. Afterwards, I explain to our friends where we are and to whom this mansion belongs. It is the residence of Arthur Kalden, who until 1929 was known by his real name of Israel. But Herr Arthur Israel was inspired to become a Nazi, disowning his origins in order to retain his immense wealth, his castle, his factory, his hunting domains, his servants and his parkland. He became a Nazi, sporting a fine uniform decked with eight stars. Today Arthur Kalden, formerly Israel, is living in his gardener's cottage, while the Americans disport themselves in his castle and entertain French women political deportees. Tomorrow (I have been solemnly promised) Herr Arthur Kalden will be in prison. And tonight we are going to dance in his drawing room!

We resolve to shatter the globe into a thousand pieces, and build a new world in which Nazis like Kalden will have no voice.

Between bursts of jazz, the radio broadcasts the whoops and cheers of delirious crowds, now in Paris, now in London, and we join in, shouting for joy. And then we dance. I danced on 11 November 1918, too, but in 1918 I didn't know what it was to suffer and to witness the suffering of others. Now that I know, I dance more intensely, laugh more intensely – and hate more intensely.

In the course of our work, I have got to know a young American. He is only twenty-four, but is already a man of remarkable character. Highly cultivated, he has seen a great deal and understood a great deal. His way of speaking, which is unusually florid and colourful, reminds me of my son Pierre, so I decide straight away that Mike is my adoptive son, the child of my heart. He was born in Berlin, and his father, Arnold Zweig, is a celebrated German writer, while his mother is an artist.

When Mike was thirteen, his parents escaped with him to Palestine in the nick of time. That was in 1933, when Hitler had just come to power. Mike Zweig spent a few years in Palestine, in one of those wonderful children's republics; then at eighteen he left for the United States, where he worked as a pilot for an airline company. When war broke out he joined the army. He can lapse into Berlin street slang at the drop of a hat, and when he gives the Germans a dressing down he does so in the local dialect. Dumbfounded, the Germans ask him timidly if he isn't really a German? 'German?' Mike retorts loftily, '*Mein Gott*, I'd die of shame! I'm Jewish!' Mike says that he has noticed that this simple declaration tends to cast a slight chill over proceedings . . .

Last week Mike arrested an SS man. This man had on his person a letter that he hadn't yet been able to deliver. In it he boasted of having personally tortured and killed eighty Russians. Seeing that he was trapped, and harbouring no illusions as to the fate that lay in store for him, the SS man asked Mike to let him embrace his wife and children before he died. 'And you, did you let those Russians embrace their wives and children?' was Mike's only reply.

We spend hours talking, Mike and I. He settles himself on my divan in such a comical fashion, curling up like a little dog. We talk about our fathers: his father, the writer Arnold Zweig, was outside Verdun in 1916, when my father, Charles Humbert, senator for the Meuse, was inside Verdun. And now here we are, the two of us, their children, chatting on my divan at Wasserburg about the reorganization of Germany and of the rest of the world. How should we deal with Germans? Take up the cudgels, show neither pity nor weakness, an eye for an eye and so forth? We trot out all the old clichés, and naturally are full of fighting words!

Ever since we were freed, Madeleine and I have longed to explore the forest around Wanfried, but the Americans have strongly advised us not to go on our own. Today is Sunday, and Mike is here with a friend. With the protection of their khaki uniforms, we can at last go for a walk on the wooded hill behind Wasserburg. After walking for half an hour we come to a clearing, and in the clearing is a little bar. 'Great!' exclaim our friends. 'Maybe we can get a beer!' But as we get closer we see that only the skeletal shell of the bar remains: everything has been looted, ransacked, senselessly smashed. The glasses have been pulverized and are now a shimmering heap in the middle of the floor, and the tables and chairs have been reduced to matchwood. We stand and stare, silent and rather awkward. 'The Poles have been everywhere, looting everything,' I say. But Mike bends down and picks up a chewing-gum wrapper: 'The Poles don't chew gum from Philadelphia. Well, now we know. When American soldiers are drunk, it's not just town halls that they smash up.'

At this point the owner of the bar arrives. She fled when the Americans arrived in Wanfried, and now she's back. Seeing her business in ruins, she starts to weep and moan. Mike is upset, and full of tender concern: 'My poor dear woman, it's terrible.' And gently he consoles her, offering her advice as to how to report the matter, where and to whom. He has tears in his eyes, and I see his right hand reaching discreetly for his pocket book. I have been watching him, waiting for this crowning gesture. With a smile I intervene, reminding him of our resolutions of barely an hour earlier: take up the cudgels, no weakness, no pity. Mike is a civilized man, with the tender heart engendered by civilization. I like Mike, and with the same perfect understanding as earlier we discuss the principle of individual cases. We agree that after all this poor woman cannot in all conscience be held responsible for Hitler, Buchenwald, Oradour . . .

Wanfried, 15 May 1945

The officers of the CIC in Eschwege are howling with laughter. We ask to share the joke. Spluttering and snorting, they explain that they have just sent packing the fourth German this morning who wanted to enlist in the US army. It's only just ten o'clock, and our friends are speculating on the number of 'volunteers' there will be by this evening. When the fourth applicant appeared, the interpreter was moved to enquire as to the reason behind this sudden enthusiasm for the American army. 'We want to help you defeat the Russians,' came the reply, and it was all the Americans could do to convince the man that the Russians are and will remain their friends and allies.

This rumour of war between the United States and the USSR is spreading through the region like wildfire. Yesterday evening Frau Wolff, one of the 'good ladies' of Wanfried, assured me with great earnestness that we should impose a blackout, as any minute now the Russians were going to launch an attack, a *Terrorangriff*. We laugh, and then Lieutenant Donnellan decides with us that it is time to clip the wings of these absurd rumours, and that it would also be interesting to know who is starting them and who is spreading them.

The roads are choked with the wretched and dispossessed of every nationality, trailing baggage and children. Our refuge, soup kitchen and hospital are proving more and more indispensable. We have left the running of all this entirely to the Germans, and we have always been confident that they are making a splendid job of it. Matron, the finest and bravest of women, has lost three sons at the front, along with any illusions she might have had about the Nazi regime.

I ask her why, given her compassion and skills, she did not set up something like this in the days before I myself drew attention to the overwhelming need for it? She pulls a foolish face as she tells me that it was simply impossible for her to take such an initiative. Madeleine and I both put the same question to several other Germans, but always with the same evasive and inconclusive response. Finally, my dogged persistence elicits an answer: 'All our charitable work was National Socialist charitable work, so we couldn't carry on with it.' Not a single one of these wretched halfwits had the gumption to help the refugees, because for them charity came under the heading of Nazism; not one of the poor fools had the sense to replace the swastika with the red cross! No, they all said, we had to wait until we were given the order, and you were the only person who could give that order; it couldn't come from a German. So they had to wait for French women to tell them not to leave their fellow Germans to die from exhaustion and starvation by the side of the road. Only when the orders came from us, short and sharp, could they set about nursing and feeding them.

The chief of the district health department appears, with a German Red Cross lady in tow, to offer me his official thanks for founding these two useful little enterprises. How delightful to have this doctor clicking his heels before me! He stresses that our initiative is the only one of its kind within a radius of two hundred kilometres. I allow myself the pleasure of yelling at this chief medical officer, in front of his high-ranking nurse, that he should be ashamed to belong to a country where the people have to wait for an enemy political prisoner to give them the order to do their duty as professionals and as human beings! He takes it all without a word.

The saddest thing about our new role as informers is that we almost never hear what happens to the quarry that we flush out, and most of the time we never even see it.

Yesterday Dr Braun came to tell me that the mayor of a neighbouring village had just revealed to him that Martin Bormann, Hitler's notorious henchman, had hidden important documents in his family castle at Lüderbach. We dispatch the Americans there without delay, but it appears that only a fluke would lead them to hidden documents in such a rabbit warren of a building. Shame!

But today we had enormous fun, like children playing at cops and robbers. For weeks now we have known that the mayor of Schwebda was hiding in the woods. Purely by chance, Pierre Dupont happened to be passing his house, and stopped to have a look. Oh joy! The bird had come back to his nest! We did an about-turn and raced off to Eschwege at ninety kilometres an hour to fetch the police – and this time the charming Herr Heinrich Bernhard, *Ortsgruppenleiter* (local section leader) of the National Socialist Party, will not return to the woods.

Another prize catch we hope to make soon is Herr Friedel Albrecht of the *Pferdeverkehrsgesellschaft* (horse-drawn transport company) of the Third Reich. We know that our information has already put the president of the German Automobile Club behind bars, when he thought he was safe in Eschwege.

Pierre Dupont is currently on the lookout for the return to his native Eschwege of Karl Pfetzing, an SS diehard who volunteered for Buchenwald and who has not yet returned home. And then there is Dr Heilmuth Pippart, a 'doctor' at Buchenwald, of whose learned skills we hope sooner or later to deprive his profession.

As innocent as newborn babes, the Americans are happy to employ any German who has a tolerable grasp of English. They seem touched to discover that there are people who know how to speak their language here, so far away from home, and too often entrust them with missions that are no business of the Germans. Recently we have drawn attention to at least four individuals among these interpreters who can boast a fairly glorious Nazi past.

Not a day goes by without our hearing the tale of another German family's sufferings. The bullying and persecution suffered by children who refused to join the Hitler Youth pierced their parents' hearts like daggers. The lives of those who did not support Hitler (though who didn't go to the lengths of opposing him) seem to have been strewn with traps and pitfalls on a daily basis. As for anti-Nazis – Catholics, democrats, communists or others – the world is only now beginning to understand what they have suffered.

Everywhere I go I hear the same cry: 'We hated Hitler!' Often, too, this is a declaration of faith and completely sincere. But when I ask why they didn't get rid of this hated figure, the reply is always the same: 'We couldn't! Our hands were tied!' To which I reply, 'Were your hands tied more tightly than ours?' I know that the circumstances were different, but I can never resist the satisfaction of telling them that we preferred to risk our lives rather than continue to live under Hitler. The Germans are a spineless lot on the whole, lacking any ability to reason things through or view them with a critical spirit; and they suffer from a total and absolute lack of initiative, inculcated by their educational system down the centuries.

Schellhase's voice still rings in my ears, and I have asked myself the same question a hundred times: 'Will we get the help we need to build a new, decent Germany?' There is a sentiment, all too frequently heard already, that sadly seems to sum up the situation as far as many French people are concerned: 'We should make them suffer'. It is a sentiment that fills me, a former political deportee, with dread. Yes, we should make the Nazis suffer, and in many cases we should put them beyond suffering for good. But as for the rest – the Germans who have already suffered so much, those whose cruel fate it was to be weak and spineless, who didn't know how to resist or couldn't do so, who were condemned to wait until the most hideous war and occupation by foreign powers brought them deliverance – if we 'make them suffer' we run the risk of producing another Hitler, of fomenting a backlash that would be absurd and tragic in equal measures. The anti-Nazis are holding out their hands (sincerely for the most part) to their official enemies, whom they see not as friends exactly (let's not exaggerate), but at least as trustworthy and currently all-powerful helpmeets. Now if these helpmeets are truly committed to building a new world, then in my view they have only two alternatives: either they abolish the German race altogether (and the crematoria are still in full working order), or else they work together with those Germans who are demonstrably of good faith. Punish the guilty without mercy, re-educate the young. The Germans are eager to learn, and are flexible and accommodating (to a fault!). They absolutely need a firm hand, but let justice be meted out without anarchy, and above all – oh, above all – without stupidity!

My over-active imagination often presents me with a scenario that must already have been played out many times. We now know with certainty that from January 1945 and perhaps earlier, raw recruits were assigned to the SS whether they were willing or not. We also know how Allied soldiers deal with the SS, and with every justification. But how many recent recruits, forced into the SS against their will, have found themselves confused with the true fanatics? What about the unfortunate brother of a young communist, Frau Kotulan of Langenhain, himself a communist forced into the SS against his will? What fate can have befallen him?

I have it on unimpeachable authority that French prisoners of war in the region of Schwelm in Westphalia were officially forbidden to point out to the American forces any anti-Nazis or other Germans who had treated prisoners humanely. They were also prevented from leaving affidavits expressing their gratitude to particular individuals. These vetoes were imposed by the French officers responsible for repatriating them. It is quite superfluous, I'm sure, to spell out the reasons that might induce Vichy officers to issue orders of such a perplexing nature.

Wanfried, 4 June 1945

We have been told that we will soon be going back to France. For us, as for most of the other prisoners, the joy of returning home is tinged with apprehension at what we will find when we get there, or rather what we will not find. It's been so long since we had any news from our families and loved ones! Are they dead or alive? Are our homes still standing? Without wanting to paint too black a picture or to expect the worst, we know with certainty that major changes lie in store for us in France. Life has gone on without us, and now we are suddenly about to reappear like ghosts – and the living are always a little afraid of ghosts. If we are honest, we are all rather dreading the moment of return, which is now looming so close.

Wanfried, 6 June 1945

The three of us have been to Eschwege to say goodbye to Captain Landes. First, I thanked him for a sight that has just given me enormous pleasure. This morning we passed the Jewish cemetery in Eschwege: under a blazing sun, a group of well-known Nazis were weeding the paths, mending broken headstones and repairing tombs that had been desecrated. Their overseers were two Germans recently released from a concentration camp and still wearing their striped uniforms. The work would be done well, and *schnell, schnell*. As I watched this scene with malicious satisfaction, Pierre whispered in my ear: 'You see the tall one over there, moving the black marble headstone? Look closely, it's Karl Schumacher, head of the DAF (*Deutsche Arbeits Front*) for the whole region and a notorious bastard.' Karl was hot and sweaty, and his elegant suit was not designed for the hard labour to which he was being subjected today. I smiled, knowing that under my arm, in my bag, I had a file drawing him to the attention of the Americans. In a few hours' time, I knew, he would be under lock and key.

It was rare (and how often had I regretted it) for us to have the pleasure of seeing the quarry we were responsible for flushing out. Today we could admire this one in the sunshine, a fine specimen with hard, cruel eyes and a mastiff's jaws.

As he congratulated us again on our work, Captain Landes handed us a copy of a positively eulogistic citation that he has sent to the War Ministry in Paris. We certainly were not expecting anything of the sort, and we were genuinely touched by his appreciation, so warmly expressed. After leaving him we went to say goodbye to Lieutenant Donnellan, our boss in the CIC. He too showered us with praise. He gave each of us a little note saying that thanks to our work he had been able to arrest a number of prominent Nazis and war criminals. On Pierre's note he added that he was a credit to the French army. Now that really did make me happy!

On our return to Wasserburg, we find Dr Braun waiting for us. Despite all our efforts, the Americans have removed him from office. He is a broken man, and we are distressed to see how distraught he is. He is a man of little strength. He joined the Nazi Party to keep his job, and he has risked his own life to protect a number of anti-Nazis and Jews. I have questioned witnesses to this, and held irrefutable proof of it in my hands. But Captain Landes will admit no double standards, and all mayors who were Party members (which is to say all of them) have been stripped of their office. So Dr Braun finds his place taken by a farmer who is a fine man and a good social democrat, certainly, but who is also famously incompetent. While Dr Braun might 'officially' have been a Nazi, I shall always have fond memories of a man who, though perhaps a little too 'flexible', had superb management skills and was unfailingly scrupulous and deeply humane. As we say our farewells, Dr Braun presents me with a lovely engraving of the town hall at Wanfried. He has inscribed it with a quotation from Goethe and the following dedication: *To Mme Agnès Humbert, a native of France, in memory*

of those days in April 1945 when she devoted herself with courage and
maternal care to our town and to the foreigners who needed her help.
This gift fills me with pride and emotion, and quite spontaneously and without thinking I embrace Dr Braun. Who would
have thought that one day I would embrace a German, and a
member of the Nazi Party to boot!

Kassel Displaced Persons Camp, 9 June 1945

So at last we are at Kassel Displaced Persons Camp. We of
the 'Holy Trinity', as we like to call ourselves, remain
indivisible. Madeleine, Pierre and I have decided to return to
Paris together; Pierre will go on from there to join his young
wife, who is waiting for him at Néris, and to meet his son,
who is nearly five years old and whom he has never seen.

A displacement camp for some one thousand people of different nationalities is a very curious place. We live in a building
that has been reduced to nothing more than its (extremely
dilapidated) floorboards, walls and roof. There is no shortage
of bugs, by contrast. The Poles have stripped out everything,
smashed everything, but sadly they have left the bugs. The
American soldiers (all fifteen of them, poor things) manage
as best they can, and supply us with excellent food twice a
day. In the evening there's a cinema and dancing. If the Poles
try to kill each other, the Americans try to intervene. The
'sanitary orderly' told me that yesterday evening two Poles
were fighting it out with an axe; he tried to separate them,
narrowly missed being sliced by the axe and ended up being
showered from head to toe with the blood of one of the combatants. The lad puts his heart and soul into his work, but he's
starting to get fed up with it and is feeling homesick for his
native New York. Captain Mary, the camp commander, faces
unimaginable obstacles head-on, with courage and composure.
But he too has had enough, and says to me with a half-smile,

'If I don't see another Pole for fifty years that'll be soon enough for me!'

You could devote an entire book, meanwhile, to the heroic devotion of the French doctors, Dr Rougier and Dr Sirot, and to that of their charming French matron. Together they have created an ad hoc hospital entirely from scratch in a bombed-out and semi-ruined building. They have scavenged every pair of tongs, every table, every surgical knife from the rubble of Kassel, bringing it all back in their car to the hospital that they have constructed over the beds of the typhoid patients they are treating, and for the most part curing, in conditions that have to be seen to be believed. It's almost enough to make one proud to be French.

Tonight I am watching the dancing. It makes a colourful scene: a cosmopolitan melting pot of every possible nationality, with everyone dancing with everyone else, and everyone talking to everyone else in that pidgin dialect, that German Esperanto that is such a delight to me.

I don't feel like dancing; I'm too sleepy. I chat half-heartedly with Pierre. His eyes are swollen with bug bites and I've been teasing him all day. But now he doesn't seem to feel like joking any more; he appears awkward and embarrassed, as though he wants to say something but doesn't quite know how to begin. I pinch myself awake, force myself to listen to him. He is asking me to forgive him, saying he's sorry, pleading some cause. I have to make an effort to wake up properly, pinching myself again, as I can tell that Pierre is saying something serious. Again he asks me to forgive him for deceiving me, for having hidden the truth from me, and he explains in short, awkward sentences that he couldn't say anything, otherwise it would have been – curtains. And so Pierre Dupont confesses to me that he is not Pierre Dupont at all, but Hans Eric Diehl, a socialist from the Saarland and political refugee in France, awaiting naturalization in 1939. A volunteer in the French army, Pierre Dupont always made sure he was in the front line. Taken prisoner, he was sent first to

Stalag IX at Ziegenhain, and shortly afterwards to Wanfried, where he waited patiently while quietly compiling the information for which the Americans had given him that little note, ending up with the words 'Pierre Dupont is a credit to the French army.' Indeed he is. By his courageous example, Pierre Dupont has proved, yet again, that in the end national frontiers exist only as lines on maps. There are just people: those who fight for civilization, and those who fight against it. Just those two camps, no more. Boris Vildé was Russian, and so was Anatole Lewitsky; Pierre Walter, born in Metz to German parents, chose France, and Georges Ithier was Panamanian by birth. We say they died for France; I believe they died for France *as well*.

On 11 June 1945, the three of us clamber into the back of an American truck. The driver is a French soldier: a dapper little Parisian, warm, cheerful and friendly. Chatting to him, I feel as if I am in Paris already. We'll be there 'for real', as children say, the day after tomorrow, in the morning. We bed down in the lorry, stretched out on top of bundles and bags and pummelled by all the lumps and bumps. I wake up often and think back to all that has happened, to the adventure that for me is reaching its end tonight. I think of my friends, I think of Pierre Dupont, asleep beside me and keeping me warm. I think of the words of the prophet Isaiah over three thousand years ago: 'They shall beat their swords into ploughshares, and their spears into pruning-hooks; nation shall not lift up sword against nation, neither shall they learn war any more.' This is what we have been fighting for, what we shall continue fighting for, so that one day there will be no more war. At this point in my profound philosophizing the driver lifts a corner of the tarpaulin, sticks his head through and shouts: '*Allez*, on your feet, you lot! Jump to it — we're in France!'

Wanfried, April 1945
Paris, January 1946

Afterword by Julien Blanc

For many years *Notre Guerre*, now translated into English as *Résistance*, was out of print and unobtainable. Yet on first publication in 1946 it caused a considerable stir. In its pages, Agnès Humbert described a struggle against Nazi oppression that lasted nearly five years, from the first tentative moves of defiance towards the German Occupation in Paris in the summer of 1940, to slave labour in Germany and liberation by the American army. Her story, which also included a year in French prisons and – perhaps most remarkably of all – an insider's view of the genesis of one of the first organized Resistance movements in Occupied France, was narrated in a style striking for its immediacy and intensity.

Historians were immediately aware of the importance of this testimony, and its value has continued to be recognized ever since. Works by both academics and Resistance veterans citing Humbert as an authority, especially on the earliest forms of anti-German dissidence, are legion. All are unanimous in praising the accuracy and precision of her account. *Notre Guerre* thus came to occupy a paradoxical position: an invaluable historical source, frequently quoted over the decades, but soon available only to a select band of initiated readers, inaccessible to a wider public and generally consigned more or less to obscurity.

Agnès Humbert was fifty-one when she published her book.

Born in Dieppe in 1894, she was the daughter of Charles
Humbert, a career soldier who, as a lieutenant in 1892, married
Mabel Wells Annie Rooke, daughter of an English 'professor of
music' who lived as part of the thriving expatriate community
in Dieppe. Having launched himself on a political career with
some success, Humbert became deputy for the department of
the Meuse, then senator from 1908, the year in which he also
divorced Mabel.

In January 1916, when she was twenty-one, Agnès Humbert
married the Egyptian-born artist Georges Sabbagh, who served
in the British army during the First World War. Both were
pupils of the Symbolist painter Maurice Denis, and after their
marriage Humbert continued to paint under the name Agnès
Sabbert. In 1917 and 1918 they had two sons, Jean and Pierre,
and in 1934 they were divorced. Trained as a watercolourist,
Humbert went on to study art history at the Ecole du Louvre,
followed by postgraduate diplomas in philosophy and ethnography. In 1936 she published a well-received monograph on
David, *Louis David: peintre et conventionnel*. The following year
she joined the staff of the newly created Musée des Arts et
Traditions Populaires, the France-focused sister museum to the
Musée de l'Homme, also housed in the Palais de Chaillot.
There she quickly became the closest colleague of the museum's
first director, Georges-Henri Rivière. A woman of the left and
militant anti-fascist, she was an enthusiastic supporter of the
government of the Popular Front, taught at the Université
ouvrière (workers' university), and contributed articles to *La
Vie ouvrière* (Workers' Life) under the pen name of Delphine
Girard. Her political commitments also found expression in
her professional life, in which she was involved in projects to
collect photographic documentation on the social movements
and strikes of 1936. A research trip to Russia in the summer
of 1939 to study Soviet museums and culture confirmed her
attachment to the communist cause.

So when war broke out, Agnès Humbert was at forty-three already a mature woman, a seasoned campaigner with a solid political grounding and a penetrating and practical understanding of the machinations of power. From the pages of her book there emerges a warm and powerful personality, committed, passionate and generous, driven by deeply held convictions to which she remained unwaveringly loyal, and defined by her absolute candour and honesty. A woman of intellect, able to analyse any situation with lucid intelligence, Agnès Humbert was also a woman of action, never afraid of concrete engagement.

A *unique document*

Both its structure and the mysterious history of its composition make *Résistance* a document of radical originality. The two opening chapters, covering the debacle of defeat, the first months of the Occupation and her involvement in the fledgling Resistance movement, are the transcription of Agnès Humbert's personal diary, which she kept from June 1940. Amid the chaos of the exodus from Paris, and afterwards in the chapter called 'Paris under the Swastika', she kept a virtually daily record of her impressions and activities. This spontaneous account, direct and unmediated, comes to an abrupt end on 13 April 1941, two days before her first interrogation by the Gestapo. It does not resume until the very end of the book, with her liberation by the American army four years later, in April 1945. The tenth and last chapter, 'Hunting the Nazis', returns once more to an almost daily rhythm, tracing in a more or less extempore fashion her work alongside the Americans in the weeks following Germany's defeat.

In the seven much longer chapters that form the core of the book, Humbert describes her imprisonment, the 'Musée de l'Homme' trial in January and February 1942, and the long months and years of her deportation to Germany and her life as a slave worker. Most of the book was therefore written after the event. Unable to keep a written record of her impressions following her arrest (with the exception of a brief period during her trial in February 1942, when she managed to scribble a few notes on a volume of Descartes), she re-created her experiences afterwards, relying on her memories alone.

Résistance thus juxtaposes two distinct types of writing – the raw spontaneity of the diary entries and the more considered reflections drawn from memory – corresponding to two distinct time frames. Between the breathless, astonishingly dense period of the early days of the Resistance (7 June 1940–13 April 1941) and the first weeks after her liberation in Germany (4 April–9 June 1945), there hangs the long hiatus of her imprisonment and deportation, during which time seems to be abolished or suspended. It is this hybrid structure, combining two literary genres that are usually quite distinct, that makes *Résistance* unique among such memoirs. And it is almost certainly this unclassifiable quality that for so many years discouraged French publishers – normally so eager to publish any text touching on the history of the Resistance – from bringing out a new edition. Yet it is this highly individual structure that lends the narrative a powerful unity and irresistible momentum. The reasons for this are several.

First of all, there is the razor-sharp precision of Humbert's memory, of her detailed recollections of people, places and events. 'I remember everything as clearly as if it were written in notebooks,' she wrote: everything was recorded in her memory as it happened, and all she had to do was slowly turn the pages.

To preserve the immediacy and spontaneity of this raw material, she committed these experiences to paper with astonishing speed. Unlike many other witnesses of this period, who waited years or even decades before taking up their pens,

Humbert began writing immediately after her liberation, when she was still in Germany in early April 1945. In the small town of Wanfried in the region of Hesse, she began to piece together her memories, to reconstruct her experiences of the previous four years and to write. After her return to France in June 1945 she carried on writing, and by January 1946 her work was complete. Published in May 1946 under the title *Notre Guerre* (Our War), it was one of the very first accounts of the war years to enter the public domain. Between the experience of these events and the writing of them, the bare minimum of time had elapsed.

To the photographic precision of Humbert's memories and the speed of her transcription may be added – as a third unifying factor – her style. Her great achievement was the way in which she maintained the same tone – vivid and impassioned, entertaining and moving – throughout the book, while at the same time scrupulously observing the rules governing a journal. Thus she was consistent in using the present tense throughout, in systematically locating events by time and place, and in punctuating her memories throughout with vivid anecdotes that both drive and add insights to the narrative.

The last unifying factor, but by no means the least, is the subject matter itself. As indicated by the original subtitle, *Souvenirs de Résistance*, the book's real subject is the Resistance itself. Wherever she may be, whether in freedom, prison or slavery, it is this constant struggle that Agnès Humbert describes. Making use of whatever weapons and methods she could, she refused ever to lower her guard, and kept up a perpetual and unremitting battle against Nazi oppression. Every page of her narrative breathes a dogged refusal to give in, an implacable determination to keep up the struggle.

Although the numbers of former Resistance members who chose to commit their impressions and the detail of their daily lives to paper are small, they do exist. Jean Guéhenno in the

Occupied zone (*Journal des années noires, 1940–1944*, Paris, 1947) and Charles d'Aragon in the south (*La Résistance sans héroisme*, ed. Guillaume Piketty, Paris, 2001) are two notable examples. But nowhere in their memoirs do we find any explicit reference to their involvement in the Resistance. Drawing a veil over their clandestine activities, they are scrupulous in avoiding all mention of names, meetings or actions. The risks and difficulties of clandestine activity impose a tangible climate of prudence and restraint. In these writers, fear of the police and the desire to protect their companions generated a constant process of self-censorship. Their writing acts as an unusual filter, concealing as much as – if not more than – it reveals.

In a field dominated by the unspoken, Agnès Humbert's diary is striking for the way in which she flouts these conventions. Far more than a mere sympathizer or fellow traveller, Humbert was committed heart and soul to the struggle against the Occupation, playing a leading role from the very start in the summer of 1940. The unique quality and value of her account lie above all in the astonishing candour with which she describes her activities. Where other diarists are obstinately discreet, keeping deeds and identities buried deep in their memories, she recounts every last detail, entrusting her reader with the full, unvarnished truth. Uncompromising in her description of her despair after the debacle of defeat and of her absolute need to react and fight back, she is equally forthright in her descriptions of the people she encountered, the very first acts of defiance they planned together, the contacts they set up and so much more. In the hands of Agnès Humbert, the Resistance emerges from the shadows of its taboo status to take centre stage.

Methodically, over a period of nine months, she documented every action undertaken by members of her group. In so doing, she created a portrait of the genesis of one of the very earliest Resistance networks in the Occupied zone, its first tentative steps, its early progress and successes, its trials and problems and ultimately its fatal setbacks. Recording people and events with the veracity of a documentary film, Humbert's journal provides the sights, sounds and textures of a vanished era and a secret war. Over half a century after the events it describes, it plunges the reader into the atmosphere of that first year of the Occupation, into the minds of the first Resistance members and into the heart of a powerful organization in the throes of coming into being. This experience of total immersion in those early days, at the very inception of the Resistance, is one of electrifying immediacy. From her unique point of view, Humbert offers vivid glimpses of a world long gone, that has left few traces of its existence.

By its very nature memory is selective, inevitably favouring some events to the detriment of others. Surviving members of the Resistance are no exception to this rule, and their earliest memories of this remote period tend to blur and fade, sometimes vanishing entirely beneath more recent or more striking images. Jean Cassou offers an illuminating example of the way in which clandestine fighters with a long record of Resistance activity tend to downplay the significance of their early actions. Cassou's case is all the more telling for the fact that before he left for the south and a clandestine career of great influence he was one of the leading members, with Agnès Humbert, of this pioneering Resistance group. In his autobiography, *Une vie pour la liberté* (Paris, 1981), Cassou recounted his early engagement with the Musée de l'Homme network under the heading 'La débâcle'; the following chapter, entitled 'La Résistance', starts with his arrival in Toulouse in April 1941: eloquent testimony to the relative importance in Cassou's recollections of these different stages in his Resistance work.

Armed with her notes taken in the heat of the action, Agnès Humbert was able to avoid the pitfalls of selective memory. Although her accounts of her imprisonment and slave labour in Germany form the longest sections of her book, the Resistance activities she undertook from the summer of 1940 to the spring of 1941 are neither sacrificed nor suppressed. Quite the contrary: the descriptions she gives of them are of documentary precision, never for a moment lapsing into vagueness or all-purpose generalizations. Day by day, contact by contact, we follow every real and concrete step in the development of what was within a few months to be one of the first and most important Resistance networks in Occupied France.

The diary: questions and enigmas

About the existence of this diary of the early days of the Resistance there can be no doubt. Beyond this one fact, however, questions multiply. How, when and where did Agnès Humbert write it? Once it was written, where did she keep it? Did she make changes before publication, and if so what were they? On these and other questions, she maintained a total silence. The 1946 edition contains neither preface nor notes nor any background information. We are given only one brief, tantalizing reference in the text: 'On 13 April my diary ends.'

The first question that arises is whether or not the 1946 edition reproduces the complete text of the original diary. Given the chronological leaps in some places (sometimes of as much as a month), it seems likely that there has been some process of selection. And given Humbert's constant concern to cut straight to the quick and to avoid overloading her narrative with unnecessary detail, it is reasonable to conjecture that she may have excised certain passages, in particular concerning her private or family life. This point is by no means insignificant. If cuts have indeed been made for this reason, they will have appreciably modified the balance of the text as a whole in favour of the Resistance, so ensuring it that emerged as the principal theme of the book.

Did Humbert rewrite or recast the raw material of her diary with a view to publication? Every diarist is prey to the temptation to rearrange or modify their writings before publication. Did she succumb? Only a comparison with the original manuscript could yield any definite answers. And the original manuscript appears to have vanished without trace. A slightly earlier version by Humbert of her journey with Sénéchal and their Gestapo interrogators (see p.53–4) does however suggest that in *Notre Guerre* she may have sought – in the traditional fashion of the Resistance – as will be seen later, to absolve the young man of any suspicion of having 'talked'.

Other questions also arise. Where and how did Humbert conceal her diary? How did it elude the Gestapo when they searched her home? On this point, too, the author is silent. Perhaps it lay 'quietly hidden under the stair carpet', along with 'the *Résistance* file, with its 400 names and addresses'. Whatever the case, fortunately the Germans never found it.

'Impetuous and reckless by nature'

Beyond these unanswered questions, the very fact of the existence of a diary of this kind under the Occupation points to a trait that was key to the author's character: the intensity and integrity of her commitment, in this as in everything she undertook in her lifetime. Jean Cassou, who knew her well, described her in *Une vie pour la liberté* as 'a woman of a strong and energetic temperament, impetuous and reckless by nature'. To this woman incapable of doing anything by halves, the notion of a secret diary that deliberately withheld the truth would have been inconceivable. The candour of her diary entries is a faithful reflection of her character. Under the circumstances, this innate inability to conceal her true feelings constituted a serious breach of the most elementary safety precautions: it is impossible to suppress a tremor of horror at the thought of what would have happened if the diary had fallen into German hands. There can be no doubt that it would have provided damning evidence for the prosecution, with devastating consequences not only for its author but also for the many others whose clandestine activities she revealed with such scrupulous honesty.

Unlike Jean Guéhenno and others who were understandably struck dumb with terror at the very thought that the Germans might lay hands on their notes, Agnès Humbert details her Resistance work without giving a second thought to the possibility that her writings might be read by hostile eyes, or to the disastrous consequences that would surely follow. On the sole occasion when she evinces a glimmer of awareness (heavily laced with irony) – 'We must exercise the utmost caution, it appears; specialist police have arrived from Berlin. Pass it on!' – she simply carries on with her diary regardless.

But above and beyond the remarkable personality of Agnès Humbert, this lack of prudence was also one of the founding characteristics of the Resistance in its earliest infancy, invented from scratch as it was by complete novices in the field of clandestine operations. Necessarily unprepared and with no particular predisposition towards this type of activity, constantly obliged to think on their feet and improvise, they learned the extreme difficulties of their struggle from experience in the field, and ultimately paid dearly for their commitment. When she managed to reach London in late 1941, Madeleine Gex Le Verrier, former editor of the foreign affairs magazine *L'Europe nouvelle*, drew attention to the damage being caused by the impetuousness of her fellow Resistance members. In a report to the Free French intelligence services in February 1942, she lamented the lack of organizational skills, the amateurism and the inexperience of these pioneers in the field. As eloquent testimony she cited the case of 'one of the women who worked on the first broadsheet entitled *Résistance*, who thought it was a clever idea to type "Vive de Gaulle" on the five-franc notes that she used to pay for her shopping'. It comes as no surprise to learn that this foolhardy creature was none other than Madeleine Gex Le Verrier's old friend Agnès Humbert.

The opening pages of *Résistance* stand apart as an eye-witness account of peerless power and searing truth, while at the same time forming a seamless introduction to the wider narrative. Driven by the momentum of describing events at first-hand and as they unfolded, Agnès Humbert's text possesses the detailed precision of the most valuable historical sources. So many and varied are the subjects she raises and the themes she explores that it would be vain to attempt to enumerate them all; rather we will focus on a handful of her essential themes.

Collapse, despair, recovery

Along with millions of her fellow countrymen and women, Agnès Humbert experiences the mass exodus from Paris and the spectacle of defeat, 'this monstrous thing' that leaves her 'too exhausted, too disheartened . . . just numb'. The collapse of France, the cataclysm that was to create such trauma and lay the foundations for all that was to come, hits her with brutal force, toppling her mental equilibrium to the point where she feels she will 'go mad, literally'.

But where others are prostrated by depression for a long time to come, Agnès Humbert quickly pulls herself together and rallies her forces. A brief spell of utter dejection gives way almost immediately to a determination to act. It is at Vicq-sur-Breuil in the Vienne, on 20 June 1940, that 'by a pure fluke' she hears General de Gaulle's appeal broadcast by the BBC: 'It is thanks to that "crackpot" that this evening I decided not to put an end to everything. He has given me hope, and nothing in the world can extinguish that hope now.' A month later, while wondering how to 'continue the struggle and "pull through"', she reaches a turning point: 'The people of Paris are rebelling already. So that's decided then: I'm going home!'

It is naturally to Jean Cassou that she turns immediately. On 6 August she hears he is back in Paris, and has only one thought: 'I have to see him, I have to see him now.' She knows of his past political activity, as she was there too. Companions in misfortune during the exodus, they deepen their friendship on those terrible roads. Together they look on helplessly as a young girl of sixteen dies, run over by a French army truck in flight. Over her lifeless body a lasting bond is forged between them: 'Jean Cassou and I knew each other already and have a lot in common, but this half-hour together at the side of a dying girl has bound us together with deep bonds of comradeship. We both know it.' It was with him that defiance and refusal stiffened into positive commitment.

Genesis of the Resistance, Paris 1940–41

As she plunges into the troubled waters of the first acts of defiance, it is in her descriptions of the emergence of the very first Resistance cell – it hardly needs saying – that Agnès Humbert offers some of her most remarkable and illuminating insights.

The first surprise is the startling speed with which these first dissidents began to organize among themselves, starting from scratch, thinking on their feet, making it up as they went along. As early as the first half of August 1940, Cassou and Humbert, determined to 'do something', decided to 'form a group of ten like-minded comrades . . . to exchange news, write and distribute pamphlets and tracts and share summaries of French radio broadcasts from London'. To make up this prototype cell they recruited from among their friends and colleagues: the Emile-Paul brothers, whose publishing house in the Latin quarter was to host their first meetings; the writer Claude Aveline; Marcel Abraham, academic and former member of the cabinet of Popular Front minister Jean Zay; Colette and Jean Duval; Simone Martin-Chauffier; and the Egyptologist Christiane Desroches. Most of the members of this 'conspiracy' were old friends and acquaintances; men and women of letters who moved in the same milieu, they had often – in articles in magazines and newspapers and on political committees – campaigned together for Republican Spain and the Popular Front, and against movements of the far right and the threat of fascism. These social networks and connections established before the war were now to play a decisive role.

Driven by what Jean Cassou described as 'moral revulsion', they had one basic essential in common: a refusal to accept defeat, and a visceral, instinctive, urgent rejection of the Occupation. Humbert is sickened by her first encounter with members of the occupying forces as she crosses the demarcation line. The same revulsion is recalled by Boris Vildé from his prison cell in November 1941: 'The first time I saw German soldiers in Paris after my return, it was with a stabbing pain in my heart that reminded me how much I love Paris, how much I love France.' Remembering 'the unreal spectacle of German troops goose-stepping up the Champs-Elysées', Cassou, meanwhile, is overwhelmed by feelings of violation, loss and indignation: 'But they have no right! The flame of the Unknown Soldier, Rude's "Marseillaise", the Arc de Triomphe, Victor Hugo – they all belong to me!' It was this ubiquitous presence of the occupying forces – loud, ponderous, inescapable – that accounted very largely for the speed with which these instinctive decisions were taken and the first initiatives began to assume a concrete shape.

The early activities of the 'Free French in France', as Claude Aveline dubbed the group, focused naturally on counter-propaganda, as the 'chitchat' of the first weeks gave way rapidly to the distribution of tracts, followed by the group's composition of its own texts. On 25 September 1940, they used a roneo machine to reproduce several thousand copies of a pamphlet entitled *Vichy fait la guerre* (Vichy wages war), in which Jean Cassou castigated the Vichy government for its actions at Dakar, where for the first time 'French soldiers fired on other French soldiers'. The very existence of this pamphlet testifies to the remarkable progress made by the group in the space of barely a month. The roneo machine – 'none other than the one belonging to the Musée de l'Homme!' as Humbert notes with delight – was a find of fundamental importance, enabling them to broaden their perspective and seriously entertain the notion of publishing a proper broadsheet, as she describes as early as 1 September.

Birth of a 'nebula'

Elsewhere in Occupied France, both in Paris and in the provinces, other early cells also sprang up at this time. In a remarkable article published in 1958, Germaine Tillion, herself a prominent figure in the early history of the Resistance, stressed the importance of these 'small, autonomous entities' which 'multiplied like microbes in tropical waters' to the north of the demarcation line in the summer of 1940. She also showed how these first scattered cells very quickly established contact with each other through a process of 'crystallization', in which 'each crystal, via its many facets, touches an infinite number of similar crystals'.

Under Boris Vildé's decisive leadership, the Musée de l'Homme group lost no time in starting to draw together these scattered initiatives. Agnès Humbert provides a detailed account of the way in which the 'Free French in France' made contact with the Musée de l'Homme. In late September 1940, Cassou learned from Dr Paul Rivet, director of the Musée de l'Homme, that a group was already 'at work' there. After an interview with Rivet, Humbert was 'put in contact' with Vildé, designated as the 'leader of anti-German activities at the Musée de l'Homme'. Contact was thus established between the two groups, which had so much in common that they seemed almost to form a single entity. Sociologically, intellectually and politically, they were almost indistinguishable. And there was one more factor in favour of this link between the two: through her work at the Musée des Arts et Traditions Populaires, Agnès Humbert was a neighbour and virtually a colleague of the researchers at the Musée de l'Homme.

In the autumn of 1940, Vildé set up contacts with a multitude of cells, including, among many others, groups set up by lawyers at the Palais de Justice, by staff at the American Embassy and by firemen in Paris, as well as very active groups in Béthune, in the Pas-de-Calais, and in Brittany. Thus around the hub of the Musée de l'Homme there developed a complex and fragmented 'nebula', drawing together numerous different initiatives, all of which were in more or less regular contact with the centre. Through these many different types of operation, the Musée de l'Homme network rapidly began to work actively in all fields of clandestine activity, from disseminating propaganda and collecting intelligence to helping escaping prisoners of war.

These links could not be established between different groups without the offices of go-betweens, who were crucial to the success of the process. This was the role in which Agnès Humbert was quickly to prove herself indispensable. It was she, as we have seen, who through Rivet enjoyed the 'delightful prospect' of introducing Cassou and Vildé to each other. Henceforth she would prove an enthusiastic liaison agent and recruiting sergeant. It was she who set up contacts with Roger Pons, an airman who was to supply the group with military intelligence. And it was she who recruited Pierre Brossolette and entrusted him with the editorship of the broadsheet *Résistance*, and who supplied Boris Vildé with valuable contacts in Toulouse, in the persons of Georges Friedmann and Léo Hamon. The list of contacts she brought to the group is impressive, and the pages of her diary are peppered with references to meetings and rendezvous. Through her work in setting up these links she thus helped the organization to both grow and diversify.

An underground broadsheet

Vildé planned an underground broadsheet very early on, declaring on 25 September 1940 that 'the first thing we must do is start a newspaper', so endorsing an earlier idea of Humbert and Cassou.

As a member of the editorial team that met at the home of Simone Martin-Chauffier, Humbert quickly elected herself the typist, responsible for typing up the articles and composing the pages by hand, ready for reproduction on the roneo machine by 'the mysterious gentlemen who supply the paper and organize the printing'. So vivid is her description of the editorial process that we can almost smell the ink on her hands. Within two months the first issue of *Résistance*, four roneoed pages dated 15 December 1940, was ready. Four more issues were to follow, the last in late March 1941.

Production of the newspaper required tremendous ingenuity at every stage, coupled with a dogged but nimble tenacity capable of avoiding the many potential traps and pitfalls along the way. Given the veritable minefield of obstacles that faced all early underground publications in the Occupied zone, bringing out five issues of *Résistance* in the space of four months was a remarkable achievement.

The principle aim of *Résistance*, not surprisingly, was to counter German propaganda by diffusing information that contradicted the heavily censored and controlled contents of the legitimate press. In *Le Temps mort* (Paris, 1962), Claude Aveline described their role as publishing 'a true account of the latest news, explanations as necessary, acts of defiance and rallying calls, every possible reason for retaining an absolutely unshakeable hope and optimism'. To supply information for the articles, Aveline went on, 'Vildé would bring the raw materials, newspapers from England, America and Switzerland', which he obtained via the American embassy in Paris. Alongside lengthy features on military developments and the international situation, *Résistance* also contained articles on specifically French concerns, such as the German stranglehold on the French economy, abuses of power by the occupying forces and the oppressive effects of cultural collaboration, not forgetting a review of the clandestine press. Impressively closely argued, authoritative and rich in information, it was notable particularly for the strength of its research and its supporting evidence.

Editorials occupied the whole of the front page and were more general in scope. Every issue championed the idea that France was not defeated as long as there were daily acts of resistance and refusal. But in order that the country should be reborn in 'purity and freedom', the Resistance should organize and develop, avoiding disorganized actions and displaying an iron discipline and constant vigilance. These instructions, constantly hammered home, were given in the name of a mysterious 'National Committee of Public Safety' which assumed responsibility for overseeing all efforts, coordinating initiatives and choosing leaders.

In comparison with much of the rest of the clandestine press in the Occupied zone at this period, *Résistance* displayed ambitions that raised it to another level and put it ahead of its time. Where other publications limited themselves on the whole to news and propaganda, Vildé's broadsheet situated itself from the outset within an organization, presenting itself as the expression of a clandestine structure that was already established. Conceived from the start as a vehicle not only for disseminating information but also for recruiting new members and unifying existing ones, *Résistance* delivered a clear message: an organization was already in existence, guided by leaders who were resolute, responsible and fully aware of the order of essential priorities; in order to be ready to act tomorrow, in short, it was essential to organize today.

When it came to Vichy, the paper's position was more complex than is often suggested. Certainly no one involved in its production entertained the slightest illusion regarding Pétain and the nature of his regime. As Laurent Douzou and Denis Peschanski have stressed, they were 'implacable opponents of Vichy . . . who rejected violently and out-of-hand both Pétain and his policies as two sides of the same coin'. Humbert does not bother to conceal her distaste for this 'puppet administration' that 'can't last for ever'. Nor does she spare Pétain himself, this 'small-time Franco'. These were the political views shared unambiguously by the whole editorial committee and every member of the Vildé group; yet they found almost no expression in the pages of the newspaper, which was extremely circumspect on the subject. Not until the third or fourth issues did the leader writer, in each case Vildé, attack Vichy, though not Pétain himself. This restraint was above all tactical, taking account of the fact that most people even in the Occupied zone at this stage still had 'their eyes closed' and retained a deep attachment to the victor of Verdun. The prudent line adopted by *Résistance* therefore aimed at a judicious handling of the majority view and a gradual education of public opinion.

Although careful to avoid any frontal attack on Pétain in their early issues, the editors of *Résistance* prepared for battle against the French head of state very early on. Humbert notes: 'From today we start collecting evidence against the "old man": passages from Poincaré's *Mémoires*, Lloyd George and Clemenceau.' This project was short-lived, owing to the premature demise of the publication in late March 1941. But it was an approach that was to prove highly successful in the Occupied zone, and was used widely in other underground newspapers and tracts.

Throughout its brief existence, *Résistance* reiterated its calls to take action and to refuse to accept defeat, exhorting its readers to 'do something, take actions that will be positive in their effects, that are considered and purposeful'. In the absence of more precise instructions, this message might be interpreted as being modest, purely symbolic and without any real significance for the course of events. We would be seriously mistaken, however, in reducing these early expressions of internal dissent to the level of 'chitchat', 'stupidities' (in Cassou's own description), or inconsequential trifles. In this field we should always be wary of over-hasty judgements, especially those that are reached *a posteriori*. At this period, the medium mattered more than the message: the very existence of a clandestine newspaper mattered more than what was written in it. There are many examples to illustrate the tremendous gulf that frequently exists between the judgements we make today and the reactions of French patriots in 1940 who were longing to do something.

For people disorientated by the collapse of their country and looking for a way to react, the psychological impact of these early publications cannot be overestimated. By their existence, however fragile, the first underground newspapers were tangible proof that not everyone was resigned to defeat, and that there were some whose souls revolted at it. Given the small circulation of these publications and the crushing domination of the German-controlled press, these first ventures into counter-propaganda may seem derisory. None the less, they set an example to follow and offered real encouragement to act. The simple fact of appealing for acts of defiance in the name of a clandestine organization, therefore, in itself elevates these publications far above the level of mere trivia.

Boris Vildé

Among the portraits drawn by Agnès Humbert, one figure is outstanding. Boris Vildé was a Russian immigrant who had been naturalized as a French citizen in 1936 (after arriving in France as André Gide's protégé), a thirty-three-year-old linguist at the Musée de l'Homme specializing in polar civilizations, with a highly promising career as a scientist ahead of him. According to Humbert, he was 'a child of the Revolution' whose 'life has been one long and extraordinary adventure', a verdict echoed by Vildé himself in his prison cell on 18 September 1941: 'If I am honest, I must confess that I am a born adventurer.'

Taken prisoner in the Jura on 17 June 1940, Vildé managed to escape despite being wounded in the leg, covering several hundred kilometres on foot before eventually getting back to Paris. Living at the Musée de l'Homme, where he was reunited with Yvonne Oddon and the recently demobilized Anatole Lewitsky, he flung himself body and soul into fighting the Occupation. Within an astonishingly short time he was leader of the Musée de l'Homme group, before being recognized almost immediately as leader by all the cells attached to his own organization. From Paris lawyers to patriotic Breton fishermen, from the group of railway workers and firemen set up by the medieval historian Robert Fawtier to the airmen of the Héricault group, loyalty to Vildé was unanimous, with not a single dissenting voice. Everyone was at his disposal, no one challenged his authority. Humbert summed up perfectly the general attitude towards him: 'We have put our trust in Vildé, and we must be guided by him.'

Charismatic and exceptional figure though he was, Vildé is by no means presented by Humbert as a 'superman'. On 15 April 1941, the day of her arrest, Humbert catches a glimpse of a much thinner man in an office in the feared Gestapo headquarters at rue des Saussaies, who gives her 'a long look of inexpressible sadness'. Later on, when the 'Musée de l'Homme' trial is about to start, she finds him 'aged' and 'his beautiful golden hair has fallen out in handfuls'. Vildé is no more immune than anyone else to the physical ravages and psychological burden of prolonged imprisonment. While stressing his great qualities, Humbert is careful never to place him on a pedestal.

The young academic from the Musée de l'Homme is not the only major figure in the Resistance with whom Humbert comes into contact. Through her we also encounter Pierre Brossolette and Honoré d'Estienne d'Orves (Jean-Pierre). The great merit of her narrative is that it shows these evocative figures as ordinary members of the Resistance, before their martyrdom elevated them to the mythical, inaccessible status of iconic figures. At the time when Humbert was writing they had not yet been raised to the pantheon of Resistance heroes, suspended in the brilliance of their posthumous glory. We therefore see them in a different light, in their day-to-day struggle against the Occupation, before the thunderbolt struck.

Resistance: a woman's vantage point

Written as it is by a woman, *Résistance* sheds a uniquely revealing light on the role of women in these early days of the Resistance, and in the clandestine struggle in general. This is not to imply that women are usually absent from or invisible in accounts of the period: in their writings, veterans of the Resistance, historians and journalists all pay ritual tribute to the role of women in the Resistance. All are unanimous in saluting their devotion, their clandestine work without which nothing else would have been possible, their sacrifice and in many cases their martyrdom. But once the obvious has been stated in the accepted fashion, the curtain is brought down and women are all too often relegated to a position of secondary importance. A refreshing departure from the norm in its point of view, Agnès Humbert's account gives salutary pause for thought.

Taken at her own word, she consistently underestimates her contribution. She reduces her role at the heart of the Musée de l'Homme network to 'my humble duties: typist, secretary, go-between and runner'. And when it comes to the first working meetings of the newspaper's editorial committee, her account of the distribution of labour is not, we feel, untinged by irony: 'Simone Martin-Chauffier brought us a tray of tea . . . The men wrote and talked, while I typed up their articles.' She strikes a similarly self-deprecating note in March 1941, when her friends urge her to make her escape to the southern zone: 'Besides, why would anyone be interested in me? I've done so little and been so careful.' Given what we know of her commitment, her activism and her key role at the centre of an organization in whose growth and spread she had played a major part, her reaction is hard to credit. The gulf between the image that she presents of her own role and what we know to be the reality is constant. Humbert seems to be incapable of measuring the true value of her contribution, or of viewing herself as anything other than a minor player. This self-deprecating approach betrays the deeply ingrained attitudes towards the place of women in a society dominated by men. Even a woman as highly educated, independent and liberated as Agnès Humbert could not escape these deep-seated social stereotypes. Her account contains numerous references to divisions of labour dictated by gender, summed up perhaps by her description of herself (a description accepted by some at face value) as the group's 'typist'.

Humbert's position as a prominent figure constantly at the forefront of events is not exceptional, moreover. In the remarkable story of the Musée de l'Homme network, she was far from being a lone woman amid a cohort of men. From Yvonne Oddon, veritable alter ego of Vildé and Lewitsky, to Germaine Tillion, working alongside Paul Hauet and responsible for her own 'sector'; from Sylvette Leleu, garage owner in Béthune, to Sister Hélène Studler in Nancy, both of whom established highly effective escape routes; from the young secretary Jacqueline Bordelet and the writer Simone Martin-Chauffier to the coolly aristocratic Countess Elisabeth de La Bourdonnaye, women were an outstanding presence throughout the movement. Fulfilling a wealth of different roles, responsible at the highest levels, setting up and often running their own groups, these women played an active part at every level and in every field. This widespread contribution by women forms another of the unique features of the Musée de l'Homme group, deserving of the highest recognition while remaining largely inexplicable. Reduced to suggesting hypotheses, we naturally turn to the indomitable personality and doughty temperament of Agnès Humbert and her female companions, characteristics that are certainly beyond dispute, but that nevertheless do not wholly account for the scale of their contribution.

Although drawn from different social backgrounds, all these women worked, and nearly all of them – at a time when less than half of all French women went to work – were financially independent. They tended to be cultured and well educated, and a number of them had been actively engaged in left-wing politics before the war. Faced with the crucial decisions of 1940, these strong, principled women showed no hesitation. Their disproportionately high numbers – in key positions, moreover – at the core of the trail-blazing Musée de l'Homme group, may be related also to another factor, more conjectural perhaps, but one that should not be overlooked. In the summer of 1940, some one and a half million French soldiers were being held as prisoners of war, not counting those awaiting demobilization. Men were therefore largely absent at the moment when the first initiatives took shape. And in their absence, women provisionally stepped into the void and took matters in hand, only to step aside discreetly as men gradually returned to fill positions of responsibility and the Resistance became more structured. Yvonne Oddon, for instance, did not wait for Vildé and Lewitsky to return to Paris during the month of July before launching into action and establishing initial contacts with the American embassy and with Lucie Boutillier du Rétail, who from her home in the sixteenth arrondissement was already helping prisoners of war to escape. Thus the debacle of defeat brought about a partial and temporary redistribution of roles, before deeply rooted social conventions gained the upper hand once more.

In these first months of the Occupation, finally, when as Claire Andrieu has pointed out, 'people's psychological make-up was of more importance than their social background', patriotism was without question the overwhelming force driving these early dissidents. This love of France, a love of an elemental strength that we struggle to understand today, was the crucial and deciding factor; this was the profound commitment cited as their motivation and justification – at the end of their trial and in front of the members of the German military tribunal – by Sylvette Leleu, Yvonne Oddon and Agnès Humbert. For Agnès Humbert, patriotism was a family tradition and honour; after the verdict is pronounced she declares: 'Despite my lies, I believe I have conducted myself with honour as the mother and daughter of officers.'

Adopting a style in direct opposition to both the gossipy garrulousness and the lofty heroic lyricism (or lyrical heroism) so often adopted for memoirs in this field, Agnès Humbert remains unfailingly modest and down to earth throughout her text. With graphic portraits and pithy dialogue, forensic focus and telling detail, she weaves a narrative of such force that it holds the reader spellbound from beginning to end. And there is one more outstanding feature that sets her text apart: the humour – irony or sarcasm, ridicule or mockery – that is spun into its very texture, cultivated in all circumstances and used as a weapon of subversion. However real the threat, however deep the despondency, her sense of humour rarely fails her.

This adamant refusal to strike heroic poses, this ability to see the funny side of everything, this irony and self-mockery that swiftly quash any tendencies towards taking oneself seriously and that brook no hint of self-pity: none of this, remarkably, is unique to Humbert. A similarly 'debunking' sense of humour and the same constant refusal to draw attention to her own gruelling experiences and extraordinary achievements are also characteristic of Germaine Tillion.

In the aftermath of the war, these women became the indispensable vectors and guardians of memory: returning from their ordeals in greater numbers than men, they bore witness, set up associations for the survivors of deportation and concentration camps, and oversaw the administrative 'winding up' of the files on the Musée de l'Homme network. They mobilized to keep alive the memory of all those who did not return, and fought against the dangers of forgetting. But when it came to the public accolades accorded to war veterans, they were conspicious by their absence. Shunning the glare of publicity from a natural sense of discretion, avoiding public platforms and decorations, they turned the page and in many cases quietly slipped back into their former lives.

Fraternity

Although essentially an individual commitment driven by personal choice, active resistance was also by its nature a collective engagement. This elision between the individual and the collective is a constant presence in Agnès Humbert's text. Her own modesty goes hand in hand with a palpable admiration for her companions, and the portraits she draws of them are imbued with a warm generosity of spirit. Far more than mere friends, her fellow members of the Musée de l'Homme group are her adoptive family, freely chosen by her and united by deep bonds of fraternity.

This fraternal solidarity, these bonds that were literally 'unto death', brought with them a joy in being together and fighting side by side, the potency of which fills the pages of Humbert's journal. In the context of these perilous times that were to destroy so many of these rare spirits, joy may seem a strangely inappropriate term. Yet many who were there have drawn particular attention to this aspect of the struggle. In 1953 a nostalgic Jean Cassou recalled: 'For me there is one word for this time in my life: happiness.'

Humbert evokes not only the dangers but also the sheer fun of those early days, when these early pioneers laid the foundations of the Resistance movement in a spirit of joy, elation and intense excitement. She communicates their infectious enthusiasm and exhilaration, anticipating 'like excited children' the prospect of flyposting the walls of Paris with her home-made stickers. Describing the inaugural meeting of the editorial committee of *Résistance*, she notes how Cassou, Abraham and Aveline are 'quite emotional, though it was all undercut with typically Parisian backchat and leg-pulling'. A little later on, in late January 1941, she describes a meal they have arranged for Georges Friedmann, a moment of conviviality and pure lightheartedness when 'for three hours we left all our cares behind and just had fun'. Their delight in each other's company, in being together in the heat of the action, is manifested in these shared jokes and a childish playfulness.

Unexpectedly, laughter is never far away, constantly erupting on the page – no matter what the circumstances – and illuminating Humbert's narrative. Even in the dark days of March 1941, when arrests were multiplying and whole sections of the organization collapsing about their ears, she and her friends 'still managed to find something to laugh about'. Far more than a mere nervous reaction to defuse the pent-up tension, this laughter was an expression of the fundamental optimism that fired the pioneers of the Resistance. At a time when Germany was victorious on all fronts and apparently invincible, and when its dominion was more acutely felt with each passing day, they never lost their hope that liberation was not far away. This belief in the future, this unshakable, heartfelt faith was an absolutely essential weapon in their arsenal, without which nothing was possible. In March 1941, for instance, Humbert writes: 'It is so inspiring to know that there are thousands and thousands of Parisians, anonymous and unknown, working like us – often better than us – to organize a resistance movement that soon will become a liberation struggle.' One of the merits of her text is that it reveals the light of this hope – fragile, frequently obscured but stubbornly tenacious – that shone out in the dark night of the Occupation, restoring flashes of colour to the bleak grey monochrome that tends otherwise to dominate our image of the Resistance.

Repression

Agnès Humbert paints a lively picture of the development of this embryonic Resistance. All too soon, however, it was to come up against a merciless process of repression: in some senses this was the price it paid for its meteoric growth and dazzling success. Soon her diary entries are punctuated by a long litany of arrests and imprisonment, culminating in April 1941 with her own. German repression was swift in coming, efficient and ruthless.

On 8 January 1942, the nineteen accused in the 'Vildé affair' (and not the eighteen counted by Agnès Humbert on that day) were put on trial by a military tribunal in the prison at Fresnes. The Germans were scrupulous in doing everything by the book. The extremely detailed cross-examinations were to last nearly a year. The presiding judge was Captain Ernst Roskothen, a lawyer in civilian life. The accused were represented by French

lawyers chosen by themselves. But despite all this it soon
became clear that this was a show trial, with the verdicts never
in doubt. The prosecutor, 'unctuous, obsequious, oily and
stupid', made no secret of his determination to secure the
maximum sentences. In the face of the growing number of
attacks on the occupying forces, the German authorities took
advantage of this opportunity, one of the first major Resistance
trials, to make a terrifying example of the accused. The prisoners
were charged with aiding and abetting the enemy by spreading
anti-German propaganda, and with espionage, though in most
cases this charge was later dropped. Humbert is at pains, nevertheless, to pay repeated tributes to the correct attitude and the
humanity of Roskothen, a point on which all those present
were unanimous. She notes the 'intelligent and distinguished
air' of this 'honest man' who 'respects and admires the men whom
he is about to condemn to death' and 'delivers an astounding
eulogy' in their praise. Roskothen's courtesy, impartiality and
often kindness were confirmed by many other members of the
Resistance whose path crossed his during the course of the
war. On the liberation of Paris in August 1944, Roskothen
was arrested and interned. No fewer than twenty-six members
of the Resistance petitioned for his release, including Agnès
Humbert. She also sent him several cordial letters, and on the
publication of *Notre Guerre* in 1946 sent him a copy, inscribed
'Au Président Roskothen qui m'a envoyée au bagne . . . Sans rancune'
(To Judge Roskothen who condemned me to forced labour . . .
Without rancour).

Be that as it may, the harshness of the sentences handed
down was extreme: ten of the accused were sentenced to death
(three women, whose sentences were commuted to deportation
with 'suspended' death sentences, and seven men, who were
executed by firing squad at Mont Valérien), three were given
prison sentences and six were acquitted or discharged.
Humbert's sentence was five years' imprisonment, to be served

in Germany. The severity of the penalties imposed was a cruel reminder of the cost of direct opposition to the occupying forces, even if only in the form of propaganda in the first months of the Occupation. Even at that early stage, those who resisted in the Occupied zone were potentially laying down their lives.

The description of the trial is especially poignant, as Humbert relates the final words and gestures of those who are about to die. In the dramatic moments before and after the verdict, on which Roskothen's own memoirs (see pp. 316–21) throw an equally startling light, the courtroom was filled with an extraordinary atmosphere that she describes with great delicacy. Though written after the event, her account relies on her memories and also on notes that she managed to scribble on an edition of Descartes that afterwards went everywhere with her (and that is now in the possession of her grandson, Antoine Sabbagh). 'We are in a state of euphoria, and everything seems unreal . . . It is hard to credit the state of mind we are all in.' Hard to credit indeed, as the accused, some with their lives at stake, still contrived, in full view of the courtroom and of their dumbfounded prosecutors, to 'risk a few whispered jokes about this "game of hangman"'. Right up to the very end, as though a final manifestation of freedom and defiance, laughter holds its own. On 12 February, by which time the defendants' position was clearly without hope, Agnès Humbert noted on her Descartes: 'We were all laughing as we left, as though after a lecture, or better still an exam.'

The striking picture Humbert paints is of men and women finding the resources within themselves to transcend their circumstances and attain a breathtaking degree of serenity. The prison diaries kept by Boris Vildé and Pierre Walter, as well as numerous surviving letters written by others condemned to death, bear eloquent testimony to a painful process of reflection that led to a sense of detachment from life, allied with an

acceptance of and familiarity with death. The admirably high
morale maintained by the accused also manifested itself in their
constant care to avoid compromising anyone else and their
determination to refute the charges. With his unflagging
attempts to exculpate the others and his insistence to the end
on his status as leader, Vildé set an incomparable example in
this respect. Even the Germans could not fail to be impressed
by this dignity and acceptance in the face of death, a noble
bearing commonly found among Resistance members. At the
heart of Humbert's narrative, rubbing shoulders with the laughter and the *joie de vivre*, the shadow of death and of those who
have died is a constant presence. Dedicated to 'the memory of
my Comrades . . . executed by firing squad at Mont Valérien
on 23 February 1942 . . . [to] Pierre Brossolette . . . [and to]
Emile Müller', the pages of Agnès Humbert's diary are filled
with all the pathos of a Greek tragedy, with their ranks of
men and woman struck down in their prime, destroyed by an
implacable destiny. Her book is above all else a tribute to
those who died. It was for them, with them constantly in her
thoughts and in the determination that they should not be
forgotten, that she bore witness so swiftly after the events.

Prison

Inserted between Humbert's description of her active resistance
and her account of the trial is a detailed chronicle of prison life
in France. Although the reader has the impression that the diary
continues, it is at this point that we leave it behind. For a
total of eleven and a half months, Humbert is incarcerated in
the prisons of Cherche-Midi, La Santé and Fresnes. This long
interlude, occupying a good quarter of the book as a whole,
might appear by its subject matter to be more conventional
than what has gone before, conforming to the all-too-common
experience of imprisonment among Resistance members in

general, and the early trail-blazers in particular. Virtually every memoir of the Resistance published after the war featured an episode of prison life.

Being deprived of their liberty came as a shock of great violence for which nothing could prepare them. On 15 April 1941, Agnès Humbert was brutally thrust into a different world that had all the appearance of a funeral vault. Although on the day after her arrival she confesses that 'prison life is a complete mystery to me', she rapidly assimilates the timetable and noises, rituals and secret codes that are so particular to this unfamiliar universe. In solitary confinement and subjected to a 'regime of extreme harshness' for several months, she is plunged abruptly into a world devoid of any human company or distractions of any kind, where she suffers perpetual hunger; stifling heat in summer, when the vermin proliferate and the slop bucket fills the air with its evil stench; glacial cold in winter that freezes the damp oozing from the walls; and the howling and wailing of women tormented beyond all endurance. To keep her sanity, Humbert escapes into a dream world and invents games that would seem ridiculous to 'people on the outside' who 'live in a different world': the ball she makes out of the paper wrapped round a lemon is 'an inexhaustible source of pleasure', and 'organizing slug races is a great entertainment'.

But most importantly, she quickly breaks down the frozen barrier of loneliness to become part of the 'clan' of Resistance prisoners. It is here, in her descriptions that make what was virtually a parallel society accessible and tangible to those who have never experienced it, that Humbert demonstrates once more her striking originality. Using the quasi-documentary style that is her signature, she shows how active resistance was not quashed by arrest and imprisonment. On the contrary, she portrays prison as a place where, far from dwindling away, transgression and rule-breaking form an essential part of daily life and even find new forms, such as singing and shouting slogans. By means of a thousand and one stratagems, communication between prisoners – via the gaps under cell doors or cunningly opened fanlights, or through the walls when the guards' backs are turned – is constant and widespread, from cell to cell and floor to floor. News of the progress of the war penetrates the prison walls, as do orders issued by de Gaulle from the BBC radio studios in London. When, on 11 May 1941, it is announced that 'General de Gaulle has called for an hour's silence from three o'clock', 'a thoughtful, total silence' falls throughout the prison, broken after an hour by a thunderous rendition of the 'Marseillaise', 'that seems to swell, becoming a tangible, palpable presence' to the point where 'the walls will burst apart and the roof will fly off'.

In this closed world, totally apart, camaraderie and solidarity among the prisoners assume an importance of life-saving proportions. Prison is also a time and place that fosters friendships of an exceptional intensity, generally between prisoners who have never so much as glimpsed each other's faces. In this regard, the bond that develops during the Cherche-Midi days and nights between Agnès Humbert and Honoré d'Estienne d'Orves deserves a particular mention. A prisoner before Agnès, awaiting trial and cherishing no illusions as to the fate that awaits him, 'Jean-Pierre', as he is universally known, is the guiding spirit of prison life.

As with Boris Vildé and Pierre Brossolette, the picture Humbert paints of 'Jean-Pierre' is far removed from the monumental figure of d'Estienne d'Orves the hero that has become more familiar to us. In place of the devout, austere crusader, we discover a sunny, cheerful figure, ever attentive to others, always with a sympathetic ear, a reassuring older brother who keeps up everyone's morale and dispenses advice and encouragement with unfailing generosity. Without ever setting eyes on each other, he and Humbert, who for a brief period occupy neighbouring cells and are able to talk to their hearts' content, develop a relationship of astonishing closeness. Between these two people whose backgrounds, beliefs and personalities were so utterly different there grows up a profound friendship. Its ability to foster relationships such as this, which would have been highly improbable under any other circumstances, is another remarkable feature of the singular phenomenon of the Resistance. Prison, synonymous with isolation and withdrawal from society, in Agnès Humbert's narrative is transformed into a place of communion and communication.

Deportation

The third and last part of the book, tracing Agnès Humbert's experiences as a slave worker in Nazi Germany, is by far the longest. In March 1942 she was deported to the fortress of Anrath, near Düsseldorf, to start serving her sentence of five years' imprisonment. For three interminable years as a political prisoner, from April 1942 to April 1945, she lived the gruelling life of a slave labourer in the factories of the Third Reich. Taking into account the time she had already spent in French prisons, she was to spend virtually four years in prison – a high price to pay for an active Resistance career lasting just ten months.

In her detailed descriptions of the calvary she endures, she draws attention to the little-known sufferings of deportees forced to work as slave labourers in Germany. For seventeen months, from April 1942 to August 1943, she experiences the hell of the Phrix rayon factory at Krefeld, where kommandos of women prisoners from Anrath are sent to work. Already weakened by her long incarceration in France, she suffers terribly and perpetually from hunger. Nicknamed 'Gandhi' by her fellow prisoners, by May 1943 she weighs a mere forty-nine kilos, as opposed to her normal sixty-five. Living in an exclusively female world, she is forced into close proximity for the first time with common criminals. The promiscuity of this life is at first almost unbearable for her, and she has harsh words for these amoral creatures, with their 'wretched faces, vicious and primitive', a collection of 'gallows birds': thieves, syphilitic prostitutes and murderesses.

But worst of all, of course, is the forced labour that the prisoners have to endure, which is nothing other than a modern form of slavery. Treated as a workforce to be exploited at will, the prisoners are subjected to a regime of close surveillance by guards and overseers who include among their ranks sadists and torturers. The most trivial misdemeanour is greeted with a rain of blows and an array of other punishments. The working day is endless and the pace infernal for the undernourished women. For eight hours solid they are forced to stand at their machines, repeating the same mechanical gestures, not allowed to stop or even to drink, while the artificial silk dust in the air parches their throats. Accidents are a daily event. Dressed in rags and without the slightest protection, the prisoners have to handle acid and viscose that cause terrible burns, especially to the hands and eyes. The unhealed wounds become infected and ooze pus. After six months of this treatment, Agnès Humbert's hands are 'well and truly pulverized'.

On two occasions only does her will-power falter. In January 1943, physically at the end of her tether, with a gaping wound on her foot and virtually blinded by the acid vapours, she is on the brink of giving up: 'Shamefully, my thoughts turn with a twinge of envy to my comrades now laid to eternal rest in the cemetery at Ivry.' In the weeks that follow her pain is unbearable: 'I howl like a dog at the moon . . . back at the house I collapse into my bunk, where I drift in and out of consciousness for five days and nights.' On another occasion, probably in April 1943 (in the endless tunnel of suffering at Krefeld, she uncharacteristically loses her sense of time), she collapses and confesses, 'Yes, I bang my head against the wall', before finding a miracle cure for the pain of the wounds on her hands: her own urine.

In order to survive this hell, to overcome her exhaustion, ill-treatment and illness, Agnès Humbert demonstrates a character of steel and courage equal to any ordeal. Two other factors also help her to endure. The first is the decisive power – once again – of friendship. Isolated in the midst of common convicts, Humbert loses no time in seeking out the rare political prisoners she can find in her early days in Germany, saying immediately to Kate, a young Belgian woman whom she meets at Anrath on 10 April 1942, 'Let's stick together, you and I, whatever happens.' With Kate, Henriette, Denise and others, Humbert rediscovers the virtues of being a member of a 'clan' and the mutual support she has experienced before. Alongside this fraternity, another factor that gives her a reason to endure and to keep hoping is her continuing resistance. Throughout her life as a deportee, resistance by whatever means possible remains a relentless pursuit, now taking on the new form of sabotage. Immediately upon her arrival at Krefeld, she sets about studying 'the theory and practice of sabotage', before passing on to practical applications and industriously rendering quantities of reels of rayon filament unusable. This obstinate refusal to contribute in any way to the German war effort was to remain an article of faith until the very end: at Hövelhof in Westphalia, where she has to make wooden crates for ten hours a day, she takes care to shear off the shafts of the nails she uses, so that the crates will 'rapidly disintegrate'.

The destruction of the Phrix factory, symbol of her interminable ordeal, by Allied bombs on the night of 22 August 1943, comes as a cause of jubilation and immense relief. From now on the conditions of her life improve considerably. After several moves and periods in a succession of different factories in Westphalia (first in Hövelhof and then in Schwelm) where the living and working conditions are infinitely better than at Krefeld, she finishes up in March 1945 at Wanfried in the region of Hesse. On 3 April 1945, when the Americans finally surround the town and liberation has come at last, her first thoughts are for her comrades at the Musée de l'Homme: 'My thoughts turn to Vildé, Lewitsky, Walter and the others. This is what they died for, so that Nazism should perish. And now, before my very eyes, the beast is slowly dying . . .'

No sooner has the advance guard of the US Third Army arrived in Wanfried than Agnès Humbert embarks on important work with them. With her fluent German and English, her knowledge of the inner workings of the Nazi system of imprisonment, her natural authority and her irrepressible energy, she rapidly makes herself indispensable to them. Concentrating their own efforts on military matters, they put her in charge of the town administration, local prison camps and the provision of shelter, food and first aid to refugees. From 15 April 1945, she sets about collecting political intelligence and is active in setting up a local denazification programme. The consummate ease with which, after four years of imprisonment and forced labour, she manages to shed her identity as a political prisoner and become a 'Nazi hunter' is truly astounding. It is there, in Germany, that – after a struggle she has continued unabated since June 1940 – Agnès Humbert's war ends.

A *vector of memory*

Many concerns are raised nowadays, and not without reason, regarding the ways and means by which the history of the Resistance can be passed on to future generations. This is a matter of no small significance. What lies at stake is the preservation of a part of history and the safeguarding of its memory, lest it should fade or even vanish altogether.

The reasons for this concern are not hard to find.

Over sixty years on, memories of the Resistance – fragile, scattered, vulnerable, sometimes liable to attack – appear at risk, particularly at a point when the rare surviving witnesses are gradually disappearing, overtaken by the inexorable march of time.

In this struggle against 'the shortening of memory that is death' (in Jean Cassou's phrase), it is essential that we revisit original documents, and reread with care the texts with which we think we are familiar. With its warm sympathies and cool intelligence, its detailed descriptions and its evocative sense of atmosphere, Agnès Humbert's narrative of her experiences is one of these essential texts. Bringing her five-year struggle against the Reich alive in terms that make it both real and familiar, it is an antidote to oblivion. The fact that this important first-hand account is now available to a wider readership in translation is a matter of celebration for all those who strive to ensure that this remarkable piece of history should not be forgotten. *Résistance* offers us privileged insights into the workings of the Resistance and opens up previously unknown worlds. With her narrative, Agnès Humbert has created an invaluable tool for perpetuating knowledge and understanding. And she has fulfilled the last wish of Boris Vildé, expressed in his letter to his wife Irène, written just hours before he and his six comrades in the Musée de l'Homme group were executed by firing squad: 'Our memory must not become the pretext for any hatred towards Germany. My struggle was for France, not against the Germans. They are doing their duty as we have done ours. All that matters is that our memory should live on when the war is over. And whatever may happen, our comrades from the Musée de l'Homme will not forget us.'

After her return to Paris in June 1945, described by her son Pierre Sabbagh (see p. 322–3), Agnès Humbert refused to return to her old post at the Musée des Arts et Traditions Populaires.

Instead, she joined Jean Cassou at the new Musée National d'Art Moderne, set up in 1947 to replace the Musée du Luxembourg. Continuing her involvement in politics, she became a founder member and president of her local group of the broadly left-wing 'Combattants de la Liberté' (Fighters for Freedom), and accepted an invitation to become the president of the women's organization 'Les Amies de la Paix' (Friends of Peace). In 1949 she was awarded the Croix de Guerre. That same year she organized an exhibition of French art in Vienna, and afterwards travelled in Yugoslavia, publishing her impressions and her admiration for Tito – which earned her expulsion from 'Les Amies de la Paix' and denunciation in the Communist daily *l'Humanité* – in 1950.

Her health weakened by her wartime experiences, she spent her final years living in the village of Valmondois with her son Pierre, by then a prominent figure in French television. She continued to write on art until her death; in 1963 she contributed the introduction to the catalogue of an exhibition of works by Maurice Denis at the Musée Toulouse-Lautrec in Albi. The exhibition, which included a painting entitled *Portrait de Pierre Sabbagh et de sa mère, 1919*, was still running when she died, on 19 September 1963. She is buried in the cemetery at Valmondois.

*

This is an edited version of Julien Blanc's introduction to Notre Guerre *by Agnès Humbert (Editions Tallandier, 2004). Translated by Barbara Mellor.*

Appendix: Documents on the Resistance

Germaine Tillion on the birth of the Resistance
(*from* Sisters in Resistance)
Indignation can move mountains . . .

France in 1940 was unbelievable. There were no men left. It was women who started the Resistance. Women didn't have the vote, they didn't have bank accounts, they didn't have jobs. Yet we women were capable of resisting . . .

Honoré d'Estienne d'Orves (in the Prison du Cherche-Midi)
I had no idea that there were so many women in prison in France for their patriotic actions. It's quite magnificent.

Editorial of the first issue of Résistance, *15 December 1940*
OFFICIAL BULLETIN OF THE NATIONAL COMMITTEE OF PUBLIC SAFETY
Resist! In our anguish at the disastrous fate that has befallen our nation, this is our heartfelt cry. This is the cry of every one of you who is not prepared to accept this catastrophe, of every one of you who wants to do their duty.

But amid your feelings of isolation and helplessness, amid the current turmoil of ideas, opinions and approaches, you wonder where your duty lies. First and foremost, to resist is to keep heart and head. But above all it is to do something, to take actions that will be positive in their effects, that are considered and purposeful. Many people have tried, but have been discouraged by their apparent impotence. Others have formed groups, but often these groups have also felt isolated and powerless.

Patiently, doggedly, we have sought these groups out and brought them together. Dedicated and determined, they are already many in number (more than an army in Paris alone), and they have understood the importance of organization, of working out a modus operandi, of adopting discipline and leaders.

The modus operandi? Get together at home with people you know. Choose your leaders. Your leaders will find men of experience who will guide their activities, and who will report back to us at different levels. In order to coordinate your endeavours with those of unoccupied France and all who are fighting alongside our Allies, this Committee will take command. Your immediate task is to organize yourselves, so that when you receive the order you will be ready to resume the struggle. Recruit men of determination, choose them with care, and surround them with the best and finest. Give heart and resolve to those beset by doubt and those who no longer dare to hope. Track down and watch those who have disowned their country and who betray her. Meet up every day to pass on information and observations that may be useful to your leaders. Be ruled by iron discipline, constant vigilance and absolute discretion. Beware of those who are reckless or feckless, loose-tongued or treacherous. Be neither boastful nor too trusting. Make every effort to supply your own needs. We are working to muster the means of action that we will later pass on to you.

In becoming your leaders we have sworn to sacrifice all – pitilessly and relentlessly – to this mission.

Unknown to each other yesterday, strangers to the political infighting of assemblies and governments, independent French men and women above all, chosen for the action to which we are sworn, we are united in a single ambition, a single passion, a single desire: to bring about the rebirth of a pure and free France.

Gilberte Brossolette on Agnès Humbert, from Il s'appelait Pierre Brossolette

Agnès Humbert was to become one of the very first French deportees. Her time [in imprisonment] was to be one of the lengthiest in the history of the camps. She managed to survive, sustained by her remarkable strength of spirit, despite spending so much time in a factory where chemicals bit into her hands more deeply with each passing day . . .

We got to know her in November or December 1940, Pierre and I, with all her exasperatingly lunatic schemes, her sublime foolishness and her recklessness that was as formidable as it was worthy of admiration and respect . . .

Her hostility towards the occupying forces was impulsive, impetuous, pugnacious. And militant. No banknote ever passed through her hands without being smothered with anti-German slogans. She would write and print tracts, then stuff handfuls of them down her stocking tops. Afterwards, in shops and queues, she would whip up her skirts, discreetly fish out her incendiary leaflets and distribute them all around with an infectious grin.

She was working with feverish intensity for what was later to be known as the 'Musée de l'Homme' network, then better known as the 'Français Libres de France' [Free French in France], by analogy with the Free French in London.

The network had come into being spontaneously in September 1940. It is with justice, therefore, that it is described as a pioneering group. For so many other groups that were later to come into being, to spread and grow, it showed the way. It was crushed by a series of arrests.

It had all started with meetings between Jean Cassou, Claude Aveline, Marcel Abraham and a few others who wanted to fight, with words and pamphlets, against the 'Pétain myth' and its damaging effects on public opinion. Very soon they were joined by a tall blond young man. This was Boris Vildé, a member of the scientific staff at the Musée de l'Homme. He advocated the creation of a modest bulletin.

They set to work with other patriots: Lewitsky, Colette and Jean Duval, Christiane Desroches, Jean Aubier, Maître Jubineau, Yvonne Oddon, Jacqueline Bordelet. And, of course, the omnipresent Agnès Humbert, nicknamed – with infinite affection and admiration – the 'runner' . . .

Another account by Agnès Humbert of the rue Monsieur-le-Prince episode, from Pierre Brossolette: Héro de la Résistance *by René Ozouf (February 1946, three months before the publication of* Notre Guerre*)*

For six hours I am 'grilled' at rue des Saussaies . . . The Gestapo know about our meetings at Jean Duval's house, at 30 rue Monsieur-le-Prince. One of our comrades who had been arrested must have admitted it under torture . . . I deny it. The chief interrogator gives orders for me to be driven with the comrade who has talked to the house of our friends (which I naturally swear not to know). Then I realize that it is Tuesday, and it is six o'clock: the day and time of our meeting at the Duvals'. All our friends will be there. I make the comrade who accompanies me understand that I have denied everything. The car stops at the corner of rue de Vaugirard and rue Monsieur-le-Prince. The driver watches me in his rear-view mirror; one Gestapo man keeps his eyes on me, while the other accompanies my comrade outside the Duvals' house. I assume an air of detached indifference . . . I think about Brossolette, who is upstairs and who greets every ring of the doorbell with: 'Watch out! It's the Hun!' This time he'll say it again, but it won't be so funny . . .

I'll never know what happened. Probably my comrade denied what he had said, went back on his statement . . . This was only 1941, and the Gestapo still hesitated to search an entire house, especially as no one knew the name of the Duvals . . . and clearly they had no idea what floor the apartment was on. Moreover, the concierge at this time was never there in the afternoon . . . After a few minutes the Gestapo man came back with my comrade, and we left for Cherche-Midi. I learned afterwards that our friends, all of them, were waiting for me at the Duvals' . . .

Gilberte Brossolette's account of the same episode, from
Il s'appelait Pierre Brossolette

During those tragic days, Pierre [Brossolette] narrowly escaped falling into the clutches of the Gestapo. He never knew. I myself knew nothing about the episode until after the war, when Agnès Humbert returned from deportation.

Among the members of the group arrested with her was a boy of sixteen [*sic*] known by everyone as the 'Kid'. He put up a brave resistance to his interrogators, but the Gestapo worked out from a note in his notebook that other 'conspirators' held frequent Tuesday meetings in a block of apartments on rue Monsieur-le-Prince. Fortunately, they never found out the number, of the apartment of Colette and Jean Duval.

Three Gestapo officers took Agnès and the Kid to keep watch with them on rue Monsieur-le-Prince in an unmarked French car. They were counting on a more concentrated expression, a barely suppressed reflex, or a revealing start of recognition at the approach of their friends and accomplices.

Agnès understood what the manoeuvre was about, and fixed the Kid with a steady stare. During the whole two hours of their dreadful ordeal she kept her eyes on his, to make him understand that he must not move a muscle, to ensure that he too gave no reaction.

Then one by one Simone Martin-Chauffier, Pierre Brossolette and a few others, including Léo Hamon, who was in the occupied zone to set up a liaison with the southern zone, walked past twice, once in each direction. Not to mention the Duvals, who appeared on the doorstep to show them into their apartment.

At that moment the poor child could have saved his life with the mere blink of an eye. But, with the support of his ally and exacting guide, he held out. On 23 February 1942, surrounded by his six older comrades – the young academics of the Musée de l'Homme – he would climb the path up Mont Valérien to the clearing where executions were carried out. And for that last, never-finished chorus of 'La Marseillaise' his voice would be as firm as theirs.

Judge Ernst Roskothen's pre-trial interviews at Fresnes, December 1941

> *Roskothen's account is written in the third person, with all names changed. Roskothen is 'Amels', Gottlob is 'Looh', Vildé is 'Kustos' and Agnès Humbert is referred to throughout as the 'museum expert'.*

Before presiding over the major trial of Gaullists at the prison of Fresnes in Paris in 1942, Amels has to spend many weeks familiarizing himself with the numerous files . . . Early one morning he is driven out to the prison, in order to acquaint himself personally with the prisoners accused of espionage and giving assistance to the enemy . . . It is an inhospitable December day, wet, cold and gloomy, with mist lying in the valleys to the south of the city. Amels is relieved when his journey in the rattling military vehicle ends at the huge complex of prison buildings . . .

> *Roskothen has to pass through a large vaulted hall filled with a rabble of disreputable-looking German servicemen, arrested the night before for brawling, etc. The sight fills him with dismay.*

It takes the whole morning to meet the main protagonists individually . . . Amels enquires about all the prisoners' state of health, which often gives cause for concern. This is especially true of the women. Dishevelled and unmade-up, they look ten years older than their true age, with pale, lined faces, unkempt hair and shuffling gait. Rarely do they complain, however, or express any personal wishes. Amels knows he must work quickly to establish contact, especially as he has no interpreter . . . This trial is going to be complex, largely because of the personalities of the chief defendants.

First comes Kustos, leader of the first, larger group and custodian of an esteemed Paris museum of ethnology: a Russian émigré, long-naturalized French, blond and in his prime, with a young French wife. The beard that he has grown in prison makes him look like the young Edouard Manet. A distinguished scholar, he appears very relaxed despite his difficult position. He has spent his time in prison working on his Sanskrit and Japanese, and this has helped to distract him. Another prisoner from the same museum is also there: an impressive dark-blonde Frenchwoman, spirited and unbroken, a writer and the mother of a naval officer. Then comes a Parisian lawyer about the same age as Kustos, Jewish with a German-sounding name. It goes without saying that Amels treats him and the others with equal courtesy. The lawyer declares openly that he has worked against Hitler because he is 'a Frenchman, a Jew and a socialist'. The youngest in this group is an eighteen-year-old accused of acting as a courier in the spy ring. A French officer's widow who is from the same northern French homeland tells Amels that she undertook her spying activities in order to avenge the death of her airman husband. Her fellow accused from the Lille area is a headteacher who was severely wounded in the Great War and can move only with the aid of a surgical corset . . .

If the accusations are confirmed, all these people – clearly without exception selfless idealists and patriots – will be fighting for their lives. Many of them will die. Amels reflects on this as he leaves, walking down endless corridors all reeking of that unmistakable prison stench. The large vaulted hall is now empty and has been swept spotlessly clean. The ghosts of the night have vanished.

Extracts from Ernst Roskothen's account of the Musée de l'Homme trial

Paris now has its major trial of Gaullist groups, on trial for disseminating information and aiding and abetting the enemy. Inside the makeshift wooden shack in the courtyard at the prison of Fresnes, where the trial is to be held in early January 1942, the walls received a much-needed coat of green paint a few days ago. A brand new cast-iron stove is burning at full strength already, but it cannot heat this large bare room. The heat escapes through the leaky roof, and the bitterly cold outside air forces its way in. The exceptionally hard frost is of almost unprecedented severity.

Inside, a long Reich war-flag with a swastika covers one end wall, reaching down to the cracked wooden floor. In front of it is a long plain wooden table for the judge, prosecutor and official recorders, with files piled up on it. Behind the interpreter's chair is a large map of France to clarify the various espionage missions. The eighteen accused will be seated on three rows of chairs.

On the opening day of the trial, 8 January 1942, the members of the court are brought in early by military bus from Concorde to Fresnes, rubbing their hands against the cold as they stride through the prison gates. In the hut in the courtyard the iron stove is glowing but does not yet give off much heat. The accused are brought in, frozen stiff in their overcoats, headscarves and mufflers, and directed to their places. In an adjacent room, meanwhile, the judge Amels greets his juniors ... and suggests that at the start and finish of proceedings they should give military salutes, touching their caps only. They both agree. They too are of the opinion that the court should appear neutral and politically unbiased.

When the judges enter the courtroom all those present, including the prosecutor Looh and the numerous defence lawyers robed in French black lawyers' gowns trimmed with ermine, rise to their feet ... When Amels asks the court to sit, something startling and impossible to credit happens. On the journey there, Amels had noticed that under his military coat Looh was wearing – most unusually for that period – a sabre. Then he had thought no more about it. But now he and the whole room are forced to look on as Looh, still standing in front of his place at one end of the judges' table, conspicuously and ceremoniously unbuckles his sabre and, as though throwing down the gauntlet, brings it crashing down on the table. Fortunately, the files deaden the metallic clash. This dramatic gesture, clearly intended to strike fear into the hearts of the accused, rather misfires.

After an initial moment of alarm, Amels decides that it is best to ignore it completely. The assessors, meanwhile, act as if nothing has happened. The accused are quite speechless: perhaps they are wondering whether this proverbial sabre-rattling is part of some ritual associated with Teutonic war trials. Accused number 7, the dark-blonde museum expert, has sufficient self-assurance and humour to greet this futile charade with a sardonic laugh. Another of the accused seems to scoff quietly and two others cough, but this could be because of the cold. The French defence lawyers give a display of icy aloofness . . .

Roskothen describes the weeks of interrogation of the accused, during which he endeavours to treat them with courtesy and consideration, while the prosecutor displays an attitude of virulent and undisguised anti-Semitism towards 'the Paris lawyer'. The court interpreter fails to translate the most offensive of his remarks, and Roskothen himself is scrupulous in addressing Nordmann as 'Herr Nordmann'.

The comportment of the accused is quite outstanding. All of them do everything they can to protect each other from the burden of guilt. They also try not to deny or embellish their statements to the police, and they allow mistranslations and misunderstandings to go unchallenged. Many of them appear quite reconciled to the unknown fate that awaits them if found guilty, and they refuse to bow under the strain. Quite the reverse: they exude calm, composure and dignity. Some of them declare that long before they were arrested they discussed openly the great risks they were taking: 'Most of us will see each other again in prison,' they would say, and 'Many of us will be shot' . . .

After several painstaking weeks, it is established, for Amels at least, that one row of the accused consistently and in the full knowledge of what they were doing carried out espionage on behalf of both the British and Gaullist forces. Kustos and the messenger personally met up with enemy agents in both occupied and unoccupied France, for the purpose of handing over secret information . . . These reports concerned German military activities in northern France and – much more seriously – the U-boat bases in the region of St Nazaire, including the subterranean bunker. In Paris there was a 'dead letterbox' for secret documents in a hotel on the boulevard des Italiens. Some of the accused were also engaged at this time in writing and duplicating several editions of the anti-German tract *Résistance*, of which they circulated thousands of copies in the Paris area by a great variety of means. Because these tracts were clearly an incitement to armed revolt against the occupation . . . they may be considered as aiding and abetting the enemy . . . Under martial law, the death sentence is mandatory. For this reason, the judge and lawyers consider it advisable to examine the particularly serious espionage evidence from the St Nazaire area *in situ* . . .

When the main trial is re-opened at Fresnes, Amels presents his findings from this journey. There is a deathly silence in the hut . . . Where it has been established that espionage is proven, Looh demands the mandatory and legally binding sentence of death. This is the case for Kustos, his messenger René, a young photographer from the Riviera, and among the women the officer's widow and the professor's wife . . . For others, such as the museum expert, there are prison sentences of varying terms . . .

When Amels arrives in the hut at nine o'clock on the day when he is to pass sentence, he is deathly pale, as the museum expert, an acute observer, will later note in a book she writes. It grieves him to be obliged to sentence upstanding men and women, people to be admired for their patriotism, integrity and humanity, to penalties of such severity . . .

The death penalties are handed down to those named by the prosecutor. The judgements and the reasons behind them take nearly three hours to read out. Exhausted, the judge leans back in his chair and asks for a glass of water. Then something else startling and unbelievable happens, especially in a trial that started with sabre-rattling. Kustos gets to his feet and in French says: 'On behalf of all the defendants, I thank the court for the fair and chivalrous way it has dealt with this case. In expression of this, I ask your honour's permission to shake his hand.'

Amels steps down from the bench. Deeply moved, without a word, he reaches out his hand to Kustos, who has taken a step towards him. Both men are thinking: 'May tyranny and subjugation, whether from within or without, one day be banished from humankind.' There is a long silence in the courtroom as the lawyers and main defendants return to their seats. Everyone is moved, even Looh, it would seem. Amels brings the sitting to a close. It is not a moment too soon for him: he needs air.

As the defendants are led back to the main building, the museum expert, who has been sentenced to several years' imprisonment, makes a solemn vow, despite her distaste for excessive displays of feeling. She later described this in her book *Notre Guerre*: 'I am sure that I will live in freedom again when the war is over. Then we will have our revenge. I will always think back on this trial with respect. Should I ever find myself sitting in judgement on my enemies I will strive to demonstrate the same degree of fairness.'

Ernst Roskothen on the dismissal of the appeals and the executions
Later the same afternoon, [the judge] hands his judgement in the Fresnes trial, typed and signed by him, to Senior Judge Dorer, together with the appeals. Dorer passes them on to the 'Grand Master of the Court', the military commander in France, at the Hôtel Majestic.

The court recommends commuting the death penalty most importantly for eighteen-year-old René, 'a young tool in others' hands', and also for the elderly headteacher, because of his severe disabilities from the war of 1914–18. The judges considered it pointless to add the names of the other prisoners sentenced to death, as this might weaken their case and jeopardize the chances of the two named men. [As far as the others were concerned,] many of those who took part in the trial, German as well as French, both thought and voiced the opinion: 'But they won't dare to shoot them, not even the people in Berlin or at headquarters will dare to shoot them in the face of public opinion.' Amels points this out to Dorer: 'Let's hope so,' he replies gravely. The defence has already entered its pleas for clemency. Added to these are petitions from respected French intellectuals such as François Mauriac, Paul Valéry and Georges Duhamel. The Finnish General Mannerheim, military commander in the war against the Soviets, has sent a telegram seeking clemency for Kustos, whose mother was Finnish.

A few days later, Roskothen is summoned by Dorer, who informs him that the death sentences have been confirmed and all the men are to be shot. The order was signed by Field Marshal Wilhelm Keitel in Berlin. Roskothen reflects that, not for the first time, Keitel's action will cause severe friction between the occupying powers and the French people. He believes that Keitel and his colleagues cannot have read his report through properly in the time, and that even in the conditions of a terrible, ruthless war the laws of justice and humanity should apply.

Just after seven o'clock the next morning [23 February 1942], a convoy of vehicles can be heard climbing the hill up to the old fortress at Mont Valérien, near Paris. The sun has not yet penetrated the mist, which obscures everything. But German voices can be heard issuing orders. After a pause there rises a ringing chorus, loud and clear, of *'Vive la France!'* Then a salvo of shots resounds through the morning stillness. A glimmer of sun breaks through the clouds. After more German commands and the sounds of vehicles leaving, it is still again on this wintry wooded hillside.

Soon afterwards, Amels meets his colleague Looh in the hotel lobby on place de la Concorde. Helmet in hand, Looh has just been dropped off by a military vehicle. Amels surmises at once that he has come from the execution. Walking up to him, Looh salutes and says, 'They all died bravely.' Amels has never seen him so solemn or respectful.

On Agnès Humbert's letter to Ernst Roskothen, 1946

> Roskothen recounts that on Victory in Europe Day, 8 May 1945, he was a prisoner in England. Subsequently, he was taken to France, where he was told he was to be given his freedom because a number of former prisoners had of their own volition written favourable reports about him. It had been established, and agreed by the International Red Cross, that he had upheld international law and carried out his patriotic duty and fulfilled the duties of his office in a humanitarian manner, often putting his own life at risk. While the necessary bureaucratic steps were taken he remained in a prisoner-of-war camp at Noisy-le-Sec. Allowed to spend Christmas with 'the Countess' (possibly Elisabeth de La Bourdonnaye) in Paris, he discovered a pile of letters from former prisoners, including one from Agnès Humbert:

But what is really moving is the letter that the museum expert, recently arrived back in Paris after her imprisonment in Germany, writes to the man who once sat in judgement over her, who on 17 February 1942 at Fresnes gave her a lengthy prison sentence.

'In those terrible days when I was a deportee,' she writes, quite as much the spirited socialist as before, 'I often thought that all Germans should be killed. But then I thought again and again of your words at the close of the trial: "Those who fall in this cause should feel no shame. They have acted out of patriotic feeling, not for financial reward. These verdicts do not impugn their honour. France will owe them recognition and gratitude." It was this memory that kept me on the path of conscience and drove away my hatred. *De toute façon, Monsieur le Président, entre nous deux, c'est reglé* [At any rate, your honour, between the two of us the score is settled].'

On Agnès Humbert's absence and her return from deportation, by her son Pierre Sabbagh (*from* Encore vous Sabbagh!, *1984*)

I never wanted to be a war correspondent. But I wanted to find my mother, a woman worthy of the highest admiration, unassailable in her strength of character and will, and in her absolute integrity. I wanted to find her out of passion and visceral necessity, because she was my mother.

From 1940 she had been part of the first – almost certainly the very first – Resistance group, with Jean Cassou, Claude Aveline, Vildé, Lewitsky. Then came betrayal, imprisonment at Cherche-Midi and Fresnes, and the Musée de l'Homme trial. Death for some of them. For her, perhaps because she was a woman, deportation.

Nearly four years had gone by since then. I absolutely had to find her alive. Nazism was on its knees. To find her, to save her, I had to be among the first. I quickly realized that only war correspondents could circulate freely.

It was a crazy quest. I knew it was. All the more so because I had not a shred of information. Where should I look? . . .

> *Entering Germany with the advancing American army, Pierre comes upon a ruined house where, amid the rubble, his army boot sets off the mechanism of a child's musical box.*

I taped a report about this episode, which I remember ending with the words: 'I dedicate this recording of a German child's musical box to you.' It was never broadcast. Censorship!

I knew all about censorship by that time. In order to talk about the war without appearing to do so, I had come up with the idea of sending a daily letter to my mother. Not my own mother, sadly, but the mother of a French soldier on active duty. To all mothers, to the mothers who had not received any letters, who would never again receive any letters.

In the wake of the Americans, the British, the French, the Canadians, the Poles, I advanced into Germany. What I saw I tried to forget. What I experienced I prefer to deny. Back in Paris, dazed and worn out, disillusioned with man and his destiny, I went home; in other words, back to my mother's apartment. I opened the door. There she was, surrounded by long-haired, transparent creatures, deportees like her. They had been delivered home by the Americans. She was alive. Sunlight filled the house. I was alive again.

Alas, the horrors that my mother had endured had ravaged her health, and we lost her tragically early.

On political commitment: Agnès Humbert's introduction to Vu et Entendu en Yougoslavie (1950)

I have never been a member of any political party.

My education and personal tastes have made me a 'woman of the left', deeply attached to Democracy and Liberty. When the time came, I was prepared – like tens of thousands of other French people – to sacrifice all my thoughts, my feelings and my life for these ideals, over a period of four years.

Having survived the scourge of Nazism, I was fortunately in sufficiently robust health to return to my job in the museum service, of which Pétain had deprived me from October 1940. Freed from all family obligations, as my sons were now established, I decided on my return from slave labour in the Third Reich to devote the leisure time left to me by my engrossing profession to fulfilling the duty of a 'survivor'. This duty appears to me perfectly clear: with my friends, to carry on the struggle to see established in France the revolutionary ideals of the Resistance.

RÉPUBLIQUE FRANÇAISE

Guerre 1939-1945

CITATION

DECISION N° 840

Le Secrétaire d'Etat aux Forces Armées "GUERRE" cite :

à l'ORDRE du CORPS d'ARMEE

- **HUMBERT Agnès** -

" Grande patriote, fait partie de l'équipe des fondateurs du
" réseau " MUSEE de l'HOMME " (Hauet Vilde) assiste le 10 Aout
" 1940 à la première réunion clandestine du groupe Jean CASSOU.
" Collabore à la publication et à la diffusion du journal
" Résistance " et transmet des renseignements militaires.
" Après l'arrestation du groupe " MUSEE de l'HOMME "(12 Fé-
" vrier 1941) continue à faire paraitre le Journal " Résistance"
" Arrêtée le 15 Avril 1941, condamnée à cinq années de réclu-
" sion, le 18 Février 1942 pour " aide à l'ennemi ". Est déportée.

Cette citation comporte l'attribution de la CROIX DE GUERRE
avec étoile de VERMEIL.

Elle annule et remplace celles accordées antérieuremert pour
les mêmes faits.

POUR AMPLIATION   Fait à PARIS, le 1er Octobre 1949
L'Administrateur civil de
    2° Classe BOUZOU   Signé : Max LEJEUNE .
Chef du Bureau "Décorations "
    P.O. le Capitaine LAMOTHE

Translator's Notes

Chapter 1: The Fall of the Third Republic

p.1 Musée des Arts et Traditions Populaires: Established in 1937, the museum housed collections devoted to French folk art and traditions. It shared the Art Deco buildings of the Palais de Chaillot, built as the architectural showpiece of the 1937 Exposition Universelle (World Fair), with its sister museum, the Musée de l'Homme (Museum of Man). Both were manifestations of the movement towards public education fostered by the socialist Front Populaire. In its celebration of 'primitive' art and its insistence on the unity of the human race, the Musée de l'Homme stood in opposition to the doctrines of Fascism and National Socialism. The author was appointed to the staff of the Musée des Arts et Traditions Populaires in 1937, and quickly rose to become the close associate of its first director, Georges-Henri Rivière.

p.2 Georges Friedmann (1902–77): Marxist intellectual and sociologist, known for the humanist sociology of work he founded after the war.

p.3 M. Jaujard: Jacques Jaujard (1895–1967): director of the national museums of France. From 1938 he organized the evacuation from Paris of major art collections both public (notably those of the Louvre) and private (particularly those belonging to Jewish collectors).

p.3 the sun is blanketed by a thick black fog: A year later, Terence

Phelan, writing for the Fourth International, recalled this phenomenon and how it was produced: 'Paris as it fell was tragically beautiful. Late on the afternoon of Wednesday 12 June, the petroleum and gasoline reserves in all the suburban refineries were set on fire by retreating French troops. Paris was ringed with monumental and sinister columns of jet-black, oily smoke. These, meeting at the zenith, far above the white cumulus clouds, slowly blotted out the sun, and spread a black pall over the doomed and deserted city. The blotting out of "the city of light" by that cloud was a sort of grim apocalypse.'

p.3 Pierre: Pierre Sabbagh (1918–94), the author's younger son by the painter Georges Hanna Sabbagh (from whom she was divorced in 1934). In the hope of finding his mother in Germany, he became a war correspondent in 1944. He subsequently went on to become a major figure in French television.

p.4 Chambord: The chateau of Chambord was one of the most important destinations for works of art evacuated from Paris before and during the war.

p.4 Jean Cassou: Jean Cassou (1897–1986) was a towering figure of French cultural, political and artistic life both before and after the Second World War. When the Musée de l'Homme network was broken up he escaped to Toulouse in the free zone, but in December 1941 was arrested and imprisoned. During his imprisonment he composed, without benefit of pen or paper, his celebrated *33 Sonnets composés au Secret* (33 sonnets composed in secret), published clandestinely by Les Editions de Minuit in 1944 under the pseudonym Jean Noir. In August 1944 he was shot and left for dead by the last German convoy to leave Toulouse at its liberation. Awarded the Médaille de la Résistance and the Croix de Guerre, Jean Cassou was also appointed (among many other honours) Compagnon de la Libération and Grand Officier de la Légion d'Honneur.

p.6 Maman: The author's mother was Mabel Annie Wells Rooke (1869–1943), from an English family who formed part of the large British expatriate community in Dieppe.

p.6 Jean: Jean Sabbagh (b.1917), the author's elder son by Georges

Hanna Sabbagh. A lieutenant in 1940, he retired from the French navy as a rear admiral.

p.7 an appeal by a French general: On 17 June 1940, faced with the knowledge that Pétain and the French government in Bordeaux would seek an armistice with the Germans, General Charles de Gaulle – formerly a junior member of the government and favourite of Pétain – fled to Britain, technically making himself a deserter. In August 1940 he was court-martialled *in absentia* and sentenced to death. Once in Britain he went immediately to London, where he asked Churchill for permission (granted without hesitation) to use the BBC to address the French people. Declaring that the war was not over, that France was not alone and that victory was still possible, he called on the French people to rally round him: 'I, General de Gaulle, now in London, call on all French officers and men presently on British soil or who may be in the future, with or without their arms; I call on all engineers and skilled munitions workers presently on British soil or who may be in the future, to get in touch with me. Whatever happens, the flame of French resistance must not and shall not die.' The text of de Gaulle's Appeal of 18 June was to be printed in its entirety in the second issue of *Résistance*. Following a minute's silence in honour of Resistance members who were executed, it is now read out every year on 18 June as part of the official ceremony at the France Combattante memorial at Mont Valérien.

p.8 still a naval officer on board the *Ville-d'Ys*, currently in Newfoundland: Following the defeat of France, there was consternation in Britain regarding the future of the French fleet. On 3 July, following the French rejection of their attempts at negotiation, British forces destroyed the squadron of warships stationed at Mers-el-Kébir in Algeria, thus effectively scuppering the French navy. The reference here is presumably to the Saint Pierre et Miquelon archipelago, a diminutive French territory lying some 30 km off British-administered Newfoundland. Telegrams from the islands' administrator, Baron Gilbert de Bournat, to the Vichy Minister of Colonies referred to 'British pressure to rally to the

British or Gaullist causes', in response to which Vichy dispatched the gunboat *Ville d'Ys* to St Pierre with orders to fire on any British ship approaching within 30 km of the islands. When the *Ville-d'Ys* left St Pierre, on 1 November 1940, de Bournat complained, 'This departure, immediately interpreted as an abandoning of the colony by France, gives new hope to the dissidents, who secretly decide to take advantage of 11 November to organize a large demonstration, get rid of me and proclaim their support for de Gaulle.' On Christmas Eve 1941 vessels from the Free French navy seized the official Vichy buildings in St Pierre, and in a referendum on Christmas Day the population voted overwhelmingly to rally to the Free French.

p.8 the Romain Rolland play *Le 14 juillet*: Romain Rolland (1866–1944), Nobel Laureate for literature and a lifelong pacifist and socialist, was a dedicated opponent of Fascism and Nazism.

Chapter 2: *Paris under the Swastika*

p.9 crossing the demarcation line at Vierzon: Under the terms of the Armistice (22 June 1940) France was divided into an occupied northern zone and an unoccupied southern zone administered by the Vichy government under Maréchal Pétain, loosely referred to as the *zone libre* or 'free zone'. There were only two ways to cross the demarcation line: unofficially with an underground guide, or *passeur*, or officially with a permit (*Ausweis*), costly, difficult and time-consuming to obtain, though there was a brisk trade in forged documents. At Vierzon, a major railway junction, the demarcation line passed through the railway station. Papers were therefore checked on trains, a process that entailed long and nerve-racking delays.

Later, members of the Musée de l'Homme group, notably Léon-Maurice Nordmann, were 'passed' across the demarcation line at Vierzon by Dr René Szumlanski and his wife Jeanne, who had their town house in the occupied zone and their country house in the free zone.

p.10 Lévy-Bruhl: Lucien Lévy-Bruhl (1857–1939), French Jewish philosopher and writer on ethnology, a founding father of the

Musée Ethnographique du Trocadéro, precursor of the Musée de l'Homme.

p.10 a certain Montandon: George Alexis Montandon (1879–1944) was a Swiss (naturalized French) anthropologist who worked at the Ecole d'Anthropologie in Paris from 1931. In the years before the Second World War he was a prominent exponent of scientific racism, and during the war he published explicit and extreme anti-Semitic works such as *Comment reconnaître un juif (How to recognize a Jew)*. He died in the Paris suburb of Clamart in 1944 following an attack by members of the Resistance.

p.10 the strikes of 1936: The election of the left-wing Front Populaire in May 1936 was accompanied by strikes that achieved a massive following throughout France and led to the signing of the Matignon Agreements between workers, employers and the government, which secured wide-ranging improvements in pay and conditions for French workers.

p.10 'the motherland': The Vichy government replaced the Revolutionary ideals of *liberté, égalité, fraternité* (liberty, equality, fraternity) with the slogan *travail, famille, patrie* (work, family, motherland), borrowed from the right-wing group Croix-de-Feu, and abbreviated disparagingly by the clandestine press to *'l'esprit Trafapa'*.

p.11 Marcel Mauss (1872–1950): Social anthropologist, nephew and collaborator of the sociologist Emile Durkheim.

p.11 Marcel Abraham (1898–1955): Academic and principal private secretary to education minister Jean Zay under the Front Populaire. Taking refuge in Toulon in 1941, he went on to help found the local cell of the *Franc-Tireur* Resistance network.

p.12 Carbonari: Secret revolutionary societies in early nineteenth-century Italy.

p.12 Emile-Paul brothers: According to Vercors (Jean Bruller), author of *Le Silence de la mer* (translated by Cyril Connolly as *Put Out the Light* in 1944) and co-founder of Les Editions de Minuit, Emile-Paul Frères were the only major Paris publishers who refused to sign the infamous *Liste Otto* of banned books, drawn up by the Nazi Propaganda-Staffel and ascribed to the French publishers' association in order to humiliate the industry. Agreeing to its terms was a condition of continuing to publish, and some 140 publishers thus felt obliged to put their name to this document, which proclaimed: 'In their desire to help create a more wholesome atmosphere, French publishers have decided to withdraw from sale those books which have systematically poisoned our public opinion; more particularly publications by political refugees and Jewish authors who, betraying the hospitality that France had given them, unscrupulously incited us to wage a war from which they hoped to benefit for selfish ends . . . The Occupying Authorities have expressed their satisfaction at this initiative taken by French publishers.' Banned authors and works included numerous French writers and German exiles, all biographies of Jewish figures, Shakespeare, Virginia Woolf and the *Book of Isaiah*. In 1946 Emile-Paul Frères were to publish the first edition of Agnès Humbert's journals, entitled *Notre Guerre*.

p.12 Stefan Zweig: A prolific Austrian biographer, playwright and novelist, one of the most translated writers in the 1930s, Stefan Zweig (1881–1942) was also a lifelong pacifist and believer in the unity of Europe. Jewish by birth (though non-practising), he was forced to flee Austria in 1938. When Richard Strauss refused to drop Zweig's name as librettist of his opera *Die schweigsame Frau* (*The Silent Woman*), Hitler boycotted the premiere and the opera was banned. In 1938 Zweig became a British citizen, and in 1941 he settled in Brazil. In despair and disillusion after the fall of Singapore in 1942, which he felt signalled the ineluctable rise of Nazism, he committed suicide with his wife Lotte.

p.13 Paul Bourget, Henry Bordeaux, Abel Bonnard: Undistinguished writers of undemanding novels. Abel Bonnard (1883–1968) was a Fascist sympathizer in the 1930s and became a minister for education under the Vichy government. After the war he was expelled from the Académie Française as a collaborator and condemned to death *in absentia*. Franco granted him political asylum, however, and he spent the rest of his life in Spain. The author's reference here is clearly ironic.

p.14 Madeleine Le Verrier: Madeleine Gex Le Verrier, formerly editor of *L'Europe nouvelle*, a journal devoted to European politics. In late 1941 she managed to reach London, where the following year she published *France in Torment*. In 1945 this was published in French by Emile-Paul Frères under the title *Une Française dans la tourmente*.

p.14 *Conseils à l'occupé*: This list of thirty-three 'hints to the occupied', composed by the militant socialist Jean Texcier (1888–1957) and published clandestinely in July 1940, was to prove hugely influential throughout France. In September 1941 it was broadcast to France by the BBC. It begins as follows:

1 Street vendors offer them maps of Paris and French phrase books; wave after wave of them arrive in coaches at Notre Dame and the Panthéon; every one of them has his little camera screwed to his eye. But have no illusions: *these are not tourists*.

2 They are the victors. Be correct with them. But do not go out of your way to please them in order to curry favour with them. Do not be over-hasty. In any case, they won't thank you for it.

3 You do not know their language, or else you have forgotten it. If one of them speaks to you in German, shrug your shoulders and walk on with a clear conscience.

p.14 Claude Aveline: Pseudonym of Evgen Avtsine (1901–92). Aveline was a prolific poet and writer. Albert Camus cited *Le Prisonnier* (1936) as his inspiration for *L'Etranger* (*The Outsider*). In 1941 Aveline left Paris to join the journalist and novelist Louis Martin-Chauffier in Lyon. The house they shared became a major centre of Resistance activity, and Aveline was one of the founders of *Combat*.

p.14 The Germans imposed Berlin time (one hour ahead of French time) on Paris on 14 June, the day they entered the city.

p.14 Christiane Desroches: Christiane Desroches Noblecourt (b.1913) was the first woman to become a fellow of the French Institute of Oriental Archaeology and the first to lead an archaeological excavation, in 1938. Working with UNESCO in the 1960s, she led the successful campaign to preserve the Nubian temples threatened by the construction of the Aswan Dam, for which she was awarded the prestigious gold medal of the Centre National de Recherches Scientifiques.

p.14 Front Populaire: A left-wing coalition including the French Socialist Party (SFIO) and Radical-Socialist Party and supported by the Communist Party (PCF). The coalition won the legislative elections of 1936, leading to the formation of a socialist government under Léon Blum. Although women were denied the vote until 1944, the Front Populaire cabinet included a number of women. After enacting many radical reforms, the Front Populaire fell apart in 1938, in the face of defeats, economic setbacks and faction-fighting, notably over the response to the Spanish Civil War.

p.15 the workers' university: The *Université ouvrière*, started in 1932, was one of the numerous public education initiatives encouraged by the Front Populaire.

p.16 *Nouvelle Revue Française*, Editions Gallimard: Founded in 1909 by André Gide among others, the *NRF* was the most authoritative of literary monthlies. In 1911 it was edited by Gaston Gallimard, who founded the Gallimard publishing house. Under the editorship of Jean Paulhan it united a group of writers who formed the beginnings of a Resistance group and who went on to work with the Musée de l'Homme network. On 1 June 1940 it ceased publication, to reappear in December of that year under German management and the collaborationist editorship of Drieu la Rochelle. By spring 1944 its circulation had melted away and it went out of business. After the war it was banned until 1953 for collaboration. Although Editions Gallimard was a signatory to the notorious *Liste Otto*, a number of distinguished editors there managed to avoid contact with the NRF and worked individually for the Resistance.

p.17 Dr Rivet: Paul Rivet (1876–1958) was a prominent ethnologist who founded the Musée de l'Homme in 1937 and was its first director. A militant anti-fascist and anti-racist, he was also one of the founders of the *Comité de vigilance des intellectuels antifascistes*. In November 1940 the Vichy government relieved him of his post at the University of Paris and dismissed him as director of the Musée de l'Homme. Deciding to accept an invitation from the president of Colombia to set up an institute of ethnology, he was smuggled across the demarcation line by Georges Ithier, escaping arrest by hours.

p.17 French soldiers have fired on other French soldiers at Dakar: General de Gaulle believed he could persuade the Vichy French forces in Dakar (where the gold reserves of the Banque de France and the Polish government in exile were stored) to join the Allied cause. A small combined British and Free French force carried out this action, in the expectation that Senegal would rally to de Gaulle as French Equatorial Africa had already done. On 23 September Free French aircraft took off from HMS *Ark Royal* intending to open negotiations, but their crews were taken prisoner; and when a boat carrying representatives of de Gaulle entered the harbour the Vichy French fired on them. When Free French forces came under heavy fire from Vichy guns General de Gaulle called off the assault, declaring he did not want to 'shed the blood of Frenchmen for Frenchmen'. Two days later the British called off their attack and Vichy was left in control of Dakar and French West Africa. This rebuttal, trumpeted by Vichy as a massive vindication of its own policies and existence, was a heavy and humiliating setback for de Gaulle.

p.18 Boris Vildé: A linguist and ethnologist at the Musée de l'Homme, specializing in the polar regions. Born in St Petersburg in 1908, Vildé fled with his family to Estonia in 1919. In the early 1930s he went to Germany, was imprisoned for fighting against the rise of Nazism, and met André Gide. In 1932 he arrived in Paris as Gide's protégé. There he met Paul Rivet, later director of the Musée de l'Homme. At the outbreak of war he was mobilized in the French Army, and in June 1940 was taken prisoner by the Germans in the Ardennes. He managed to escape, arriving on 5 July 1940.

p.18 Intelligence Service: Secret Intelligence Service (now commonly known as MI6).

p.18 distributing tracts: see Gilberte Brossolette's account, p.311.

p.20 Deuxième Bureau: The French state's external military intelligence agency. Officially dissolved on France's surrender in June 1940, it continued to operate in secret from Vichy and Lyon.

p.21 a leader of whom we know absolutely nothing: Presumably a reference to de Gaulle.

p.22 Casimir de La Rocque: Nickname coined by his opponents for Colonel François de La Rocque, leader of the extreme right-wing Croix-de-Feu movement until it was dissolved by the Front Populaire in 1936, and afterwards of the less virulent Parti Social Français.

p.22 Vige Langevin: Teacher and author specializing in folk art and music; after the war an advisor to UNESCO (with Jean Piaget) on art education for children.

p.22 *une épingle anglaise*: The French for 'safety pin' translates literally as 'English pin', hence the subversive pun. Tiapa Langevin survived the war to become a respected mountaineer.

p.22 demonstrations of 11 November: The occupying authorities had forbidden the observance of any of the usual ceremonies marking Armistice Day, which traditionally culminated at the Tomb of the Unknown Soldier beneath the Arc de Triomphe. Paris students had already planned a demonstration in support of Paul Langevin, and this now merged with the more widespread anti-German feeling. The BBC meanwhile urged the French people to take to the streets, and tracts reminded them of their patriotic duty. Plans were spread by word of mouth, and by five o'clock on 11 November large numbers of university and school students had filled the streets around the Arc de Triomphe, shouting their defiance and singing 'La Marseillaise'. The SS broke up the demonstration with extreme brutality, firing into the crowd, carrying out beatings and interrogations and taking an unknown number of demonstrators to prison. Jean Suret-Canal, then a prisoner at Cherche-Midi, recalled (in *La nouvelle critique*, 1949) seeing young students and schoolchildren being processed there on 12 November, while other prisoners heard cries of '*Maman, Maman!*' as they were beaten up in the courtyard. No definitive figures for those wounded or killed have ever been established. The Vichy police, who were also involved, destroyed all their records of the incident.

p.23 Paul Langevin (1872–1946): Distinguished physicist and humanitarian, a founder of the *Comité de vigilance des intellectuels antifascistes* and president from 1944 to 1946 of the *Ligue des droits humains* (Human Rights League). When the Gestapo arrested Langevin, it was taken as a signal that the occupying forces and Vichy were targeting French intellectual, scientific and cultural life. Langevin was imprisoned twice during the Occupation and removed from his post as the director of the Ecole de Physique et Chimie.

p.23 *Résistance*: Possibly the first use of the term in this way.

p.24 Oh Montoire!: On 24 October, at a carefully stage-managed meeting at the station of Montoire-sur-le-Loir, in the presence of Hermann Goering, Joachim von Ribbentrop, Otto Abetz, Pierre Laval and Admiral Darlan, Maréchal Pétain had shaken the hand of Adolf Hitler, so publicly sealing the 'collaboration' between Vichy and the Occupiers. This was a French initiative, understood at the time as a form of mutual, pragmatic cooperation. A week later, however, Pétain made a radio broadcast in which he announced that he had now entered on 'the path of collaboration as a positive move towards the new order in Europe [*dans le cadre d'une activité constructive du nouvel ordre européen*]', so apparently endorsing German hegemony. While the Vichy government and its officials continued to use the term 'collaboration' to indicate a rational means of coexistence, for the first Resistance publications it immediately signified subservience and treason.

p.24 Lewitsky (1903–42): Born in Russia and brought up as an impoverished refugee from the Bolshevik regime, Anatole Lewitsky was head of the European-Asiatic department at the Musée de l'Homme and a world expert on Siberian shamanism. He returned to Paris in early August 1940, having been demobilized from the French army.

p.24 Our *canard* has laid its first egg: *Canard* (literally 'duck'), slang for an amateurish newspaper or student rag.

p.24 Louis Martin-Chauffier (1894–1980): Archivist, palaeontologist, librarian of the Mazarin Library in Florence, Martin-Chauffier was also a novelist, translator and publisher of avant-garde authors, including André Gide. In the late 1930s he was also editor-in-chief of a string of weeklies, before becoming literary editor of *Paris Match* and leader writer of *Paris Soir*. In 1940 he left with the staff of *Paris Soir* for Lyon, where he joined the Resistance and from 1942 was editor-in-chief of *Libération*, one of the most important Resistance newspapers. In April 1944 he was arrested by the Gestapo and sent to Neuengamme concentration camp and afterwards Bergen-Belsen. At the Liberation he returned to France and to *Libération*.

p.24 Simone Martin-Chauffier (1902–75): Worked at the Centre des Etudes Politiques and as a translator. In Paris she sheltered Belgian youths on their way to join the Free French. By early 1942 she had joined her husband Louis (see above) near Lyon, where their house became a major Resistance centre at which the leaders of the three major local movements held weekly meetings. Claude Aveline (see above) subsequently joined them there. The Martin-Chauffiers' teenage daughters Hélène and Claudie and their twelve-year-old ward Luce also played an active part in the Resistance. Their son Jean survived Bergen-Belsen, like his father, and was later editor-in-chief of *Le Figaro*.

p.24 How wonderful it felt not to be frozen: The winters of 1940–1 and 1941–2 were among the coldest of the century throughout most of Europe. Food, clothing and fuel supplies were all in extremely short supply throughout Occupied France. In her biography of her husband Pierre Brossolette, Gilberte Brossolette remembered that of all the hardships of those winters, 'the harshest for forty years, with as much as forty centimetres of snow' in the centre of Paris, 'the most terrible was the cold that forced us to live, at work and at home, bundled up in overcoats and mufflers'.

p.25 Prison de la Santé: Built in 1867, the notoriously insalubrious and vermin-infested Prison de la Santé ('Prison of Health') was used during the Occupation to house both political and common criminals. Executions were carried out on the guillotine in its courtyard. In 1944, a revolt by prisoners was brutally suppressed by the Vichy police, with many prisoners killed.

p.29 Alfred Dreyfus: Dreyfus (1859–1935) was a talented young Jewish artillery officer in the French army who in 1894 was accused of high treason on trumped-up charges, court-martialled, cashiered and sentenced to life imprisonment on the notorious Devil's Island in French Guyana. Revealing the anti-Semitism that lay deep within the French establishment, the 'Dreyfus Affair' rocked the Third Republic and divided French society into 'Dreyfusards' and 'anti-Dreyfusards' (supporters and opponents of Dreyfus). Prominent among the former was Emile Zola, who in 1898 published a famous open letter and challenge to President Félix Faure entitled *J'Accuse!* After six years of imprisonment Dreyfus was released, pardoned, rehabilitated and awarded the Légion d'Honneur. The French Army refused to acknowledge his innocence until 1995.

p.29 La Closerie des Lilas: Legendary Left Bank café-brasserie founded in 1847 on the boulevard du Montparnasse, a popular meeting place for the Paris avant-garde.

p.29 'M. de Saint-Maur': The Mauriste order was a scholarly Benedictine order with its monastery at St Germain-des-Prés, dissolved in 1790.

p.30 *Le Matin*: Daily newspaper founded in 1883, which adopted a nationalist, anti-communist line. In 1940 it became overtly collaborationist and pro-Nazi. The last issue was published on 17 August 1944.

p.30 Nordmann: Léon-Maurice Nordmann (1908–42), prominent Jewish lawyer and associate of Léon Blum, co-founder with André Weil-Curiel of the group later known as 'Bretagne-France libre', which attempted without success to set up secure escape routes to England via Brittany, and which joined forces with Vildé in September 1940.

p.30 René Sénéchal (the Kid) (1922–42): In 1940, an eighteen-year-old accountant who acted as liaison agent between Sylvette Leleu's group in Béthune and the Musée de l'Homme network. He also guided British servicemen out of Occupied France and into Spain, probably via Toulouse.

p.31 the plague is less noticeable: The Nazis were commonly known as *la peste brune* (the brown plague). The metaphor was taken up most famously by Albert Camus in *La Peste*, published in 1947.

p.31 *haricot vert*: Literally 'French bean', one of the numerous contemptuous terms for the German occupying forces, which also included *les Fritz, les Boches, les épinards* (spinach) and *les doryphores* (Colorado beetles, as they devoured the potato harvest).

p.32 It's always a struggle to scrape together enough money: Many copies of *Résistance* appear to have been sent out by post, at the expense of group members.

p.33 I type in red letters: *'Vive le général de Gaulle'*: When Agnès Humbert's long-standing friend Madeleine Gex Le Verrier was in London in 1942, she drew up a report for the Free French secret service in which she drew attention to the dangers of rash enthusiasm and amateurism among the Resistance. Naming no names, she cited this exploit as a glaring example of the unnecessary risks they ran.

p.33 Gaston Monmousseau (1883–1960): Prominent communist and trades unionist, parliamentary deputy, wartime leader of the clandestine Communist Party in Provence.

p.34 Delphine de Girardin (1804–55): Fêted writer and chronicler of Paris under Louis-Philippe, who wrote under the nom de plume of Vicomte Charles de Launay.

p.34 Yvonne Oddon (1902–82): Chief librarian at the Musée de l'Homme and an influential and respected figure in French library studies. After the war she worked in the field of education and museography with UNESCO and other agencies in many parts of the world. For her work in the Resistance she was made a Chevalier de la Légion d'Honneur.

p.35 Georges Ithier: Freight officer for the Paris office of the Dutch airline KLM. As an interpreter working with the British army, he fought on the beaches at Dunkerque before making his way back to Paris through enemy lines. Recruited by Vildé, Ithier specialized in crossing the demarcation line with correspondence, British airmen or French Gaullists.

p.35 the submarine base at Saint-Nazaire: René Creston, another colleague at the Musée de l'Homme, was in contact with Albert

Jubineau, a lawyer and *résistant* in Saint-Nazaire, Brittany. They set up a small group to obtain detailed plans of the massive and strategically crucial dry dock and U-boat installation at Saint-Nazaire. Reproduced by the Musée de l'Homme group, these plans reached British intelligence agents. On the night of 28 March 1942, British commandos launched a raid that was to become known popularly as 'the greatest raid of all', during which the entrance to the port was rammed, and delayed explosives ensured that its facilities were put out of commission until 1947. The commandos sustained 80 per cent casualties and earned five VCs.

p.36 Pierre Brossolette (1903–44): Prominent left-wing journalist and radio commentator before the war, awarded the Croix de Guerre for his conduct during the retreat of 1940 (and stripped of it by the Vichy government in December 1943). Madeleine Gex Le Verrier, his former editor at *L'Europe nouvelle* and a friend of Agnès Humbert, suggested him to Agnès: 'You want someone who's been opposed to the Nazi regime from its very beginnings? And someone who is a gifted communicator to work on your bulletins? Well, I think I know the very man for you.' Jean Cassou described how he and Agnès Humbert found Brossolette shivering in his overcoat in the shop. Having outlined their work (noting in conclusion that they 'cherished no illusions') they received a grimly stoical response: 'All is lost, there's no hope . . . That said, since there's nothing to be done, I'm with you . . .' In December 1941 Brossolette joined the Forces Françaises Libres and acted as agent and information specialist for the intelligence network CND (Confrérie Notre Dame), before going to London in person the following year to meet de Gaulle. Over the next two years he broadcast on the BBC, carried out important missions in France and rose to great prominence within the Resistance. The bookshop on rue de la Pompe became an important clandestine meeting place, and the rabbit warren of shelves and cellars concealed plans and leaflets, reports and correspondence to be sent to London, which Gestapo searches failed to discover. Brossolette's son Claude was awarded the Médaille de la Résistance at the age of fourteen.

De Gaulle awarded Pierre Brossolette the Croix de la Libération and the Médaille de la Résistance and appointed him a member of the Conseil de l'Ordre de la Libération. In 1943, he petitioned de Gaulle for the Médaille de la Résistance for Agnès Humbert and Jean Cassou.

p.37 Pierre Walter: Alsatian photographer.

p.37 *Pantagruel*: The first printed clandestine newspaper to appear, in October 1940. The writer and editor was Raymond Deiss, a French Alsatian music publisher and owner of an offset printer, who declared in the first issue that its aim was 'neither hatred of the Germans nor rebellion, but simply the safeguarding of our age-old right to independent thought'. He brought out sixteen issues, attaining a circulation of ten thousand, before his arrest in October 1941. He was beheaded in prison in Cologne in August 1943.

p.38 Gaveau: Albert Gaveau was in the pay of Captain Doehring of the Gestapo, for whom he worked throughout the Occupation. His German-born mother was related to Doehring's secretary. No one knows how many Resistance members he betrayed. Ernst Roskothen, German judge at the military tribunal that tried members of the Musée de l'Homme group, known at the time as the 'Affaire Vildé', observed: 'We know all that Gaveau knew, and nothing but what he knew. This affair should have been called the "Gaveau Affair".' In his memoirs he noted that although Gaveau did not appear at the trial, his presence hovered over the courtroom like 'an evil spirit'. In 1944 Gaveau fled to Germany, before returning to France after the war. In 1949 he was tracked down and brought to trial. Surviving members of the Musée de l'Homme group gave evidence at his trial, as did Roskothen, who came voluntarily from Germany in order to do so. Gaveau was found guilty of treason and sentenced to life imprisonment.

p.38 These tracts explain . . . national reserves: In his memoir of this period, Ernst Roskothen, later to sit in judgement on members of the Musée de l'Homme group, describes discovering tucked into his seat at the Folies Bergère a piece of paper marked *'Recopier, faites circuler'* ('copy and circulate'). Duplicated on a roneo machine, it is headed *Libération* and reads: 'Who is to blame for the fact that we have nothing to eat? Not the British blockade, but the looting of the Boche, who are plundering everything from our country . . .' Roskothen reflects: 'It is true that the quantities of goods that our soldiers and officers take home with them on leave have to be seen to be believed. And here in Paris, conversely, I've noticed the queues outside the shops getting longer and longer . . .'

p.39 docked at Martinique: Jean Sabbagh's ship, the *Ville d'Ys*, had been disarmed at Fort de France, Martinique, in November 1940.

p.41 *'familiale'* postcards: These ready-printed, delete-as-appropriate cards (reading 'date/in good health/tired/slightly, seriously sick, wounded/killed/prisoner/dead/without news of/family/is well/ needs food, money, news, luggage/returned to/works at/starts school at/going to/Affectionate thoughts, kisses/signature') gave rise to considerable ingenuity, as Vercors/Jean Bruller (author of *The Silence of the Sea*) noted in his autobiography, *The Battle of Silence*: 'It was quite a tour de force to impart, by means of news about Baby and Granny's health, the date, place and exact time of a discreet rendezvous.'

p.44 My brother: William Humbert.

p.44 Léo Hamon (1908–93): Lawyer extremely active in the Resistance, first in the unoccupied zone (where he worked on *Liberté* and *Combat*) and from 1943 in Paris, where his dynamism and inventiveness lent the movement a new lease of life. In August 1944 he played an important part in the liberation of Paris. After the war he pursued a career in politics, culminating in his appointment as Secretary of State in the government of Chaban-Delmas.

p.45 President Roosevelt's latest speech: Probably a reference to the 'Four Freedoms' speech, the President's Annual Message to Congress delivered on 6 January 1941, which contained the following pledge: 'Let us say to the democracies: "We Americans are vitally concerned in your defense of freedom. We are putting forth our energies, our resources and our organizing powers to give you the strength to regain and maintain a free world. We shall send you, in ever-increasing numbers, ships, planes, tanks, guns. This is our purpose and our pledge." '

p.47 One of them looked curiously like Lindbergh: Charles A. Lindbergh, world-famous aviator and noted American isolationist in the years leading up to the Second World War. When her fourteen-year-old son was interrogated by the Gestapo in the spring of 1942, Gilberte Brossolette noted that one of the Gestapo officers, in plain clothes *'genre sportsmen'*, was 'the absolute image of Lindbergh as I had seen him years earlier in the offices of *Le Quotidien'*.

p.47 childhood memories: The author spent her childhood in Lorraine, a region disputed historically between France and Germany, where her father was senator for the department of the Meuse and had many German contacts, some of them controversial.

p.48 La Sûreté Nationale: French national police headquarters. From August 1940 the Nazi SD (*Sicherheitsdienst* or Secret Service) had gained a foothold in the Sûreté Nationale HQ at 11 rue des Saussaies, and torture started there early in 1941. It was the tortures of the era from May 1942, when General Oberg was head of the SS and German police in Occupied France, that made it the most feared address in Paris. People who remember it at that time still shudder at its mention.

p.54 1792: Year 1 of the Revolutionary calendar and the beginning of the 'radical' stage of the French Revolution.

Chapter 3: In the Prison du Cherche-Midi

p.55 Prison du Cherche-Midi: A military prison from its inception in 1851, Cherche-Midi was evacuated on 10 and 12 June 1940 and subsequently requisitioned in its entirety by the occupying forces. After the war it was used to house German prisoners of war. The verminous building, which stood on the corner of rue du Cherche-Midi and present-day boulevard Raspail, was condemned and demolished in 1966.

p.56 Fernandel: Popular comedy actor and singer (1903–71), famous for his lugubrious features.

p.56 Jean-Pierre: Jean-Pierre Girard was the *nom de guerre* of Honoré d'Estienne d'Orves (1901–41), Free French naval officer who from December 1940 was one of the first Free French agents in France, setting up the important 'Nemrod' network in Brittany and Paris. Betrayed by his radio operator, he was arrested with other members of the network in January 1941. Held in solitary confinement in atrocious conditions, he was put on the 'women's corridor' at Cherche-Midi in order to prevent him from communicating with his fellow accused. A prisoner in the next cell to him, Sarah Rosier, remembered how impressed he was with the number of women prisoners: 'I had no idea that there were so many women in prison in France for their patriotic actions. It's quite magnificent.' At their trial he made every effort to save his fellow accused by taking all responsibility on himself. On 29 August 1941 he was shot at Mont Valérien. The first Free French agent to be executed by the Germans, he refused to be blindfolded or bound and conducted himself with a conspicuous courage and dignity that made a great impression on his captors.

p.60 Bonsergent: On 23 December 1940, the walls of Paris were plastered with posters announcing in French and German the execution that morning of Jacques Bonsergent, a twenty-eight-year-old engineer who had hit a German soldier in a scuffle on 10 November, and who was seen as a scapegoat for the following day's demonstrations. Beneath the German posters were notices from the French police, threatening severe penalties for anyone found defacing them, which would be considered as an act of sabotage. Many of the posters were torn down regardless, and those that remained became instant shrines, decorated and surrounded overnight with floral tributes and miniature French and British flags. The execution of Bonsergent assumed symbolic significance as the moment when the occupiers first showed themselves in their true colours, with Bonsergent as France's first martyr.

p.62 Peter II has seized power in Yugoslavia: Yugoslavia had in fact capitulated the day before, on 17 April 1941.

p.63 Jacotte: Jacqueline Bordelet, a young secretary at the Musée de l'Homme, who posed as Pierre Walter's fiancée. In the police car after their arrest she pretended to sob uncontrollably, so contriving to swallow contact names and addresses.

p.63 It was the same Gestapo men who picked me up: Led by Captain Doehring, paymaster of Albert Gaveau.

p.66 GFP: *Geheime Feldpolizei*, the Secret Field Police, responsible for searches and arrests and accorded wide-ranging powers. At the Nuremberg International Military Tribunal proceedings, GFP personnel were found to have committed both war crimes and crimes against humanity 'on a wide scale'.

p.67 Elisabeth, Comtesse de La Bourdonnaye (b.1911): A wealthy aristocrat who met Boris Vildé through his father-in-law, the historian Ferdinand Lot. She put her chateau in the unoccupied zone at the disposal of the Resistance, and with her partner, Professor Robert Debré, and her son Geoffroy became an active member herself. Throughout the period of the trial she concealed at her home several Jewish children threatened with deportation, whom she had earlier rescued from the Rothschild orphanage.

p.67 General de Gaulle has called for an hour's silence: De Gaulle had launched these 'passive demonstrations' of solidarity with an appeal on 1 January 1941 for all French patriots to stay indoors between three and four o'clock. The occupying authorities were sufficiently alarmed to offer free distributions of potatoes on the streets of Paris at the appointed hour.

p.67 'Le Chant du départ': Revolutionary anthem and battle hymn of the First Republic, composed and first performed on 14 July 1794. '*La Victoire en chantant / Nous ouvre la barrière*' ('Victory sings while opening the gates for us') is the opening couplet.

p.68 the one that people sang on their knees in 1792: Barbaroux, commander in 1792 of the Marseillais troops from whom 'La Marseillaise' took its popular name, wrote in his memoirs: 'I shall always recall with tender emotion how at the last verse, when we sang "*Amour sacré de la Patrie*", all the citizens, both in their houses and on the streets, fell to their knees.' Jean Renoir featured this scene in his film *La Marseillaise*, released in 1938.

p.68–9 'Le Galoubet' . . . 'La Petite Tonkinoise': A medley of popular songs and sea shanties. 'Brave marin', about a brave sailor coming home from the wars, would have been particularly poignant in the circumstances, as would 'Solveig's Song', with its yearning chorus of 'You'll come back again'. 'Viens, Poupoule' and 'Elle était souriante' were light-hearted romantic songs of the Belle Epoque; 'La Petite Tonkinoise' was one of Josephine Baker's successes.

p.70 Fossés de Vincennes: The moat of the Château de Vincennes (a military barracks), site of the execution notably of the Duc d'Enghien in 1804 and Mata Hari in 1917.

p.71 it was on General de Gaulle's orders that he returned to France: D'Estienne d'Orves had returned to France against the better judgement of de Gaulle, whom he had persuaded to agree to the mission. Sarah Rosier, a fellow prisoner, quoted him as saying: 'Above all, when the war is over, tell everyone that whatever I did, I did alone, that no one asked me or ordered me to do it, and that particularly General de Gaulle and Admiral Muselier were opposed to my coming to France because I am the father of a large family. I came despite them; promise me that you'll tell everyone that when it's all over.'

p.72 Jean Paulhan (1884–1968): A towering figure of French literary life before the war, Paulhan was editor of the *Nouvelle Revue Française*, the most influential of French literary magazines, which he stopped publishing at the Armistice. Recruited by Vildé, he agreed to accommodate the group's noisy and cumbersome roneo machine at his house. By the time the fourth issue of *Résistance* came out on 1 March 1941, arrests of members of the group had already started, and Paulhan, judging it too risky to keep the roneo machine, reluctantly dismantled it and threw it piece by piece into the Seine. On 6 May, having found his name in a notebook carried by René Sénéchal, the Germans came to his house to search for the machine. They arrested him and imprisoned him for a week, but released him after interrogation. He went on to found another Resistance publication, *Les Lettres françaises*, and to lead the *Nouvelle Revue Française* network.

Chapter 4: In the Prison de la Santé

p.86 Senator Charles Humbert: Humbert was a colourful and controversial figure, a pugnacious self-made man who started his career in the army, ended it as a politician and newspaper proprietor and moved in high circles. He had started life as a foundling on the steps of a church, and when the woman who brought him up was expelled to Germany in 1914, her return was secured by the personal intervention of the President of the Republic. In 1917 (by which time he was divorced from Agnès's mother), Humbert was arrested at his chateau on secret charges concerned with accepting money from German sources in order to buy out the newspaper on which he worked, *Le Journal*. In return, it was alleged, he was to adopt a pro-German editorial line. When his co-proprietor through this deal, an adventurer named Bolo Pasha, was executed as a German spy, Humbert's position looked precarious. The case became a cause célèbre throughout Europe and America, with journalists relishing the flamboyant style in which Humbert conducted his own defence. As *The Times* noted in his obituary in 1927, 'he was able to show that he had no knowledge of the suspicious origin of the money Bolo supplied, and he was acquitted'. By the end of the trial he had spent seventeen months in custody at La Santé.

p.86 Medor: Character in Ariosto's *Orlando Furioso*.

p.87 the assassination attempt on Laval: Pierre Laval (1883–1945) was Vichy prime minister from July to December 1940 and again from April 1942 to August 1944. On 27 August 1941 he was injured in an assassination attempt by Paul Collette, member of the extreme right-wing Croix de Feu group, but soon recovered. Found guilty of high treason after the war, on 15 October 1945 he was executed at Fresnes. The sole journalist to witness his execution was Agnès Humbert's younger son, Pierre Sabbagh.

Chapter 5: In the Prison de Fresnes

p.91 Prison de Fresnes: Opened in 1898 on the southern outskirts of Paris, Fresnes remains one of the largest prisons in France. During the Occupation the Gestapo used it to imprison captured

British agents and members of the Resistance. Conditions were appalling, with torture and executions commonplace. Those who survived Fresnes were sent to Germany, to forced labour or concentration camps.

p.93 Andrieu (1896–1942): A veteran of the First World War who had been seriously wounded and highly decorated, Jules Andrieu was a head teacher in Béthune in the Pas-de-Calais who worked with Sylvette Leleu.

p.93 Sylvette Leleu: After her airman husband had been shot down and killed in September 1939, Sylvette Leleu sent her two young sons to stay with their grandparents and used the garage she ran as a cover for her Resistance work. With ingenuity and daring, she helped dozens of Allied servicemen to escape from local prisoner-of-war camps and drove them to Paris, where the Musée de l'Homme group would arrange safe houses, false papers and escape routes. She also received consignments of *Résistance* and doubtless distributed them in the Pas-de-Calais area. The mechanics in her garage were experts in the art of sabotaging German vehicles brought in for repair. René Sénéchal, her young accountant, acted as go-between between Paris and Béthune. When he was arrested, the Gestapo found on him a notebook and some letters addressed to Free French servicemen in London. In the notebook they found Sylvette Leleu's address, and on one of the letters they found the address of a woman who inadvertently led them to Jules Andrieu.

p.94 M. et Mme Simmonet: Alice Simmonet was a friend of Vildé's wife, Irène, and a graduate student at the Sorbonne, where her professor, Robert Fawtier, pledged half his salary to Vildé to finance his Resistance work. She helped to produce and distribute *Résistance*. Alice was arrested on 10 February 1941 with her husband Henri, head of a veterinary school, who was not involved in her work, and who was released after their trial.

p.95 the presiding judge: Captain Ernst Roskothen (b. 1907) was a magistrate before the war and refused to join the Nazi party. During the trial he attempted unsuccessfully to save

Sénéchal from the firing squad by suggesting to him that he was unaware of what he was doing, and he travelled to Saint-Nazaire to convince himself of the accuracy of the plans found in Vildé's possession, which would make a death sentence mandatory. Profoundly impressed by the patriotism, composure and dignity of the accused, he was also struck by Agnès Humbert's demeanour. As prosecutor Gottlob brandished his sabre for effect, he noted that 'Accused no. 7, the museum expert, has sufficient self-assurance and humour to greet this futile charade with a sardonic laugh.' When Roskothen was imprisoned on the liberation of Paris in August 1944, no fewer than twenty-six Resistance members – including Agnès Humbert and Yvonne Oddon – petitioned for his release, stressing his humanity, his respect for those who appeared before him and his efforts to reduce or remove the charges where possible. In 1949, when Albert Gaveau was brought to trial for betraying the group, he travelled to France voluntarily to testify against him. When Agnès Humbert first published her diaries in 1946 under the title *Notre Guerre*, she sent Roskothen a copy with the inscription: 'To presiding judge Roskothen, who sent me into slave labour . . . Without rancour.'

p.95 the prosecutor: Captain Gottlob, a devout Nazi of virulently anti-Semitic views.

p.99 Louise Alcan: Worked at the Musée des Arts et Traditions Populaires; survived Auschwitz and wrote a memoir entitled *Sans armes et bagages*, published in 1947.

p.100 The prosecutor directs his vitriol at Nordmann: One of the accused, Jean-Paul Carrier, noted that 'Gottlob was relentless and shameless in his harassment of the only Jewish prisoner, whose head he succeeded in procuring despite the flimsiness of the evidence against him.' In his account of the trial (written in the third person) Roskothen recalled that the prosecutor 'harries him with blind hate, just because he is a Jew. The presiding judge and the interpreter make every attempt to correct these improprieties. The accused are fully aware that the judge misses no opportunity to address the lawyer as "Herr".'

p.101 speeches for the defence: One of the lawyers involved later observed that these were like 'pleas for corpses'.

p.102 Last of all come the death sentences: In his account of the trial, Roskothen describes an astonishing gesture at this point: 'The judgements and the reasons behind them take nearly three hours to read out. Exhausted, the judge leans back in his chair and asks for a glass of water. Then something startling and unbelievable happens . . . [Vildé] stands up and says in French: "On behalf of all the defendants, I thank the court for the fair and chivalrous way it has dealt with this case. In expression of this, I ask your honour's permission to shake his hand" . . . Deeply moved and without a word, the judge reaches out his hand . . . Both men are thinking: "May tyranny and subjugation, whether from within or without, one day be banished from humankind." '

p.104 I return to my cell: At this point Roskothen attributes the following words to Agnès Humbert ('the museum expert'): 'I am sure that I will live in freedom again when the war is over. Then we will have our revenge. I will always think back on this trial with respect. Should I ever find myself sitting in judgement on my enemies I will strive to demonstrate the same degree of fairness.'

p.105 Hôtel Crillon: One of the most exclusive hotels in Paris, on place de la Concorde at the foot of the Champs-Elysées, occupied by the German High Command during the Occupation.

p.106 distinguished names such as François Mauriac, Paul Valéry and Georges Duhamel: Petitions for clemency were submitted by a galaxy of distinguished men of letters, academics and dignitaries within France and abroad, including Fernand de Brinon, Vichy representative to the German High Command in Paris, and General Mannerheim, commander-in-chief of Finnish armed forces. Meanwhile, Germaine Tillion, ethnologist at the Musée de l'Homme, who subsequently became the group's leader until her own betrayal and arrest in August 1941, made repeated and fruitless appeals to the ineffectual Cardinal Suhard, Roman Catholic Archbishop of Paris, and his deputy, the pro-German Canon Tricot. Roskothen's court itself recommended clemency for Sénéchal and Andrieu.

Chapter 6: In the Communal Cell

p.109   Fernand Zalkinoff (1923–42): Born into a family of Russian Jewish origins, before the war Fernand Zalkinoff had been a promising student whose ambition was to become a teacher of German. In 1940 he was an early member of the groups that in 1941 became the Bataillons de la Jeunesse, the armed wing of the Jeunesses Communistes (Young Communists). Inexperienced, untrained and few in number, the young fighters of the Bataillons de la Jeunesse spearheaded the armed Resistance movement in Paris and the surrounding area with reckless courage, with up to 85 per cent of their actions ending in failure. At their show trial at the Palais Bourbon and before their execution at Mont Valérien on 9 March 1942, Fernand Zalkinoff and the six comrades arrested with him behaved with conspicuous dignity and courage.

p.109   They were all shot on 23 February: The men were executed in a clearing near the fort of Mont Valérien, overlooking the Bois de Boulogne to the west of Paris, where altogether about a thousand prisoners and Resistance members were shot during the course of the war. The site is now a monument to the Resistance, with an eternal flame lit by General de Gaulle on 18 June 1945. As there were only four stakes for the seven condemned men, Vildé, Lewitsky and Walter volunteered to go last. The condemned men sang 'La Marseillaise' before they died, and Roskothen reported a ringing chorus of '*Vive la France!*' before the final salvo. Their dignity and courage impressed even the prosecutor Gottlob, who immediately afterwards reported to Roskothen, who had never seen him so solemn or respectful: 'They all died bravely.' Father Franz Stock, chaplain to the prison of Cherche-Midi, observed that he had seen many Frenchmen die, 'but none so well as these'.

p.110   Rachel has been taken away: After the war, Marcel Degliame, a founder of the Combat Resistance movement and cousin by marriage of Fernand and Rachel Zalkinoff, reported that their father Nojm was shot as a hostage at Mont Valérien on 11 August 1942. Rachel, her mother and sister, together with an uncle and aunt, a cousin and her husband and their two children aged nine and six, were all sent to Auschwitz, where they died in the gas chambers.

p.110 Drancy: Set up by the Vichy government in August 1941, Drancy was a transit camp to the north-east of Paris from which Jews rounded up by French police on Nazi orders, together with smaller numbers of Roma people, homosexuals and Resistance members, were transported to extermination camps. The camp was notorious for its overcrowding, lack of sanitation, inadequate rations and the brutality of the French guards, infamous for separating children from their parents. The capacity of the camp was 4,500 prisoners, but from August 1941 to August 1944 it processed some 70,000. It is believed that some 2,000 of these survived.

p.110 *Michel Strogoff*: Novel by Jules Verne, published in 1875, describing the epic voyage of Michel Strogoff, courier to the Tsar, from Moscow to Irkutsk in eastern Siberia, to warn the Tsar's brother of imminent invasion by the Tatar hordes.

Chapter 7: Forced Labour

p.111 Anrath Prison: Under the Third Reich, the prison at Anrath, ten kilometres south-east of Krefeld and forty kilometres north of Cologne, was designated for female political prisoners under the *Nacht und Nebel* ('Night and Fog', a phrase borrowed from Goethe) directive issued by Hitler on 7 December 1941. A year later, Heinrich Himmler issued instructions to the Gestapo regarding the application of *Nacht und Nebel* to political activists in the Occupied territories: 'An effective and lasting deterrent can be achieved only by the death penalty or by taking measures which will leave the family and the population uncertain as to the fate of the offender. Deportation to Germany serves this purpose.' In a list of slave labour camps and prisons published by *Défense de la France* in 1946, Anrath was classified among the 'most murderous'.

p.112 the prison director is a sadist: Dr Bodo Combrinck, a lawyer and low-ranking member of the Nazi hierarchy, was the notoriously brutal director of the men's prison and women's penitentiary at Anrath – to which the Nazi regime sent large numbers of political prisoners – from 1939 until the arrival of the American army on 2 March 1944.

p.112 Bécassine: A popular comic-book character, a Breton girl in traditional dress with an innocent air and short plaits.

p.121 'Hommes: 40; chevaux en long: 8' ('Men: 40; horses lengthwise: 8'): These were the markings that appeared on the closed railway wagons in which prisoners were transported from Drancy to extermination camps, one hundred to a truck.

p.131 Sikorski: General Wladyslaw Sikorski (1881–1943), prime minister of the Polish government in exile and commander-in-chief of Free Polish forces.

p.132 Ukrainian girls, so young they are still virtually children: In January 1942, Erich Koch, appointed by Hitler to rule Ukraine, had closed all universities and schools with students over fifteen years of age, and ordered all students and teachers to be deported to Germany, there to be 'worked to death'. The German army also kidnapped young adults off the streets of Ukrainian towns and cities and sent them into slave labour. It is estimated that over two million Ukrainians were forced into slave labour in Germany.

p.133 A terrific air raid over Cologne: On the night of 30 May 1942, Cologne was the target of the first of the RAF's 'thousand bomber raids' under Bomber Command AOC Arthur 'Bomber' Harris, in which nearly 900 bombers dropped just under 1,500 tons of bombs in 90 minutes.

Chapter 8: At the Phrix Rayon Factory

p.148 the Phrix rayon factory: In 1939, Germany's rayon industry was the most important in the world. As cotton and wool became increasingly scarce, wartime Germany relied heavily on the rayon industry, with army uniforms containing a high percentage of rayon.

p.149 carbon disulphide: Described as smelling like 'rotten radishes', carbon disulphide is extremely volatile and easily absorbed through inhalation.

p.151 founded on human suffering: Occupational studies of workers in the rayon industry have shown that inhalation of carbon disulphide increases the risk of heart and blood vessel disease, of serious eye problems and of toxic effects to the nervous system.

p.156 'La Concon': *Con* in French is a term of disparagement approximating to 'bloody idiot' or (in the feminine) 'silly bitch'.

p.158 the landing at Dieppe led to nothing: The Allied landing at Dieppe on 19 August 1942 was intended to foster German fears of an attack from the west, and to serve as an opportunity to test the Allies' seaborne invasion capabilities. The raid was a disaster, with over a thousand Allied lives lost.

p.164 Stalingrad has fallen: This was in fact only the beginning of the Battle of Stalingrad (Volgograd), one of the largest and bloodiest battles in human history, and turning point in the Second World War. After tremendous losses on both sides and massive sacrifice and suffering by the population of Stalingrad, it was to end in crushing defeat for Germany on 2 February 1943.

p.177 *souris grise*: 'Grey mouse', a French name for women auxiliaries of the *Wehrmacht* (after their grey uniform).

p.180 Louis Jouvet (1887–1951): Actor, director, designer, technician, one of the most influential and respected figures in French theatre at this period.

p.184 Now it's Duisburg going up in flames . . . now Essen: On 21 January 1943 the Allies' Combined Bomber Offensive was launched, aimed at the 'progressive destruction and dislocation of the German military, industrial and economic system, and the undermining of the morale of the German people to a point where their capacity for armed resistance is fatally weakened'. On 5 March, Bomber Command opened the battle of the Ruhr, a series of heavy attacks on the Ruhr region that were to last until July 1943, with Duisburg, Essen and Krefeld among the principal targets.

p.190 The Allies have captured Tunis!: By 13 May 1943 the Allies had secured a victory in the hard-fought six-month Tunisia campaign.

Chapter 9: The Fall of the Third Reich

p.210 the Allies had landed in France: D-Day, 6 June 1944.

p.210 Paris was liberated!: The Resistance began the battle for liberation on 19 August 1944; the occupying German garrison surrendered on 25 August. Toulouse was liberated on 19–20 August, Lyon on 2–3 September.

p.212 Our life there was lived to the perpetual din of gunfire: December 1944 saw two major German military operations in this area. The battle for the Roer river, between Cologne and Aachen, was described by German radio as 'the most terrible and ferocious battle in the history of all wars'. According to *Time* on 11 December, German troops fought 'as if it were the Meuse, the Marne and the Somme of the last war all rolled into one'. On 16 December, the Germans launched a major counter-offensive in the Ardennes that was to become known as the Battle of the Bulge. For this massive onslaught, Field Marshal von Rundstedt, German commander-in-chief in the west, ordered his troops to 'give their all in one last effort' as 'everything was at stake'. 'December's tragic interlude' is perhaps a reference to the author's frozen grief for her mother's death.

p.215 Allendorf: Allendorf bei Kirchhain was a subcamp of the Buchenwald concentration camp complex. From 1944, women were sent to Allendorf from Auschwitz in order to carry out highly dangerous work making explosives and handling chemicals of extreme toxicity. Allendorf was part of a secret munitions centre covering some 600 hectares, the largest in wartime Europe. Decontamination of the site was eventually declared complete only in March 2006.

Chapter 10: Hunting the Nazis

p.226 Burghers of Calais: In 1347, during the Hundred Years War, Calais was besieged by the English army for eleven months. According to Froissart's *Chronicles*, six burghers of Calais offered themselves as hostages to the English army in exchange for the freedom of their city. This incident of heroic French patriotism inspired Rodin's famous sculpture, commissioned by the mayor of Calais and completed in 1888. Depicting the rich merchants as they leave the city gates, stripped of their wealth and at their most vulnerable, it is a monument to heroic sacrifice rather than to victory.

p.227 where the concentration camps are in this region: Buchenwald concentration camp, some 110 kilometres to the south-east, was liberated by the American Third Army on 11 April 1945, two days after its soldiers pulled out of Wanfried.

p.235 'Fatty': Presumably a reference to Roscoe 'Fatty' Arbuckle, American silent screen comedian. 'Babbitt' was the eponymous middle-aged anti-hero of Sinclair Lewis's satire on American values and mindless conformism, published in 1922.

p.244 Dr Ley: Robert Ley (1890–1945) was a prominent Nazi who in 1932 became head of organization for the NSDAP (National Socialist German Workers' Party). After Hitler banned all German trade unions and arrested their leaders in May 1933, Ley set up the *Deutsche Arbeitsfront* (German Labour Party or DAF), imposing himself as dictatorial leader of 25,000,000 workers and confiscating union funds to fund the 'Strength through Joy' movement. Arrested by American troops at his mountain home near the Austrian border, Ley was tried before the International Military Tribunal at Nuremberg and sentenced to death. He hanged himself in his cell before the sentence could be carried out.

p.244 Martin Bormann: Hitler's immensely powerful private secretary was with him in the Führer's bunker from 28 April and witnessed his will. Evidence that Bormann left the bunker and died in the ruins of Berlin remains contested. He was tried at Nuremberg *in absentia* and condemned to death.

p.251 Where are they? . . . Yvonne Oddon: After being moved from one German prison to another, Yvonne Oddon (1902–82) was sent to Ravensbrück concentration camp on 20 November 1944. Released under the terms of an exchange negotiated between the Red Cross and Heinrich Himmler, she had arrived back in Paris just twelve days before this entry, on 14 April 1945.

p.252 Too late, the true reason . . . dawns: The implication here seems to be that the local German population had made unfounded complaints about the Russians in order to mask their real grievance, which was the Russians' efficiency in gleaning and supplying information about local Nazis.

p.256 Jehovah's Witnesses: Jehovah's Witnesses were subject to intense persecution under the Nazi regime; estimates put the proportion of active members arrested and tried for their beliefs at 50 per cent and the proportion sent to concentration camps at 10 per cent.

p.257 Hitler is defeated!: In January 1945, as the Russians advanced towards Germany across Poland and the Allies bombed Berlin to devastation, Hitler retreated to his bunker. There on 20 April he celebrated his fifty-sixth birthday – by now, according to a military aide in the bunker, a 'sick, prematurely old man' – with a macabre party and inspection of boy soldiers. In the small hours of 28–29 April he dictated his will, and shortly afterwards he and Eva Braun were married. On the morning of 29 April, news was brought to him of the execution of Mussolini and his mistress by Italian partisans. A day later, the Russians had reached the heart of Berlin. On the afternoon of 30 April, Hitler committed suicide, biting on a capsule of prussic acid and shooting himself in the temple.

p.257 we heard General de Gaulle's speech: In the early hours of 7 May 1945 the Germans signed an unconditional surrender at Reims. Victory in Europe was declared simultaneously in London, Moscow and Washington on 8 May. De Gaulle's speech that day began: 'The war is won! Victory is ours! Victory for the United Nations and Victory for France!' The short speech contained the following passage: 'As her flag is once more bathed in rays of glory, France turns her thoughts and her love first of all to those who have died for her, and then to those who have fought and suffered so greatly in her service. Not a single brave deed by her soldiers, sailors and airmen; not a single act of courage or self-sacrifice by her sons and daughters; not a single ordeal suffered by French men and women taken prisoner; not a single death, not a single sacrifice, not a single tear shall have been in vain!'

p.258 Arthur Kalden: Kalden died in a prisoner-of-war camp in 1945.

p.258 Arnold Zweig (1887–1968): Pacifist, socialist and prolific writer, best known for his First World War tetralogy and his correspondence with Sigmund Freud. In 1948 he was invited to return to the Soviet Zone (later the German Democratic Republic), where he played a prominent part in public life until his death.

p.260 Oradour: On 10 June 1944, soldiers of the Der Führer regiment of the Second SS-Panzer Division Das Reich massacred 642 men, women and children in the small town of Oradour-sur-Glane near Limoges. The ruins of the town have been preserved as a monument to those who died. In 1999 a Centre de la Mémoire was added to this site, dedicated to the victims of all war crimes.

*

Translation of document on p.324:

HUMBERT Agnès

– Outstanding patriot, one of the founders of the "MUSEE de L'HOMME" network (Haute/Vildé), present on 10 August 1940 at the first clandestine meeting of the Jean CASSOU group.

– Collaborated on the publication and distribution of the broadsheet "Résistance" and transmitted military intelligence.

– Following the arrest of the "MUSEE de l'HOMME" group (12 February 1941) continued to publish the broadsheet "Résistance".

– Arrested on 15 April 1941, sentenced on 18 February 1942 to five years' imprisonment for "aiding the enemy". Deported.

Bibliography

Andrieu, Claire, 'Les résistantes: perspectives de recherche', Le Mouvement social, no. 180, July–September 1997

d'Aragon, Charles, La Résistance sans héroisme, ed. Pikkerty, Guillaume, Editions du Tricorne, Paris, 2001

Aveline, Claude, Le Temps mort, Mercure de France, Paris, 1962

Blumenson, Martin, The Vildé Affair: Beginnings of the French Resistance, Robert Hale, London, 1977

Bouaziz, Gérard, La France torturée, Fédération Nationale des Déportés et Internés Résistantes et Patriotes, Paris, 1976

Bourderon, Roger, and Germaine Willard, 1940: de la Défaite à la Résistance, Messidor/Editions socials, Paris, 1990

Brossolette, Gilberte, Il s'appelait Pierre Brossolette, Albin Michel, Paris, 1976

Cassou, Jean, La Mémoire courte, Editions Mille et Une Nuits, Paris, 2001

— Une vie pour la liberté, Robert Laffont, Paris, 1981

Collection Défense de l'Homme, Les Témoins qui se firent égorger, Editions Défense de la France, Paris, 1946

Diamond, Hanna, Fleeing Hitler: France 1940, Oxford University Press, Oxford, 2007

Foot, M.R.D., Resistance, Eyre Methuen, London, 1976

Gex le Verrier, Madeleine, France in Torment, Hamish Hamilton, London, 1942

Guéhenno, Jean, Journal des années noires, Gallimard, Paris, 1947

Herbert, Ulrich, Hitler's Foreign Workers: Enforced Foreign Labour in Germany under the Third Reich, Cambridge University Press, Cambridge, 1997

Honoré d'Estienne d'Orves, Rose and Philippe, Honoré d'Estienne d'Orves, Pionnier de la Résistance, Editions France-Empire, Paris, 1999

Kedward, Rod, Resistance in Vichy France, Oxford Univerity Press, Oxford, 1978

—*In Search of the Maquis*, Oxford University Press, Oxford, 1993

—*La Vie en Bleu: France and the French since 1900*, Penguin, London, 2005

Krivopissko, Guy (ed.), *La Vie à en Mourir: Lettres de Fusillés (1941–1944)*, Tallandier, Paris, 2003

Langloi, Caroline, and Michel Reynaud, *Elles et Eux de la Résistance: pourquoi leur engagement?*, Editions Tirésias, Paris, 2003

MacDonogh, Giles, *After the Reich: From the Liberation of Vienna to the Berlin Airlift*, John Murray, London, 2007

Marcot, François, with Bruno Leroux and Christine Levisse-Touzé, *Dictionnaire historique de la Résistance*, Robert Laffont, Paris, 2006

Martin-Chauffier, Simone, *A bientôt quand même . . .*, Calmann-Lévy, Paris, 1976

Noguères, Henri, with Marcel Degliame-Fouché and Jean-Louis Vigier, *Histoire de la Résistance en France*, 4 vols, Robert Laffont, Paris, 1961

Ozouf, René, *Pierre Brossolette*, Librairie Gedalge, Paris, 1946

Piketty, Guillaume, *Pierre Brossolette: un héros de la Résistance*, Odile Jacob, Paris, 1998

La Presse Clandestine, 1940–1944, Colloque d'Avignon 20–21 June 1985, Conseil Général de Vaucluse

Rameau, Marie, and Claire Andrieu, *Des femmes en résistance, 1939–1945*, Editions Autrement, Paris, 2008

Roskothen, Ernst, *Gross-Paris, Place de la Concorde, 1941–1944*, published privately by the author, 1977

Sabbagh, Jean, *Georges Sabbagh*, Editions du Panama, Paris, 2006

Sabbagh, Pierre, *Encore vous Sabbagh!*, Stock, Paris, 1984

Tillion, Germaine, 'Première résistance en zone occupée. Du côté du réseau "musée de l'Homme-Hauet-Vildé"', *Revue d'histoire de la Deuxième Guerre mondiale*, no. 30, April 1958, republished in *Esprit*, February 2000

Vercors, *The Battle of Silence*, Collins, London, 1968

Vildé, Boris, *Journal et lettres de prison, 1941–1942*, Editions Allia, Paris 1997

Vinen, Richard, *The Unfree French: Life under the Occupation*, Allen Lane, London, 2006

Weitz, Margaret Collins, *Sisters in the Resistance: How Women Fought to Free France, 1940–1945*, John Wiley & Sons, Inc., New York, 1995

Wood, Nancy, *Germaine Tillion: une femme-mémoire*, Editions Autrement, Paris, 2003

Sisters in Resistance (DVD), written and directed by Maia Wechsler, Red Triangle Productions

Index

A NOTE ON THE AUTHOR

Agnès Humbert was born in 1894 in Dieppe, and married the artist Georges Sabbagh in 1916. They had two sons and were divorced in 1934. In 1936 Agnès published an influential study, *Louis David: peintre et conventionnel*, which made her reputation as an art historian. The following year she was recruited to a senior post at the newly created Musée National des Arts et Traditions Populaires, sister institution to the Musée de l'Homme. After the war she refused on principle to return to the post from which she had been sacked on Vichy orders. She was awarded the Croix de Guerre for her Resistance work in 1949, and continued to write books on art until her death in 1963.

A NOTE ON THE TRANSLATOR

Barbara Mellor is a translator specialising in the fine and decorative arts, art history, architectural history, fashion and design. Her most recent projects include *Dior: 60 Years of Style* and *The Society Portrait: Painting, Prestige and the Pursuit of Elegance*, and a series of exhibition catalogues for individual contemporary artists. She divides her time between the Scottish Borders and the Aveyron.

A NOTE ON THE TYPE

Linotype Garamond Three – based on seventeenth-century copies of Claude Garamond's types, cut by Jean Jannon. This version was designed for American Type Founders in 1917 by Morris Fuller Benton and Thomas Maitland Cleland, and adapted for mechanical composition by Linotype in 1936.